THE MAN THE ANZACS REVERED

WILLIAM "FIGHTING MAC" MCKENZIE
ANZAC CHAPLAIN

THE MAN THE ANZACS REVERED

WILLIAM "FIGHTING MAC" MCKENZIE
ANZAC CHAPLAIN

DANIEL REYNAUD

Fourth printing, 2021.

The author assumes full responsibility for the accuracy of all facts and quotations as cited in this book.

Except where the meaning is unclear, quotations from diaries, letters and other historial documents have been transcribed to retain original usage, spelling and punctuation.

Proudly published and printed in Australia by
Signs Publishing Company
Warburton, Victoria.

This book was
Edited by Nathan Brown
Proofread by Lindy Schneider
Cover and photo pages designed by Lulu Lewis
Cover photograph courtesy of The Salvation Army Heritage Centre, Melbourne, other images used by permission of the Australian War Memorial,
Typeset in Berkeley Book 11.5/15

ISBN 978 1 925044 16 4 (print edition)
ISBN 978 1 925044 17 1 (ebook edition)

FOREWORD

I have known some of the story of "Fighting Mac" since I first met him in 1973, as a doctoral student. I use "met" in the loosest possible way because, of course, William McKenzie died in 1947 and I was making his acquaintance through some of his writings and his story. I was writing about Australian Army chaplains as part of my doctoral thesis on the Australian churches in World War I. Nevertheless, even in that limited acquaintance, Padre McKenzie stood head and shoulders above most of the other Australian chaplains.

Later I began working at the Australian War Memorial and remained intrigued by the little-known story of Australian chaplains. I had discovered through Arthur Bazley, C E W Bean's devoted batman during the war and later an enormous help on the *Official History of Australia in the War of 1914–1918*, that Bean had envisaged a volume on the chaplains for inclusion in his history. But it was not to be. The *History* had to be trimmed down to the 12 volumes that Bean finally produced. So the story of the chaplains remained untold.

I tried to do something about this and, in 1986, Allen & Unwin published my book *Padre: Australian Chaplains in Gallipoli and France*. Chaplain McKenzie played a role in that book but he might, in truth, have been more prominent. I was told that a daughter lived in Perth and I wrote to see if there were any personal papers remaining that she might consider donating to the Australian War Memorial. Generously and promptly, she donated letters from McKenzie to his wife and children from the front. It was a very important donation.

Even so, the story of "Fighting Mac" remained known only to a few. I remember talking on ABC Radio in my regular Australian history slot about McKenzie. Later I took a phone call from a man who told me that he was in a management position at Rookwood Cemetery in Sydney where McKenzie is buried. This man said that there should be a significant memorial at the grave to this wonderful member of the First Australian Imperial Force. I most warmly agreed but I doubt anything was done. From time to time, I see Salvation Army Officers in my local shopping centre collecting for their various good causes. I ask them if they know of Chaplain McKenzie and his story. Invariably they say that they do not know anything about him.

So the reader might imagine my pleasure at hearing of the writing and publication of this very fine book. At last "Fighting Mac" has the biography that he so thoroughly deserved.

McKenzie was a beacon of hope in the AIF in the atrocious conditions of Gallipoli and the Western Front. His witness to his deeply held religious convictions told Australian soldiers that there were values higher than the horror among which they were living on a daily basis. McKenzie's life of practical Christianity told soldiers that even in the midst of war, all men had an obligation to be doing good to others, of caring for others, and of maintaining—insofar as was possible—the values and standards each soldier had learnt at home.

The great strength of this book, at its very centre, is the account of McKenzie's religious impulses and his spirituality. William McKenzie was not merely a "beaut bloke" and an Australian national treasure who just happened to be a Salvationist. His conversion and his fidelity to his religious beliefs underpinned his life and allowed him to make sense of that life. Here was a true soldier of Christ who would bear witness to his faith in whatever circumstance he was placed. No biography of McKenzie would be appropriate if this were not its centrepiece. Daniel Reynaud understands this and thus gives us the whole man, alive, faithful, remarkable—a servant of his God in whatever setting he was placed.

William McKenzie—"Fighting Mac"—deserves recognition and here he has it. As Daniel Reynaud writes: "If the original Anzacs revered [McKenzie], then we who revere them should pay attention to his story." Who could argue with that?

Dr Michael McKernan
Historian, author and broadcaster

Contents

Foreword v

The Man the Anzacs Revered 1

1. **The Shaping Ground**
   Biggar to Bundaberg, 1869–1887 6
2. **Salvation Army Officer**
   Melbourne to Bendigo, 1887–1914 27
3. **Making His Mark**
   Sydney to Egypt, 1914–1915 54
4. **The Legend is Born**
   Gallipoli, 1915 95
5. **Consolidating the Legend**
   France, 1916–1917 131
6. **The Hero Returns**
   Australia, 1918–1927 177
7. **Front Line Again**
   China, 1927–1930 196
8. **Culmination**
   Australia and Retirement, 1930–1947 214
9. **The Best-known Man in the AIF?**
   The Legacy of "Fighting Mac" 233

Acknowledgments 247
Bibliography 251
Index 257

INTRODUCTION

The Man the Anzacs Revered

William McKenzie was once one of the most famous of the Anzacs. He made his name early in World War I, even before the landings at Gallipoli, but it was on the peninsula that he was elevated from hero to legend. His actions in France only enhanced his standing with the men of the Australian Imperial Forces (AIF). For decades after the war, he attracted crowds of adoring soldiers and their grateful families almost everywhere he went. One historian considered that his popularity in the AIF was unsurpassed, except perhaps by Anzac commander General William Birdwood, and that his post-war fame rivalled that of Australia's wartime prime minister William Hughes.[1] McKenzie never reached a rank higher than Major and his official role involved only the 1st Brigade at most, yet his fame spread across the entire AIF without the inherent advantage of the high-profile public positions of the two other Williams.

What makes the legendary reputation of "Fighting Mac" even more incredible is that he embodied almost everything that the typical digger of the Anzac legend loved to hate. McKenzie was a chaplain, a species of noncombatant officer often held in low esteem.

He railed against booze, brothels, betting and bad language, and he ran frequent evangelistic campaigns for the Anzacs at which he forcefully appealed to them to become Christians. Despite these apparent disadvantages, he was widely known, respected and loved—even worshipped and revered. For 20 years after the war, McKenzie was a celebrity, a magnet for returned servicemen and their families wherever he went across Australia.

Yet, today, McKenzie's name is almost completely unknown outside some Australian religious circles. However, legends continue to be invented about him, adding to the inaccuracies told about him almost from the beginning. But his story needs no embroidering, and the exaggerations—often piously done by both diggers and Christians to enhance his standing among the public—diminish the truth of his real-life achievements.

How did a "wowser" become an Anzac legend? And how did a legend become a virtual unknown today? This is the first biography of Fighting Mac to sort the facts from the fiction and present McKenzie as he was.

McKenzie's first biographer was the prolific Salvation Army writer Adelaide Ah Kow, who published his story in 1949, just two years after McKenzie died.[2] Described as an "honest, gracious author who would have believed everything she wrote to be true,"[3] her biography contains considerable source material obviously obtained firsthand from McKenzie and many who knew him personally. It fills in so much that is otherwise unknown about McKenzie, especially in its wealth of small anecdotes. It is the best of the three biographies of McKenzie to date, and both a delight and a frustration to any later historian. The frustration lies in the absence of documentation behind so many of her fascinating details, especially when she quotes from a now-lost McKenzie diary. Rarely is anyone she quotes named and there is no bibliography or any other information about sources. She wrote in a popular devotional vein for The Salvation Army, and her slant is always toward the positive and occasionally the moralistic. But what it lacks in objectivity, it makes up for in lively story and warmth of tone.

The second biography of McKenzie came in the form of a booklet titled *Fighting Mac* by another Salvationist, Percival Dale.[4] It is short on new material and a considerable amount of its content demonstrably belongs to the realm of legend. As a source, it is of little value.

The third "biography" is self-published by Queensland-based pastor-evangelist Col Stringer.[5] While it suits Stringer's evangelistic purpose, it is not an accurate or reliable account of McKenzie's life.

The origins of the biography you are now reading lie in my own journey of historical exploration and discovery. I have no personal connection to Anzac. The war stories I grew up with were those of my French parents. My father was interned by the Japanese in what was then called French Indochina during World War II. Immediately after, he fought in the French army and then as a civilian truck driver during the early stages of Vietnam's war of independence. Like many war veterans, he rarely spoke about his experiences but, when he did so, it was with clinical objectivity. My mother, whose grandfather was killed in the opening months of the Great War, has more freely recalled her own traumatic experiences of the German occupation of France during World War II. My parents' respective stories showed that war can be recounted both emotionally and dispassionately—and that each communicates its own truth.

Being born and bred in Australia, the Anzac story is familiar to me, becoming "my" story by belonging to the broader Australian culture. Also familiar, having researched and published on Australia's cinema on the subject of the Great War, are the myths and legends surrounding Anzac, which have often distorted the collective memories about the men who fought. Not that the Anzac legend is composed of lies, but rather that its truths are edited to remove the awkward and uncomfortable, those other equally-true-but-dissonant facts that jar against the dominant triumphant notes of Anzac. These elisions slide over the gaps, obscuring the richness, complexity and contradictions of Anzac history.

One such gap in our public memory of Anzac is religion, on which relatively little has been written, on the assumption that there was little to say. I was drawn to this by my interest in matters both military and religious. Stories of war have always fascinated me and much of my historical research has been war-related. I have also been a practicing Christian all my life. Starting first with diaries and letters of Australian chaplains in the Great War, then moving on to searching the diaries and letters of soldiers for references to religion, I found an important trail of evidence opening up.

Among this, naturally, was the story of William McKenzie, whose wartime diary and letters had been donated to the Australian War Memorial by his family. As I explored these papers further, it seemed to me that his was a story with special qualities that deserved to be told again. My father's tendency to objective, analytical truth demanded that I attempt this as accurately as possible. My mother's emotional engagement begged that the fullness of his personality be captured as best as possible. McKenzie's experiences in religions with high expectations felt familiar to me, helping me to give a sympathetic but (I trust) not uncritical account of this key area of his life.

Further details were found in various sources, but principally The Salvation Army archives in Melbourne and Sydney. Of particular help in rounding out the story was information from descendants, especially two of his granddaughters—his eldest and his youngest—who provided family memories that filled vital gaps in the account.

The story that follows is an attempt to capture McKenzie in all his charismatic and energetic complexity, with particular focus on his war years. He was a devout man of God who became enshrined in the hearts of thousands of men who showed little other commitment to things religious. If the original Anzacs revered him, then we who revere them should pay attention to his story.

1. Michael McKernan, *Padre: Australian Chaplains in Gallipoli and France* (Sydney: Allen & Unwin), 1986, page 3; Michael McKernan, "William McKenzie," *Australian Dictionary of Biography*, <http://adb.anu.edu.au/biography/mckenzie-william-7391>, accessed December 19, 2013.
2. *William McKenzie M.C., O.B.E., O.F. Anzac Padre* (London: Salvationist Publishing and Supplies, 1949).
3. Lindsay Cox, Salvation Army Heritage Centre Archivist, Melbourne, in conversation with the author, July 26, 2007.
4. Dale's booklet lacks any publishing details at all. A copy is held in the Salvation Army Heritage Centre, Melbourne.
5. *'Fighting McKenzie' Anzac Chaplain: Tribute to a Hero* (Robina, Qld: Col Stringer Ministries, 2003).

CHAPTER 1

THE SHAPING GROUND

BIGGAR TO BUNDABERG, 1869–1887

Like so many other Anzacs—famous and not so famous—William McKenzie was born in the United Kingdom:[1] in Biggar, South Lanarkshire in Lowland Scotland, on December 20, 1869. His formative years were spent in a cottage nearby and he remained a passionate Scotsman for the rest of his days, his Australian accent acquired in his teens permanently marked by a Scottish burr.[2] He was the third child and eldest son of a family that would eventually consist of six boys and three girls. His older sisters were Anne and Henrietta. Following William were Robert, James (often known as Jas), Alexander (or Sandy), Isabella, Archibald and Evan. All were Scottish born except for Evan, who was born around Bundaberg after the family emigrated to Queensland.

William's father Donald was born in Inverness in 1840, son of William, a labourer, and grandson of Ebenezer—or Evan—a teacher of Highland descent. It would appear that Ebenezer, despite his education, was not a financial success, as his children took up labouring work. The family seems to have alternated between

Highland Inverness and Lowland Biggar. William (Senior) was born in Biggar but married in Inverness, where several of his children were born, before returning to Biggar.

At the age of 50, the ploughman William was left a very valuable legacy that promised a dramatic change of fortune for his working-class family. He told 29-year-old Donald not to renew his six-month labouring contract, as the family would not have to work for a living any more. Unfortunately, soon after, Donald's 11-year-old younger brother James caught typhus at school. His mother Isabella nursed him back to health but caught the disease herself, as did her husband. Isabella died on March 29, 1870, and William followed her on April 8. The practice of burning all the clothing of those infected meant that the papers confirming the inheritance, which the anxious William had carried in his pocket for safe-keeping, were accidentally destroyed, and Donald and his five siblings could not claim the riches that would have given them prosperity. Despite his schoolmaster grandfather and his younger brother's schooling, it appears Donald was illiterate, signing his parents' death certificates with a cross, which would have made it harder for him to pursue the legal avenues to have the inheritance restored.

Many years later—in the 1930s—the grandchildren of William and Isabella, including the junior William, would try to claim the inheritance, but they were unable to do so due to slippery lawyers and the legal window of opportunity having closed.[3] Instead of prosperity and ease, Donald was left with the added burden of a younger brother to raise, while his 20-year-old sister Jane appears to have taken on the 13-year-old Jean.[4] Without the legacy, the McKenzie children were forced to look elsewhere for their future.

Donald McKenzie married Agnes Callan—or Callen—who was born in 1844 and was a deeply religious woman with a history of clergymen in her family. She kept the home. Delving back further into the family history, it is hardly surprising to find Covenanters, preachers and other men of passionate conviction, who were prepared to suffer intense hardship rather than compromise their faith.

The William who is the subject of this book spent his early years in the town of Biggar, which lies on the margins of Lanarkshire and the Border districts, and is about 40 kilometres south-west of Edinburgh and just a little further south-east of Glasgow, and about 70 kilometres north of the English border. With ancient origins, Biggar was important as a regional market town and it had been the site of two castles, the second—called Boghall—built by the Fleming family in medieval times.

Biggar did not escape the turbulent history of the region, notorious for its lawless Border lords constantly raiding and feuding, contesting the overlordship of the Scottish monarchy. These lords frequently raided and were raided by the English, seeking to subdue their unruly northern neighbours.

In the late medieval and early modern period, the Lords Fleming were supporters of the Stewart dynasty[5] and were strategically placed to buttress the southern districts of Scotland for the monarchy. However, they were entangled in the violent politics of the era, with John—the second Lord Fleming—killed in a feud with a rival family in 1524, and his son Malcolm—the third Lord Fleming and Lord Chamberlain to King James V—captured by the English in 1542 at the Battle of Solway Moss and killed in the disastrous Battle of Pinkie Cleugh in 1547 against the same foe.

His son James—Lord Chamberlain to Mary Queen of Scots—was possibly poisoned by the French who were unhappy with the terms of the marriage treaty he helped negotiate in Paris. James' brother, John, inherited the title, the castle and the troubles. Siding with Mary Queen of Scots, he suffered with her as she was driven into exile in England and his own young family was stripped naked then expelled from Boghall Castle by his enemies. Remnants of Boghall and the earlier castle were visible in young William McKenzie's time, whose lively and combative behaviour was in keeping with the heritage of his region.

Closer to a village in size, the town itself sits in a shallow valley with hills rising gently around, dominated to the southwest by Tinto Hill, a rounded dome giving an excellent lookout over the

South Lanarkshire countryside. The River Clyde flows a couple of kilometres to the west, while southern Scotland's other great confluence—the River Tweed—runs about eight kilometres to the east. Biggar is situated on the old Roman road to Edinburgh, which branches off from the main highway between Carlisle, the last great town in northern England, and the city of Glasgow.

Just nine years before William's birth, Biggar gained its own railway station on a new line that connected to the main trunk line. The Industrial Revolution had announced itself earlier, with a coal gas factory established in 1836, which added to the little town's importance, allowing gas lighting in the streets and eventually creating enough for gas cooking and heating as well. However, its stone houses and church, with a gentle brook running through the surrounding lush green meadows, still give an air of rustic charm to the place.

Certain traditions were maintained, such as the annual Hogmanay, the New Year's Eve torchlight parade and bonfire, which is still celebrated in the town. Possibly the Riding of the Boundaries was also a regular tradition, dating from the time when clans would patrol their borders against raiders from neighbouring clans. One can imagine William taking delight in the festivals with their links to ancient Scotland. A popular saying in the region—"Glasgow is big but Biggar is Biggar"—might have been current in William's childhood, perhaps the spark for William's lifelong delight in wordplay. Certainly the town itself retains the tendency, for its new annual folk festival is labelled the "Biggar Little Festival."

McKenzie once summarised his upbringing as "porridge, the shorter catechism and plenty of lickings."[6] It seems an archetypical Scottish childhood, but suggests both that he was a handful and that his religious upbringing had little attraction for him at the time. Although living in the Lowlands, McKenzie's upbringing was suffused with dour Highland values: daily prayers, strict Sunday observance and regular church attendance, with "God first" in everything. It was a religion he later described as "rigid," which must have grated on a restless lad.[7]

The severity of Calvinist Presbyterian rectitude weighed on

him, with its predestinarian belief in God alone choosing who was saved and who was damned. The side you were on became evident through the righteous behaviour of the saved and the wickedness of those destined for hellfire, which must have hinted at a warm afterlife for William. Sundays consisted of a day at church, about four kilometres from the family home. After the morning services, the children remained for Sunday school, arriving home for a late lunch at 3 pm, which hardly can have improved young William's appetite for religion. It is no surprise that as a young man he felt little allegiance to his Presbyterian upbringing, which had failed to hold any emotional appeal. His mother is said to have worried over his wilful and disobedient behaviour, saying regretfully, "Our Wullie is a horrid ill laddie."[8] Yet it was not all scripture and the strap, for both his parents had their softer side. Donald in old age was remembered fondly by a nephew, who recalled the fun and horseplay at occasional family reunions.[9]

The "horrid ill laddie" grew up to be big for his age and, along with an enormous physical energy, he was also energetic and passionate in personality. The combination made for a combative childhood as McKenzie's force of personality collided with that of his peers. Several stories circulate about how he first got his nickname "Fighting Mac," many of which revolve around his pugilistic youth, though no document survives to confirm that he earned the moniker at this young age.

One tale tells of William being arrested by the town sergeant in the middle of a serial fight with another classmate, sharing a couple of terrifying hours in a cell with the corpse of its previous occupant, who had hanged himself. Some time later he met the classmate again, who surprised William by refusing to fight again, as he had been converted.[10] Other accounts centre on variations of playground fights, sometimes taking on the whole school or beating a string of boys older than himself.[11] It is hard to pin down any of these stories with certainty, but they all point to an energetic lad with a militant nature and a willingness to use his large size and robust physique to settle differences.

However, the nickname was not exclusive, achieving a currency in William's youth through the amazing exploits of Hector MacDonald, who had climbed from poor crofter's son to Major General Sir Hector MacDonald, war hero and aide-de-camp to Queen Victoria herself. He became a household name as "Fighting Mac" by the 1890s for his brilliant leadership in various imperial wars, which sometimes saved the reputations of high-profile generals such as Lord Kitchener. It is possible that William was badged in honour of his illustrious compatriot. It could also account for McKenzie's boyhood ambition to join the Seaforth Highlanders and make a career as a soldier.[12] Certainly, the application of the nickname during the Great War was probably influenced by its currency among the troops, especially among the strong Scottish contingent in McKenzie's battalion.[13]

Of the rest of his childhood, his first biographer, Adelaide Ah Kow, is almost our only source. She speaks of an uneven performance at school, showing his inquiring mind, his high spirits and a tendency to get into trouble. She also notes an excellent memory, for which he was famous until his final years, and a passion for poetry and history.[14] Having completed his primary education, William left school around his 13th year and began working, either for a neighbouring farmer, then driving a pony and trap for the local architect, or as an apprentice estate agent.[15] Either way, his dream of being a soldier was deferred.

In 1884—when William was 14—his parents decided to leave Scotland. Having missed out on his father's legacy, prospects at home were limited for Donald McKenzie's sons and the colonies beckoned with their great opportunities for industrious men with a pioneering spirit. Highland Scots had been emigrating for some time in response to the suppression of supporters of the Jacobite Risings in the 18th Century, and continued to leave in growing numbers in the following century as landlords conducted mass evictions of poor subsistence crofters in order to enclose fields for the higher returns of grazing sheep.

The Industrial Revolution also changed employment patterns on farms, as rural Scotland was depopulated by machinery that took over from hand farming and, in the towns, new factories offered opportunities. Some migrated to the industrial city of Glasgow in Lowland Scotland, but others moved to England, or—more commonly—to America, Canada, Australia, New Zealand, India or other British colonies. The military absorbed many unemployed Scotsmen. Scottish regiments, particularly from the Highlands, became famous in colonial campaigns around the world, helping restore their battered national reputation with their English cousins after the rebellions of the previous century. In the mid-to-late 1800s, largely middle-class Lowland Scots joined the great emigration, less under persecution than for economic, social and religious betterment.

Scots often formed the vanguard of the expansion of the British Empire, as administrators and settlers took up the economic advantages and upward social mobility offered by life in the colonies, where they frequently prospered through their habitual hardiness, thrift and industry. They took great pride not just in being British but in being Scottish. Communities with distinct Scottish identities have remained common in the United States, Canada, New Zealand and Australia. Entire regions were dominated by Scottish settlers, such as Nova Scotia in Canada, Otago in New Zealand and the Illawarra and the New England areas of New South Wales, Australia.

The missionary impulse of zealous Presbyterianism was also a strong motivator for a move overseas. Many pioneers in exploration were Scottish missionaries opening up new fields of evangelistic endeavour, followed swiftly—it must be said—by opportunistic and enterprising traders, also often Scotch. Some settlements, particularly in New Zealand, were founded by clergymen seeking to establish communities of righteous Scots, and Scotsmen were frequently behind the drive to establish schools in the colonies to ensure following generations would be literate enough to read the Bible and maintain the true Protestant faith.

In many ways, these emigrants represented core values and attitudes that underpinned the Victorian era and beyond. Religion held a place in society that might surprise the modern observer and, while its beliefs were far from universal even then, Christianity was still seen as the bedrock of civilisation. However, it was marked by deep social divisions, with the Established Churches of England and Scotland—Anglicanism and Presbyterianism, respectively—strongly associated with the ruling classes, and Non-Conformism—represented in Scotland by the evangelical branches of Presbyterianism—more commonly found among the middle classes. As church-going was strongly associated with social respectability, the labouring class was often alienated from any of the churches.

The period was marked by prominent religious reform movements of largely evangelical character initiated by people mostly from the religious and political elites and the middle classes, who refused to accept the inequity and suffering of the working class. These movements energetically sought to engage society at large and renew spirituality, as well as reforming public and private morality, believing they should and could eliminate socio-spiritual evils such as poverty, dirt, ignorance, alcoholism and prostitution. Darwinism may have rocked conventional religious beliefs regarding origins, but it also strengthened the uplifting endeavours of evangelicalism through its promotion of the idea that humanity was evolving for the better, leading to optimism about the human capacity for positive change.

It was also an era of increasing emphasis on the individual. Industrious personal endeavour was preferred over legislative or state intervention, as the actions of individuals rather than governments were seen as the key to progress. Similarly, religion became more a matter of personal conviction than of corporate behaviour. Evangelical Christianity placed great emphasis on the solitary soul's agonising wrestle with sin and of salvation through a personal relationship with Jesus. Such a victory was attained through individual prayer and Bible study, rather than through the work of an ecclesiastical hierarchy administering sacraments. This classically Victorian combination of earnestness, optimism, industry and a zeal for individual improvement would permanently colour the life of William McKenzie.

By the late 1800s, a number of organisations, formal and informal, promoted emigration and the British government published guides to prospective emigrants to help re-establish themselves in the colonies. So Donald McKenzie's decision to emigrate was not radical. It was nourished by the large network of Scots in British colonies around the world and specifically encouraged by the emigration of his own siblings. His sister Jane had moved to New Zealand in 1872 with her husband, taking the 15-year-old sister Jean with her. In 1883, his brother Evan moved to the colony of Queensland, followed by Alexander (Sandy) who arrived there in January, 1884, leaving just the eldest, Donald, and the youngest, James, in Scotland.

Teasingly, Sandy had a chance encounter with a lawyer in Edinburgh as he was preparing to leave, who recognised the name and promised to have old William's inheritance money released from Chancery—but nothing came of it. The incident persuaded Donald that attempting to recover the fortune was a waste of time and money.[16] So, a few months later, Donald decided to move as well. Later, James would join the brothers in Queensland in 1888.

Donald and Agnes set out for the "New World," with seven children—the youngest, Alexander, Isabella and Archibald, aged just four, two and one. Curiously, there is no record of Donald's eldest daughter Anne emigrating with the family. Aged about 19, she may have had employment or have been married, but the records are silent on her status and fate.

Despite the family connection to the Antipodes, Donald's first choice seems to have been Canada, the most popular destination for Scottish emigrants. Perhaps it felt closer culturally as well as geographically. Taking the train to London, the McKenzies found that unscrupulous shipping agents had overbooked the ship on which they were to sail and the authorities prevented them from boarding. They soon diverted to Queensland, aboard the 2000-ton *Merkara*, a passenger and cargo steam ship built in 1875 and operated by the British India Steam Navigation Company, which had started the first direct London–Brisbane mail run just three years earlier. They left London on September 23, 1884, arriving in

Brisbane on November 18, before transferring to the 260-ton coastal steamer *Lady Musgrave*,[17] named after the colonial governor's wife, for the voyage to Bundaberg, where William's uncles Sandy and Evan lived.

But on the voyage to Australia, William's fighting instincts had come to the fore again. According to Ah Kow, he attacked an Irish boy who was helping himself from the McKenzie's food cupboard and the fight degenerated into a contest between the rival national factions. Eventually, the ship's captain had to confine the ringleaders in order to stop the feud. It is another source for the nickname "Fighting Mac."[18] Whenever the nickname arose, William's behaviour must have added to the woes of the voyage. With three of her seven children under the age of five, Agnes did not need her teenage son causing extra problems. Presumably, the 16-year-old Henrietta provided help in minding the younger ones.

The Queensland in which the McKenzies arrived was a vigorous young self-governing colony, with a population of about 250,000 in 1884. Like many British settlements on Australia's eastern coastline, it had begun as a convict settlement around Brisbane in 1824. But convict transportation ceased by 1839 and the first shipload of free immigrants arrived in 1848. Queensland became a self-governing colony with its separation from New South Wales in 1859 and its economy received a boost from a series of small gold rushes from the late 1850s.

Another boom industry encouraged by the colonial government was sugar cane, which spread up the coast from Brisbane. A commonly-held view of the time was that the European constitution was unsuited to a tropical climate, an opinion supported by the horrific death-rates of whites from tropical diseases in equatorial Africa and the West Indies. Popular racial theories held that non-whites had more animal-like resistance to the fevers that ravaged their white racial superiors. Non-white labour was thus seen as essential as it was better adapted. The precedent had been set in other colonies, particularly those of the West Indies, where black slave labour had been used until slavery in the British Empire had been abolished, only to be replaced by its close relative, indentured labour, which could operate under near-slave conditions for minimal wages.

For a labour-intensive industry such as sugar cane, the added advantage of coloured labour was that it could be obtained very cheaply, compared to the relatively high wages of white workers in Australia. Without the cheap labour that convict transportation once offered the early colonists, cane farmers turned to the use of indentured labour, largely brought from the nearby Melanesian island groups of New Caledonia, the Solomon Islands and the New Hebrides (now Vanuatu). Some of these labourers came voluntarily; others were tricked or kidnapped by crooked shipping agents in a process known as "blackbirding."

Some 62,000 islanders—called Kanakas at the time—were brought to Queensland over about 40 years from 1862. The standard contract was for three years and many signed up again, suggesting that conditions were not intolerable. Nevertheless, the use of Kanaka labour caused controversy in Australia, partly over its resemblance to slavery, but more over fears of racial contamination, and that it would undercut white wages and working conditions. Already there had been ugly violent scenes over the presence of large numbers of Chinese on the gold-fields in Victoria and New South Wales, and Queensland had passed legislation to restrict Chinese immigration in the 1870s. A separatist movement in northern Queensland was accused by its opponents of wanting to establish a separate colony in order to create a planter's aristocracy based on black labour.[19]

Bundaberg itself was a pioneering township in 1884. Established in the late 1860s as a timber settlement about 385 kilometres north of Brisbane and about 15 kilometres inland on the Burnett River, it switched to maize in the 1870s as the sources of timber were exhausted. Sugar took over as the principal industry when maize suffered from an onslaught of diseases and pests. Gazetted a municipality in 1881, Bundaberg was surrounded by a number of small sugar plantations, with a handful of larger mills capable of producing raw sugar, the first opening in 1882.

Farming in subtropical Bundaberg was a vastly different proposition from the small-scale ploughmanship that William's father was used to in Biggar. After working for a prominent dairy farmer—Robert Hamilton—for almost two years, Donald established his own farm of about 160 hectares (400 acres) at Electra in the district of South Kolan on the Burnett River, about 25 kilometres upstream from Bundaberg. Such a landholding would have been a landed gentleman's estate by Scottish standards but nothing unusual in the colony. Although sugar cane was the principal crop, McKenzie practiced a more familiar mixed farming, with some maize, fruit trees, pineapples, horses and cattle.[20] As was typical of the district, Donald McKenzie employed a dozen or so Kanakas.[21] Grief and joy touched the family in the early years: Isabella died at South Kolan, aged about 3 or 4 of what family tradition calls cot death, although the exact cause is not known; and Evan was born around 1890, completing the family.[22]

William began working for his father but the Scotsman in Donald saw no reason to pay his own son any wages for working on the family farm, so the young man soon became restless for more independence. He had earlier earned pocket money by working a milk run with his cousin William, son of Sandy,[23] for Hamilton, the farmer who first employed Donald McKenzie, but now he wanted a better income. Aged 17, William left home to work at "Bucca Bucca," a horse and dairy farm where his uncle was the manager. Then he moved to a large dairy farm to gain experience, with an eye to setting up as a squatter himself.[24]

William's departure from home also freed him from the burden of religious rituals, such as church attendance. His devoted mother had created in her home a "prophet's room"[25] for itinerant preachers of any flavour who happened to need accommodation—and it was frequently used. Not keen on religion, William made it clear to visiting clergy that he considered them unwelcome guests. Among them was an Officer of The Salvation Army, for whom young William had some contempt. He disliked the way The Army worked with the "deadbeats and other weak atoms of humanity."[26] He was still Calvinist enough to despise people who had demonstrated their own damnation by letting themselves sink so low, feeling that they deserved their fate. Asked to show the Officer around the district, William attempted a measure of sabotage by offering him a highly-strung horse, but the Officer managed his mount without incident,[27] which must have disappointed the unhelpful McKenzie.

At one stage, William returned home but moved on to the "Hopeful" sugar farm in order to expand his horizons, vowing to become fully independent before contacting his parents again. The large plantation was seeking an overseer for its 60 Kanakas and score of Chinese workers. He bluffed the Scottish owner into thinking he was 22, still rather young for an overseer, but McKenzie's size—he was already over 185 centimetres tall and weighed a solid 82 kilograms—freshly-cultivated moustache and side whiskers, and absolute self-confidence persuaded the landowner to give him a try. Little did he know that McKenzie was only 17, but the young man justified the trust placed in him and proved to be a very good overseer, reputedly more effective than those who had preceded him.[28]

Despite his success, William was feeling homesick and a chance meeting with his mother, who was returning from an unfruitful attempt to find him in Bundaberg, allowed the young man to come home without losing too much face. It was still an uneasy reunion. William was openly questioning the religion of his parents, upsetting his mother with atheist opinions he had picked up from others. But his behaviour strayed little from the norms expected of a good Presbyterian boy and he remained a fine Christian to all outward appearances.[29]

To retain some measure of independence from his parents, William set up a room in a barn some distance from the family home where he could read and ponder at leisure. His anti-Christian opinions reflected his own searching. While the religion of his upbringing failed to capture him, he had not abandoned the possibility that there might be something in Christianity. The earnestness of his questioning had been sharpened by the death of his young sister Isabella a few years earlier.

Characteristically, his searching was not passive. William read by hurricane lantern in the barn and even attended some of the open-air meetings of The Salvation Army in town. While he was uncomfortable with their work, he found himself increasingly drawn to their activist brand of Christianity, impressed by their commitment in the face of mockery and violence. It had the passion, conviction, physicality and risk that he so clearly missed in his own religion. He had first heard Salvation Army preachers in the streets of London before leaving Britain; on his arrival in Brisbane, he had again seen them in action.

The Salvation Army was a relatively new movement. It grew out of the personal ministry of Methodist preacher William Booth, who caught a vision for working with the social outcasts often ignored by both the Established Church and the Non-Conformist churches. But it was classically Victorian in its attempts to improve the spiritual, moral and social welfare of the down-trodden, and it inherited the revivalist fervour of other Non-Conformist movements such as the Wesleyans, with its regular appeals for converts to come forward at large public meetings.

Beginning his ministry in 1865, by 1880, Booth's movement had a name—The Salvation Army—a uniform and a quasi-military organisation. Membership required taking an oath before a revered flag emblazoned with trinitarian symbols and the motto "Blood and Fire," symbolising its determined war on Satan, sin and social injustice. The Army's direct confrontation of institutions that created and sustained the cycle of poverty led to active opposition from publicans and pimps, often spilling over into violence toward Officers holding public rallies. Opponents organised themselves into the "skeleton army," disrupting meetings and assaulting Officers with missiles, sticks and fists, and Army halls were sometimes vandalised. Law enforcement officers were known to watch passively while assaults on Army meetings were in progress.

Respectable society was equally offended by this new religion that manifested itself in the streets with noisy brass bands and an effusive, emotionally-charged religious expression. The Salvation Army threatened the social order by championing the addicts, alcoholics, prostitutes and other outcasts, and allowing women equality with men, and it found itself marginalised by many respectable Christian denominations. Its demanding standards of behaviour—no alcohol, smoking, gambling or swearing, and a strict Sunday-keeping, for example—also made its members outsiders in both secular and mainstream religious circles, although it was close in attitude both to Booth's Methodism and McKenzie's Presbyterianism in this respect.

The movement came to Australia in 1880. By the time the McKenzies arrived in Australia, it had several thousand adherents and 12 Corps—as Salvation Army churches are known. Its work extended to Queensland in 1885, and a Corps established in Bundaberg on September 6, 1886. It was equally difficult in the colonies for the new movement: in Brisbane soldiers were assaulted by gangs of as many as 200 youths; and more than 100 Salvation Army workers were prosecuted over several decades throughout the colonies and the new Commonwealth on various charges of disturbing the peace.[30] But there was something in The Army's courage and conviction that piqued McKenzie's curiosity and grudging admiration.

The key turning point in McKenzie's life was his dramatic conversion experience at the age of 19. Praying and wrestling spiritually in his barn, one night in July, 1887, McKenzie had "a powerful revelation of the Spirit of God" and felt an overwhelming conviction of his own sinfulness. Fearful of sleeping lest he wake up in Hell, he was so distressed that he could neither work nor eat. Then he heard an audible voice that instructed him to go to Bundaberg and find The Salvation Army. Surprised, he looked around and saw no-one, so he ignored the impression.

But the next night and the following two nights, he heard the same voice. At 4 am on Friday, he finally vowed to go to Bundaberg on the following Sunday.[31] But being the type who never delayed in acting on conviction, he saddled his borrowed horse that day and rode the 27 kilometres into town to present himself at the theatre where The Salvation Army met.[32] Unfortunately, he chose a time when the

Corps was holding a "soldiers' meeting" to which non-members were not admitted. McKenzie took lodgings overnight and waited for the meeting the next night—Saturday, July 23, 1887.

That evening he was detained by a talkative acquaintance and, when McKenzie finally tore himself away, he rushed to the theatre just in time to hear the appeal for penitents to come forward. Spurs clicking, he immediately marched down the aisle, a walk that felt a mile long, to the Penitent-form—or Mercy-seat, as it was often called by Salvationists—the bench at the front of the hall where those seeking salvation could pray with Army soldiers. He recorded that he was struggling with his Calvinist ideas, which conflicted with the concept that he could freely choose to accept the offer of God's grace.[33]

At the bench, he was met by an earnest young Cadet—a trainee Officer—who in his eagerness promised McKenzie "a wonderful thrill" as he experienced the touch of God. Nothing happened and a disappointed McKenzie was then counselled by a wiser Officer, who pointed out that salvation was simply a contract between him and God, not necessarily an emotional encounter. He quoted the scripture, "Him that cometh unto Me, I will in no wise cast out" (John 6:37).

"Immediately," McKenzie later recounted, "my mind grasped the great outstanding fact that here I had come to God in my need, believing He was the only One who could meet that need, and that He was able and ready to do so. I said, 'I will trust God to save me now;' and with the prayer, 'God, be merciful to me, a sinner,' I rose from my knees and passed from the Hall."[34] McKenzie would always remember July 23, 1887, as his spiritual birthday.[35]

The emotional consequence of his decision burst through on his ride home the next day. Fearing his own weakness and wrestling with doubt over the previous day's events, he cried out in prayer, "O God, I do not want to make a fool of this! I believe Jesus died for me. Save me, for Christ's sake." He felt an immediate answer, a sense of transformation, of joyful assurance of his salvation and he gave a tremendous "Hallelujah!"[36]

With his characteristic urgency, he took up the challenge that The Salvation Army Captain had given him to be bold in witnessing about his faith. Being bold was natural to McKenzie and he confronted the first person he met—a tough bullocky coming the other way—in a direct and tactless fashion. Calling him a drunkard, scoundrel and waster, McKenzie urged him to go to The Salvation Army and get converted. The startled bullocky could not wait to escape. Others he met on his trip were similarly confronted, with predictable results.

McKenzie then went to church, where his father and brothers were. At the end of the service, he stood up and announced his decision to the astonished congregation. Naturally, his mother was alarmed and his father was angry. But nothing would diminish McKenzie's religious activism, having been warned that opposition would result from his decision, and he visited everyone he knew to tell them of his change of heart, urging them to do the same.[37]

The dramatic conversion of McKenzie evokes different reactions in modern readers. For many Christians, particularly those of an evangelical persuasion, his story may seem quite normal. But for those of no faith or little religious background, McKenzie's apparent direct connection with God, hearing his voice in clear, unambiguous terms, may sound more like the workings of religious extremism or mental instability. Yet McKenzie poses a dilemma for many people. He repeatedly testified of talking with God, and his spiritual life manifested many seemingly mystical elements.

Furthermore, we still have to account for a young man who rebelled against the demands of a puritanical religion, yet found fulfilment and liberation in joining another that by any standards was even more demanding of self-discipline and self-denial. For the rest of his life, this strong-willed character embraced every demand to subordinate himself to his religious organisation, which he perceived as the will of God, and did so with every appearance of joy, throwing himself into his work with a singular energetic commitment that marked him out as exceptional, even in an organisation noted for its highly committed individuals.

The overwhelming testimony of his life is that he was perfectly sane. He was almost universally admired and respected as a man and as a Christian, by those who had no religious convictions, even by many who were decidedly anti-Christian. The austere qualities of his religion that would normally mark him as marginalised in Australian society—the wowser, fundamentalist killjoy—only had a superficial impact. Instead, this man of intensely spiritual energy became one of the most popular, respected and recognisable figures in inter-war Australia, by any measure what today would be labelled a celebrity.

A useful framework for understanding the nature of McKenzie's spiritual experience in July, 1887, can be found in literature relating to men's initiation. Richard Rohr's *Adam's Return: The Five Promises of Male Initiation*[38] provides a handy synthesis of much of this, noting that initiation rites common to many cultures and religions all begin with a need for a ritual dying and rebirth, a concept that matches exactly McKenzie's dramatic conversion experience. His own sinfulness struck him forcibly before his conversion and he retained a sense of his own brokenness throughout his life, constantly returning in earnest prayer to the God of grace who forgave his sinful condition.

After his conversion, McKenzie incarnated Rohr's five lessons of the initiated man: he joyfully accepted that life was hard, that he wasn't important, that life wasn't about him, that he was no longer in control, and he was fully aware but not afraid of his own mortality. In short, he let go of what humans normally hold on to. Acceptance of these five truths liberated him into a life of fullness, compassion and action, making religion "much more of an affirmation of life itself and love's possibility, rather than a funereal fear of death, judgment and hell. True religion is always an occasion for joyful mysticism rather than a grim test of moral endurance." Of people touched by such a transformation Rohr writes, "they often grow more radiant, more flexible and more compassionate with age."

For McKenzie, it was his gateway from a legalistic, moralistic and mournful religion into one of liberation, joy and fulfilment. But there was nothing sentimental or soft about his new faith; if anything the demands of Salvationism shaded those of his old Presbyterianism.

The difference was in the change of heart and outlook in McKenzie. As McKenzie reflected years later of The Salvation Army:

> What a religion! Why, it was the real article! It meant giving up things—drink, tobacco and much else—and facing scorn and derision. It meant going down to the mud and slime; it meant living with the lowest and the worst; it meant fighting with the devil himself for the souls of men. Lo', it snatched me clean out of myself. It hit me, like a blow. It was so real, so honest. I said to myself "here's the true religion for a fighting man;" and off I went to be converted and to sign on.[39]

This empowered him to transform a religion full of do's and don'ts—of "moral endurance"—into one of "joyful mysticism," devoid of fear and characterised by joyful compassion.

1. The most notable example is John Simpson, of donkey fame, who spent only four years in Australia before dying on Gallipoli and being posthumously cast as the archetypical Australian hero.
2. On one occasion, he was described as "a Scot of the Scots" and, in 1930, he wrote of the primacy of Australia in his heart, with the caveat that "in sentiment, Scotland comes first": *War Cry*, December 10, 1898; William McKenzie, "Australia is my first love," *Melbourne Herald*, June 14, 1930, page 271.
3. Letter from William McKenzie (son of Sandy) to William McKenzie (son of Evan), dated March 7, 1937 (actually written February 27), held by author, courtesy of Rhonda Symonds. These two Williams were cousins to the subject of this biography.
4. Family papers, held by author, courtesy of Rhonda Symonds.
5. As they were then known. Mary Queen of Scots popularised the French spelling of Stuart, by which they are better known.
6. Michael McKernan, "William McKenzie," *Australian Dictionary of Biography* (Online Edition) <www.adb.online.anu.edu.au/biogs/A100299b.htm>, accessed August 13, 2013.

7. *War Cry*, February 11, 1933, page 8; William McKenzie, "Australia is my first love."
8. Adelaide Ah Kow, *William McKenzie M.C., O.B.E., O.F. Anzac Padre* (London: Salvationist Publishing and Supplies, 1949), page 6.
9. Letter from William McKenzie (son of Sandy) to William McKenzie (son of Evan), March 7, 1937.
10. Ah Kow, page 6.
11. Envoy George Hazell, podcast, <www.chr.org.au/audio/fighting-macKenzie-podcasts/MacKenzie-Track-01.mp3>, accessed July 25, 2013.
12. "Troubadour for Christ," *The Musician*, September, 1947, page 8; Harold Begbie, "Captain Mac . . . A famous Salvationist," *War Cry*, March 3, 1917, page 3.
13. Sadly, MacDonald came to a tragic end. When allegations of homosexuality were published in 1903, he shot himself in a Paris hotel. However, his fame continued and he was the subject of popular poetry, memorials and also of an ongoing myth that he in fact escaped Paris to start a new life in disguise, seen variously in Asia and Germany (as General von Mackensen!). He remains a folk hero in Scotland today.
14. Ah Kow, pages 5–6.
15. "Ivan Hoe," "The Farmer's Son who Became M.C., O.B.E., O.F.," *The Young Soldier*, February 5, 1949, page 5; Ah Kow, page 6.
16. Letter from William McKenzie to William McKenzie, March 7, 1937.
17. The *Lady Musgrave* was wrecked on the sand bar off Ballina on March 28, 1904, in a storm, but without loss of life.
18. Ah Kow, page 7.
19. Christine R Doran, "Separation movements in North Queensland in the Nineteenth Century," in B J Dalton (editor), *Lectures on North Queensland History*, Third Series (Townsville: James Cook University of North Queensland, 1979), page 93.
20. "Ivan Hoe," page 5.
21. McKenzie, "Australia is my first love."
22. Family papers, held by author, courtesy of Rhonda Symonds.
23. Just to keep things confusing, Evan McKenzie also had a son William, making a total of three cousins all called William McKenzie in and around Bundaberg at the time.
24. G J Donnellan, "Fighting Mac," *Reveille*, March 1, 1933, page 8.
25. On the biblical model of the Shunemite woman, who built a guest room for the prophet Elisha to stay in when he passed through (see 2 Kings 4:8–10).
26. "The Scot We Know," *The Scottish Australasian*, August 1918, page 6416.
27. Ah Kow, page 9.
28. Ah Kow, page 7.
29. *War Cry*, February 11, 1933, page 8.
30. <www.salvationarmy.org.au/en/Who-We-Are/History-and-heritage/Opposition-and-acceptance-of-The-Salvation-Army/>, accessed August 26, 2013.
31. Ah Kow, pages 8–9; "Tremendous Tribute-Paying at Newcastle to Commissioner and Mrs McKenzie," *War Cry*, February 27, 1937, page 7.
32. Their own custom-built Hall was opened later that year.

33. *War Cry*, March, 18, 1939.
34. Ah Kow, pages 9–10.
35. Letter to Hay, August 2, 1915, PR 85/815, Letters of Major W McKenzie 4th Bn, Australian War Memorial.
36. *War Cry*, March 18, 1939.
37. Ah Kow, pages 10–11.
38. Richard Rohr, *Adam's Return: The Five Promises of Male Initiation* (New York: Crossroads, 2004), pages 1–10.
39. Begbie, *War Cry*, March 3, 1917, page 3.

CHAPTER 2

SALVATION ARMY OFFICER

MELBOURNE TO BENDIGO, 1887–1914

William McKenzie spent two more years in Bundaberg, developing his personal spirituality and becoming active as a soldier in the ranks of his Corps. He took his devotional life very seriously, describing his early-day battling as a follower of Christ, when "he often read his Bible and prayed till two and three o'clock in the morning, weeping for joy of soul. In order that he might pray aloud and shout if so moved, he had a bed in a shed a quarter of a mile from the homestead. Here he wrestled with God and here, without any to help, he became fully sanctified."[1]

His desire was for both a transformation of his own character and a fire for the salvation of others, and the habit of long and intense personal spiritual devotion remained with him for life. William saw a direct connection between his own spiritual life and the impact of his ministry on others, often driving himself back to all-night prayer sessions, weeping over the souls of the lost, especially when the number of seekers at his services was less than he expected.[2] It is said that in the two years of his time as a soldier in Bundaberg, he brought 62 people to the same decision point for Christ that he himself had experienced.[3] Helped by one of his brothers, he held meetings in the local Methodist church to build up those who had joined him.

It was hardly surprising that soon McKenzie bent his thoughts toward becoming a Salvation Army Officer. His mother was disappointed with the news. Her dream of seeing him become a Presbyterian minister was shattered. His father was even more upset, throwing him out of the house and disowning him. Only after William came home from World War I in 1918—30 years later—was Donald able to overcome his Scottish stubbornness and admit to his son that his decision to become an Officer was the right one.[4]

Shunted out of home, McKenzie found work elsewhere but troubles accumulated. He had a bout of typhoid fever, then lost many of his goods and all his savings in a fire that burnt out his camp. It is hardly a wonder that the homeless young man of 19, prone to heights of spiritually intensity, also suffered from periods of depression at this time.[5]

McKenzie applied to The Salvation Army training home on Punt Road, Melbourne, to become an Officer and received a letter dated June 4, 1889, accepting him for training. The letter outlined the rigorous conditions McKenzie was expected to abide by. It stated that if he was found to be unsuitable he would "cheerfully return to your post among your comrades in the private ranks of the Army." It was accompanied by another printed letter that set out the strict rules for training: no criticism of superiors, no disobedience, punctuality required, steady application and so forth.[6] If the pre-conversion William McKenzie had attended, it is hard to see him surviving long under such discipline, but now he delighted in the rigours to which he was subjected.

The life of a Salvation Army Officer was no joke: William Booth had created an autocratic organisation that took its discipline seriously. Its soldiers and Officers could expect no kid-glove treatment, either from The Army or the people among whom they were expected to work. The Army demanded high standards of self-sacrifice from its recruits, promising nothing more than hardship and persecution in the service of Christ.

McKenzie's new attitude showed on the boat trip to Melbourne. His previous sea voyage had been marked by fights in defence of family and national honour; now he became the subject of jokes, which he took with a patient grace and humour that turned his enemies into admiring friends. He ran meetings on board with another Salvation Army cadet but, when the weather turned rough, a couple of sailors teased him as a "Jonah" and dangled him overboard. Despite having the brawn to answer back in his former fashion—around this time, he described his own hands as being the size of "a leg of mutton"—this time he laughed and told them their efforts would be wasted, as he was glory-bound if he drowned. The sailors' response showed that they now had some respect for this religious firebrand. Because he seemed a good sport, they pulled him back on deck.[7]

Arriving in Melbourne on June 26 as a stranger to the city,[8] McKenzie revelled in his new environment at the Punt Road Training Home. He was soon marked out as a leader of great potential, exhibiting not just intense spiritual commitment but also remarkable energy, a retentive memory, a lively attitude and an irresistible charisma. While he easily managed his studies, he was at his best when working with people. He loved with enormous passion the chance to sell The Salvation Army's newspaper, *The War Cry*, which he considered "a power for good, a weapon with which to fight evil."[9]

In the face of opposition, McKenzie was fearless. His huge size and absolute confidence made him a formidable opponent. As a trainee and later as an Officer, he regularly went into places that posed the highest risk to his physical wellbeing, especially hotels, confronting publicans and patrons alike with direct speech and action. Any abuse he received was answered with unfailing good humour as McKenzie ploughed straight on with his mission, totally undeterred. The inability of opposition to deflect him from his mission or even ruffle his spirits often captured the moral high ground in the eyes of observers and left his opponents baffled, even charmed.

When threatened with physical assault, McKenzie usually removed himself from the offender's presence and, although some blows were landed, his huge frame seemed to absorb them with little ill effect. On one rare occasion, he is recorded as having replied with a gentle violence of his own: a drunken heckler threatened to dump him in the horse trough if he didn't stop his open-air meeting outside the pub. Naturally, McKenzie continued, but it was the heckler who got the dipping—not William—after a dextrous sidestep from McKenzie saw his opponent fall in.[10]

The final six weeks of McKenzie's training involved a walking tour of rural Victoria as part of a 40-strong group of Cadets under the title of "the Royal Life Guards."[11] The group covered 500 kilometres on foot, selling *The War Cry*, conducting public meetings—often in the open air—and visiting homes of people who showed an interest. McKenzie played the E-flat bass—popularly known as the tuba—in the band, on the principle of "big man, big heavy instrument." Given The Salvation Army's reliance on brass bands as an attention-getter at public meetings, it is unsurprising that he had taken up brass instruments while a soldier in the Bundaberg Corps and he showed a talent for music that stood him in good stead during the war years.

Carrying everything they needed, the walking tour generated many blisters and pains, but it was considered good hardening up for their future life as a Salvation Army Officer, which was not supposed to be easy. McKenzie demonstrated his character in an incident outside Trentham. After a hot and dusty morning, the group was refreshed with tea and hot scones. Then they marched about 10 kilometres along the railway line in pouring rain. Near Daylesford, the Bandmaster called on them to begin playing and McKenzie realised he had left his music behind at Trentham. The Bandmaster suggested that someone else would pick it up later, to which McKenzie replied, "Indeed you won't. I left it there, and *I'm* going to walk back and get it." And so he did, all the while in the rain.[12]

On completion of his training, McKenzie was commissioned as a Lieutenant—the Salvation Army's term for ordination as a novice minister—and posted to Newcastle, one of the most challenging

Corps, on January 18, 1890. It was an industrial city, renowned for its working-man's culture in the coal mines, copper smelters and soap factory. "A tough place it was, I can tell you!" McKenzie himself wrote of it. "But in those days the Salvation Army was a target for ridicule and abuse."[13] Nonetheless he received ongoing support from colleagues, and a letter survives from one of his former Training Home mentors to inquire after the wellbeing of his soul and to encourage him in spiritual disciplines.[14]

The self-described "raw Lieutenant" was given the sole responsibility of selling *The War Cry* by his Corps Captain. His first action was to double the order for the new 16-page edition from 600 to 1200. The alarmed Corps Captain threatened him with paying for any losses from his own pocket. But the Captain had underestimated his new Lieutenant. McKenzie set out each day to various suburbs, working all day without lunch, filling up with water to assuage his appetite. Arriving home after 7 pm, he would then have dinner, his first meal since breakfast. In this way, he averaged 600 to 700 copies weekly—and he organised women from the Corps to sell the rest. He was never out of pocket, as all copies always sold.[15]

If that wasn't enough, McKenzie was also responsible for the foundation of an Outpost—a new Salvation Army church before it is given Corps status—in a Newcastle suburb. One day a Tighes Hill customer asked him if there were no souls to save in her district. Stung by the woman's challenge McKenzie immediately hired a hall, engaging it for the following evening. He held meetings there and under the Moreton Bay fig trees on a nearby piece of wasteland, on ground that was later turned into a park. The result of his labours was immediate. His first converts came on his first night, and led to the establishment of the Outpost of Tighes Hill. In 1937, as Commissioner for Eastern Australia, McKenzie visited Tighes Hill, which then boasted a flourishing Corps.[16]

The Salvation Army had a habit of moving its staff frequently—particularly junior staff—and barely four months into his appointment to Newcastle, McKenzie was posted to West Maitland (now known as Maitland) on May 24, 1890. Then came moves to Taree on

October 11, 1890, and—after promotion to Captain—to Hill Grove on February 14, 1891, as Corps Officer. Geographically, some moves were not far, but it meant starting again, building contacts and a reputation in the local community. However, McKenzie was not complaining. He adored the challenge of his work. In the meantime, his personal records in the Salvation Army files indicate how well he was regarded by his superiors. Soon after his posting to Newcastle, his first review rated him as "spiritual, devoted and loyal: fairly lively: fair musician, promising." A year later, his review read, "Splendid fellow, will make a good Captain."[17]

On May 9, 1891, he received Marching Orders to a less desirable new posting. He was sent to the staff of the *Junior Soldier War*, the Salvation Army's magazine for children, where he gained experience in magazine editing. From there, he went to another staff posting as Divisional War Office Scribe for New South Wales. In December, he was appointed Colonial War Office Scribe in Sydney, then moved to Brisbane and the Wide Bay Division—the latter including his old stomping ground of Bundaberg—as War Office Senior Scribe on May 13, 1892. In each case, the language refers to roles in various administrative headquarters of The Salvation Army.

As always, McKenzie gave his best in these positions but staff work did not suit his temperament or his passion. At every opportunity, he escaped the offices and joined in field work.[18] He would drop into pubs after work hours to talk with men at the bar, and try to sell them *The War Cry* and turn the conversations to spiritual things. It not only served his passion for the "lost," but also ensured he stayed in touch with ordinary Australian men, who often had little interest in religion. While he held strong opinions about God, salvation and sin, which he expressed in forthright terms, he also had the capacity to listen carefully and respectfully to those who disagreed with him. One of his co-workers said of him, "He believed that every man had a right to his own opinion and, though he could hold his own with ease, he listened cheerfully to the side presented by the other chap."[19]

His posting to Brisbane also allowed him to catch up with his family on occasion. Such times must have been precious as his hectic schedule and the various postings in The Salvation Army offered few other opportunities to see them. His youngest brother Evan—born in 1890—was almost a stranger to him, as he had left the area just before he was born.

After nearly two years of staff duties, McKenzie was thrilled to be returned to a Corps posting. "Glory be to God!" he wrote, "I'm glad I'm going to the Field again."[20] Associates noted that he "revelled in close contact with the people."[21] He received postings to four different Corps commands in Queensland over the next two years, beginning with Toowoomba in mid-March, 1893, then Charters Towers in November, followed by Townsville in September, 1894, and Ipswich two months later. Again, two of these appointments were tough mining towns: Charters Towers—at that stage a booming gold-mining town with a population to rival that of Brisbane—and Ipswich, also a coal town. But McKenzie poured his immense energy into the leadership of the Corps.

He began soul-saving meetings on arrival, and his journal[22] summarised his daily activities. Every night, except Tuesdays, he held public meetings either indoors or out, and these often followed long hours of visitation during the day. He was not a gifted public speaker, often searching for the right words, but could be moved to eloquence by the force of his feelings. What he did well was lead the singing, spice his preaching with wit and humour, and put his messages in simple, accessible and forcible language.[23] His animated delivery and above all his utter sincerity, which shone through everything he did, made him effective. Of course, the endless practice improved his rhetorical skills as well.

McKenzie felt that every public meeting should result in souls saved. He despaired if one closed without candidates—or not enough of them—at the Penitent-form. "*No souls*," ran a line in his diary, underlined for emphasis, and later, after successive nights without visible results, "Nobody saved. Lord help us!"[24] Yet these times were few. At such times, he would pour out his heart in prayer for hours at night, concerned that his own spiritual failings may have been a contributing factor, often weeping with intense emotion over the needs of sinners, and his preaching the next day was often fruitful. But he relied not only on earnest prayer; he was also remarkably inventive in the kinds of meetings he ran: "Never at a loss for ideas for attracting crowds, William organised meetings where bachelors, spinsters, married couples and other groups and personalities were put into the spotlight."[25] His meetings were never for the sake of it; they were always evangelistic in intent.

Several specific instances reveal something of the character of his work during these years. The Toowoomba Corps acquired the nickname the Toowoomba Tearaways, "for their pep and zeal."[26] On one occasion as he was on his way home after a heavy day's work, he heard the same voice he had heard in South Kolan, urging him to enter the house on his left. It was the home of a total stranger but McKenzie obeyed. Answering his knock was a couple in distress, with the wife in an alcoholic rage having attempted to murder her equally drunk husband. McKenzie spoke, prayed and persisted, finally persuading them to come to his evening meeting. They went—McKenzie still dinnerless—where the couple were saved. In years to come, he would meet them again, still loyal Salvationists.[27]

At Charters Towers, he found a large Corps of about 300 meeting in a hall that often attracted 1000 people. Yet the apparent prosperity was tempered by a low rate of conversions and a massive debt. Slackness and debt offended every sensibility he had, from the Scottish to the Salvationist, and he quickly organised a novel way to address both issues: a picnic on a grand scale on the Burdekin River, with a special train put on to move the crowds. It attracted 2000 attendees and produced enough revenue to nearly wipe out the debt. Having captured the attention and goodwill of the town, McKenzie organised his Corps into six companies, running open-air meetings in simultaneous locations to avoid clogging the streets with their audiences. For weeks, there was little result. But a visiting Salvation Army official reported in February, 1894, on his visit to Charters Towers, "that the Army is very much *in evidence* on this famous goldfield."

McKenzie's flamboyant style was illustrated when the major was "seized in a most unceremonious fashion" at the railway station and dropped 'in the centre of a great crowd of people, who seemed to be dressed in all the colours of the rainbow." The Officer continued his report:

> In addition to the brass band, the soldiers had provided themselves with some curious instruments, the sound produced from them being a strange conglomeration, but the object of the march was gained, the town was stirred from end to end, and the three days' meeting we were to hold thoroughly announced. All day on Sunday the attendances were A1, though the results were somewhat disappointing, as we had certainly looked forward to a great breakthrough on the part of sinners, especially when we faced that tremendous crowd at night, every seat in the capacious barracks being filled and many standing in the aisles, while numbers were unable to get admission. . . . We only succeeded in getting three to come to a decision, to which must be added a backslider in the morning meeting.[28]

While the town's sinners were not responding to McKenzie's efforts, others were stirred to action. The local authorities were not impressed with his campaigning and the Inspector of Nuisances demanded that McKenzie stop. This he was not prepared to do and, on February 17, 1894, he and his Lieutenant were arrested, the charges reading that they "unlawfully did occasion an obstruction in and upon a certain land in the said municipality." They were tried on February 23[29] and sentenced to a fine, which the Scotsman in McKenzie refused to pay, resulting in a short stay in prison with hard labour. The authorities' heavy-handedness backfired, for "they had to listen to their Army prisoners singing gospel songs every time the corps band played hymn tunes outside the gaol."[30] *The War Cry* reported:

> The "running-in" mania seems to have struck the municipal fathers at Charters Towers, and the new

> mayor is in to distinguish himself by making gaol-birds of those who are spending their lives to make bad men good and save the country the expense of their depredations. Captain McKenzie and Lieutenant Morrison have been sent to gaol for a week for a start, but they are capable of putting in a good many more if needed. At any rate, his "worship" will show good sense and sound wisdom by declaring a truce, or he will find, as a good many have before him, that it is a losing game to fight the [Salvation Army], and it is infinitely more convenient to back down voluntarily than to be compelled to do so.
>
> It is no part of our business to oppose the authorities, and we are most anxious to avoid any clashing and to work amicably with them; at the same time we are not going to quietly submit to the petty interferences of those who have a spite against us, and who wish to use that office they have been temporarily exalted to as a means to gratify personal animus and dislike.[31]

Incensed citizens held protest meetings, attended by some clergy of other denominations and men of public standing. There were problems "inside" as well. McKenzie reportedly rubbed salt into the mayoral wounds by plying his great strength to wielding the axes he was given, achieving his aim of breaking all the handles and forcing the guards to put him on the cross-cut saw instead. The net result was that they were released after eight days and attracted even greater crowds from the sympathetic publicity gained during their incarceration. A satisfied McKenzie was able to fill the Penitent-forms in his hall.[32] Persecution of The Army by civic authorities across Australia lasted another decade but faded away after its work and mission became better understood and accepted.

During his time at Townsville, a fellow officer recalled McKenzie praying all night and commenting, "I remember looking down at the town and weeping over the sins of the people. I never saw so many conversions in the open-air as in Townsville."[33] Similarly in Ipswich, an apparently thriving Corps saw no penitents in the first two weeks of his arrival. He prayed all night until, at 3 am, he felt an assurance of a revival in the town. Overcome with enthusiasm, he ran out into the dark streets, singing out in his loud voice, "A great revival is coming to Ipswich! We are going to have a revival in Ipswich."[34] A later writer noted, "He felt such a strange thing was expected of him by God, and surely enough it must have been, for many people gave up their sin as a result."[35]

The eight months leading the Corps at Toowoomba provided something personal for McKenzie that would transform his life. He met a family of German-speaking immigrants from Alsace, the disputed borderlands between France and Germany, but since 1871 under German control. The mother, Frederika Hoepper, along with three of her six boys, Johann, Carl and Ferdinand, and the youngest of her two girls, Annie, were staunch Army soldiers. Frederika's husband, Frederick, was deeply opposed to The Salvation Army, railing against it and burning copies of *The War Cry* that he found in the house. But the opposition did not deter them and they were faithful workers in the Corps, finally seeing their father join them shortly before his death.[36]

McKenzie soon began making notes in his diary about the quiet, blue-eyed 18-year-old Annie, noting his interest in her and feeling that she could be a good Officer if pushed. On her part, the tall, strong young lady only noticed that she seemed to be getting more and more Corps work assigned to her by the energetic 23-year-old Captain. McKenzie kept his feelings to himself until he wrote to her on leaving Toowoomba for Charters Towers, receiving an encouraging reply to his letter. However, the romance was largely conducted by letter as each continued on their careers in The Army, McKenzie through his Corps and then another round of Staff appointments, and Annie to Officer training in Melbourne, and then appointments in the rugged gold-mining towns of Western Australia, while still in her teens.[37] Her three brothers also became Cadets in 1903.

After a year in north Queensland, the posting to Ipswich must have been welcome, as it was about 70 kilometres from Toowoomba—still a great distance by the transport standards of the day, but a lot more accessible than Charters Towers or Townsville for a man in love. This was followed by postings to the Divisional War Office, Queensland South in June, 1895, then as Divisional War Officer for Brisbane and Wide Bay in April, 1897, allowing him to catch up occasionally with those he loved. But by this stage, Annie Hoepper was far away, already an Officer in the goldfields of Western Australia, having graduated from the Training Home in July, 1896.

Despite the absence of Annie, McKenzie typically kept himself busy. One of his tasks was contributing a column to the Queensland edition of *The War Cry*, adopting the pen-name of "Banana Fritters," referring to himself in it by his administrative title as "The Scribe." The column was a mixture of serious and social news. In one column, he notes of himself: "The Scribe put in the week-end at Sandgate. I could almost have fancied myself in Paradise as I looked out upon the calm sea in all her loveliness. The aspect was charming. We all fought hard. Conviction was apparent, but we did not get a catch." The charm of this piece on McKenzie's fishing prowess lies in its lovely parody of Salvationist soul-winning language. After his departure, he was eulogised, again with humour, as "a good, faithful and capable scribe, and very much loved by officers and soldiers. He is a true son of Scotland, and a great believer in his country, and he truly was a credit to it in very many ways, one of which was his size."[38]

The Army took a very directive approach to the careers of its Officers, among other things stipulating that Officers could only marry fellow Officers. The reason behind this was that Officers were shifted frequently without consultation and a spouse who was also an Officer could not refuse "marching orders" if they didn't want to go. This did not stop a later Salvationist writer from critiquing this process as unreasonable, "with almost blithe abandon of personal consideration."[39]

So, for McKenzie, getting married was not just a case of persuading the young woman in question, but also of persuading his superiors to make the match possible. His Salvation Army personal records have a teasingly brief statement on his social life, showing that he had a previous engagement behind him, to a certain Candidate James, sometime around his first Staff appointment.[40] Sadly, nothing more is known of this mysterious engagement or of Candidate James, but as it clearly did not continue, one can speculate that perhaps Miss James failed to qualify as an Officer—a not uncommon occurrence, given the inordinate demands of the role—making it impossible for McKenzie to marry her and continue in his calling as an Officer.

With one failed engagement behind him, he was understandably proactive when it came to Annie Hoepper. His Salvation Army service record reveals that on July 14, 1898, he received a posting to Kalgoorlie Corps, Western Australia, yet he never served in the West.[41] We do know he had been lobbying the Field Secretary to have Annie transferred back from the West. A letter from the Field Secretary dated December 21, 1897, suggests that a deal was negotiated, reading in part, "We . . . are very pleased indeed to note the spirit in which you have received our [letter] on the matter of transferring Captain Hoepper. You can depend on us carrying out our part of the contract as soon as ever possible and at the first opportunity effecting the change which you seek for the Captain."[42]

It would seem that his superiors, sympathetic to the romance, were trying to engineer them into closer proximity and that McKenzie's posting to Kalgoorlie represented an attempt that was aborted "on account of circumstances and his health," though *The War Cry* announcement discreetly gave no details about the health issue.[43] Instead, a couple of weeks later, McKenzie was posted to Horsham, Victoria, as Divisional Officer (DO) effective August 20, 1898. Annie was moved back to Victoria in 1899. They were married at Horsham on June 21, 1899.

The War Cry published an extended account of the event, along with a photo of the couple, which captures the atmosphere of the occasion with the intimacy characteristic of *The War Cry* news articles:

> Wednesday, June 21, was the shortest day of the year, but its hours were the longest to some folk I know. It

was the date of the long-thought-about, talked-about and even dreamed-about wedding of Adjutant McKenzie and Captain Hoepper.

A fine tea was given by the sisters and lady friends of the Horsham corps, but the rain fell mercilessly all day and thinned the attendance. The Town Band kindly played both at the tea and the wedding. An officers' meeting preceded the tea, when the Wimmera lasses and lads met together in high spirits and eager expectations, and were treated to a cheering and helpful address by the Brigadier on the Century Scheme. The Brigadier handed Lieutenant Gardiner her promotion to the rank of Captain, amid the cheers of her comrades.

The wedding took place in the Institute at eight p.m., and a very happy crowd came along. The proceedings were splendidly conducted by the Brigadier, who gave a reading, and those talking eyes of his quite captivated the crowd.

A trio by the C.C.O. [Colony Commanding Officer], D.O. [Divisional Officer—McKenzie himself] and an F.O. [Field Officer] proved one of the most acceptable features of the evening's programme.

Captain Gardiner spoke for the spinsters and Captain Clark for the bachelors, and expressed all sorts of good wishes for the happy couple, as did also Ensign Shepherd on behalf of the married folk. Both the Captains promised faithfully to follow the D.O.'s example as soon as possible.

The Articles of Marriage were then read, and under the dear old colours our comrades were federated for life, amid the warm and enthusiastic applause of the crowd. The Brigadier spoke in the highest terms of them both. Then came the speeches of the bride and the bridegroom. Good old "Mac" was apparently as brave as a lion, and his wife spoke with much sweetness

> and feeling amid a dead silence. Her first words to the Horsham people have made a good impression. Over a dozen telegrams of congratulation, from three different colonies, were read by the Brigadier, notably one from Adjutant Carpenter, who was married at the same hour by the Commandant. It read: "Mutual sympathy; you and I are the happiest men alive."
>
> Next morning the officers returned to their different corps, eager for the fight and praying God's double blessing upon Adjutant McKenzie and his wife. Still raining.[44]

McKenzie was also moving through the Army ranks, promoted Ensign in May, 1898, Adjutant in January, 1899, and Staff Captain in December, 1900.[45] Along with his Staff Captaincy came an appointment to Adelaide as Divisional Officer on his 31st birthday, a position that carried responsibility for supervising all the Corps of the region. In comparative terms, it might be likened to that of a bishopric in the episcopal churches and represented a considerable trust in the young Officer. The trust was not misplaced. McKenzie watched over his Division with unflagging energy and inspiration. His principal means of transport was a bicycle, although any mode was used, from walking to cars and buses, when they were available.

Many articles written by him appeared in *The War Cry*, some as devotionals or editorials, others as news reports. They include an article about backsliding—the popular term for falling away from active Christian life—an exhortation to youth and an article titled "Will You Be Saved?" His nom-de-plume in Adelaide was sometimes "Pineapple"—perhaps harking back to his Queensland days—under which he wrote a tale about a girl engrossed in picking flowers on a railway line until it was too late. While moralistic, it is competently written and typical of his style. Another pen-name, "The Thistle," evoked his Scottish roots for his regular column titled "Honey Extracted by 'The Thistle'."[46]

His news reports give some idea of the nature of his work. In one he speaks of "a rattling open-air on Saturday night of the right sort:

a fine muster of soldiers, a large crowd of people, and a splendid case of conversion at the drumhead." He tells of the conversion of a commercial traveller who had been drinking three nights in a row: "It was truly a casting out of devils, and my, didn't he jump and shout when the work was done." The man's wife came to tell them the next day that he had prayed all night and the next night he gave a testimony. McKenzie then organised a big social tea to celebrate the Duke's birthday.[47] "It was a glorious success. . . . We had a monster musical meeting at night, followed by a coffee supper; a big crowd attended. The whole thing was a triumph for Adelaide."[48]

In another article, he outlined his adventurous travels of the previous weeks, including the Self-Denial week—The Salvation Army's annual fundraising project that called on the community to join Salvationists in denying themselves some pleasurable thing and donating the money saved. During that week in 1902, McKenzie was touring his division, often riding by night and holding meetings by day. One night, lost in the dark, he rode into a pothole and landed head first over the handlebars. He noted, "It was a very awkward fall, and left a few marks, but then it was Self-Denial service!" But he compared his trifling tribulations with how the farmers were "almost without hope" because of the severe drought.

He recorded overnight rides of 40 miles (about 65 kilometres) to Quorn, 25 miles (40 kilometres) to Port Augusta, and a 30-mile (almost 50-kilometre) ride through the ranges, starting at midnight, which he found "not very inspiring, for if an accident befell you the chances are you would lie some considerable time before help came. However, our Heavenly Father was good, and in two and a half hours I was safely home. . . . I rode 260 miles [about 420 kilometres] on the bike last week, and this week will put that distance out of sight."[49]

With the South Australian economy in tatters due to drought and mining failures, McKenzie laid down a challenge to his Southern Division workers to better the fundraising efforts of the Northern Division. The North published its response in *The War Cry*: "All right, McKenzie: it is a fair thing—twenty-four corps each. We have pluck enough to keep the mighty Mac at the feet of the North. Just read these lines, ye would-be Southern champions!

"Ah Mac, my man, ye are unco rash,
The Northern chicks ye canna thrash:
We'll beat ye bad, aye, leave ye deed,
For in our veins flows conq'ror's bluid.
(Bagpipe accompaniment; no tune necessary.—Ed.)"[50]

Of personal interest was the announcement of the dedication of the first McKenzie child, born on April 10, 1900, and named for his grandfather Donald, with the middle names of William Booth, which nicely captured both his father's name and the name of the founder of The Salvation Army, with whom he shared a birth date.[51] Colin Campbell would follow on June 27, 1901, then Gordon Lindsay on March 22, 1903, and Jean Gregor on July 5, 1904, and lastly Mavis Hinemoa on December 22, 1908. Her middle name was a tribute to McKenzie's time in New Zealand, the name of a legendary beauty in a romantic Maori myth.

But fatherhood did little to stop the time and energy he poured into his work and this cast an extra burden on Annie, who raised the children on her own for long periods of time while McKenzie's focus went into travelling around the Corps. It was she who maintained the strong rituals of family devotion, instruction and prayer during his frequent and sometimes prolonged absences. Fortunately, she was tough, resourceful and eminently practical. Enormously competent, Annie was a meticulous housekeeper who kept a row of tins on her mantelpiece. When the meagre Salvation Army salary would arrive, minus whatever McKenzie had withdrawn for other purposes, Annie would assiduously divide up the rest into her tins. First and foremost was the tithe tin, into which 10 per cent was faithfully placed. Next was groceries, then clothes, then books—which were an important, almost revered, part of the McKenzie household—then other tins for things such as travel and charity. She spent wisely and well, insisting on getting the best-quality goods she could with the money available. Typically, she would buy a top-quality suit for Donald, which would be passed down to Colin then Gordon, and finally—with a little remodelling to make it more feminine—it would belong to Mavis.[52]

Ah Kow describes Annie as a tower of strength for a husband of impulsive nature. He had an enthusiastic commitment to work that pushed the limits of endurance and a tendency to bouts of depression. His hatred of debt made him reduce his own salary to a bare minimum at times in order to relieve the depression-struck finances of his parishes, which added to Annie's burdens. When he returned—often exhausted—she was at hand to give him rest, and moderate his more impulsive decisions.[53] This is as close as Ah Kow comes to criticism of McKenzie and, given her tendency to cast things in the most positive light possible, it suggests that he was not always an easy man to live with. This was not through any malice, for he was famously gentle and acquaintances claimed never to have heard an angry word from him or a cross word between husband and wife.[54]

The difficulty lay more in his child-like enthusiasm and sincerity, his energetic and impulsive disposition, which tended to depression in the periods that followed the intense emotional highs he experienced in his ministry, and the unreasonably high standards of behaviour he set for himself and his family—a legacy of his Victorian-era Presbyterian upbringing that he was not able to forsake. For example, the strict observance of Sunday meant that the family made an eight-kilometre walk each Sunday from their home in Camberwell to the Salvation Army citadel in the centre of Melbourne, then back after the services, in order to avoid paying for public transport. However, Annie's commitment to her God, denomination and family was rock-like, matching that of her husband, and she had no expectation of an easy life. Her consistent attitude was one of trust in God to get her through every challenge and a calm acceptance of—or more accurately at times, resignation to—whatever was thrown at her.[55]

Naturally, McKenzie threw himself into fatherhood with the same abandon he gave everything else. On his homecoming from a trip, there was usually something special: a little welcome home ceremony and special tea, or a rambunctious father pretending to be any variety of spirited animal with his children tumbling all over his back in riotous laughter. "O Daddy," Mavis cried once in this playtime, "you're marvellous! We love every square yard of you." While Annie maintained the continuity of the spiritual atmosphere of the home, they were a genuine team in ensuring a disciplined yet warm family atmosphere.

McKenzie's letters to his children reveal a capacity to adapt his language and subject matter to the age of his audience, and they were always couched in affectionate and tender terms. His letters frequently enjoined the children to spiritual devotion, but they also contained delightful descriptions and humorous anecdotes. On his sons, he impressed the highest standards of chivalry toward women, especially their mother and sister.[56] But McKenzie also had another welcome domestic advantage not common to men of his generation: he considered no job that needed doing as beneath his dignity. He would take a scrubbing brush to a grimy new home or cook a meal with his usual panache, when Annie was unwell, giving the dish a fancy French name to add the flavour that his culinary skills failed to impart.[57]

Similarly in his profession, he would plunge into any task that needed doing on his arrival at a Corps, no matter how menial, whether it was cleaning a filthy stove, painting a Corps barracks or chopping wood.[58] One of his singular qualities was his complete absence of self-consciousness and his capacity to be entirely in the moment without thought to his dignity. He would join in any singing with gusto, his powerful voice unrestrained by situation, or take up any children's or young people's activities with the same simple energy, playing cricket with girls in an orphanage or covering himself with treacle in a treacle bun competition.

His actions were often a source of merriment for onlookers but their amusement was usually joined by his own hearty laugh, especially at his own expense. And he loved humour, using it constantly to oil the wheels of human relationships and as a way of easing into a spiritual conversation, which he could do with utter naturalness in almost any social context.[59] His enthusiasm for God was also expressed in uninhibited fashion: "Outside the hotel bars and billiard saloons, he emphasised his message, leaving no-one in any doubt as to which side he was on. With shouts of 'Glory! Hallelujah!', gesticulations of delight, and a few dancing steps, he sought to impress everyone with the joys of Salvation fighting."[60] In almost all situations, his overriding concern was the salvation of others, to which everything else—especially his own feelings, dignity, comfort or personal needs—was of secondary importance.

But other family matters must also have occupied McKenzie's attention during these years. In 1900, a flood wiped out his father's farm at Electra and he was forced to start from scratch on a new property at nearby Pine Creek. In 1903, his mother Agnes died. While his responses to these events are unrecorded, they must have impacted this emotionally sensitive man.

After two years in Adelaide, he was specifically requested to join the Waterloo Corps in central Sydney, as part of a Special Corps Appointments in great centres of population.[61] Waterloo had a particular challenge on its hands with the inner-city poor around Redfern and Waterloo, and he served there from mid-January, 1903, until he was posted to the Ballarat Division in early December. His work in that district was headlined in *The War Cry* as "Still attracting the drunks" and praised for its revivalist preaching,[62] and he contributed many pieces himself to *The War Cry* during this time.

After almost two years in central Victoria, he was appointed editor of the New Zealand *War Cry*, sailing in December, 1905, on the *SS Warrimoo*.[63] In the meantime, he had been promoted to Major and was given some editorial work at the Melbourne headquarters before leaving for New Zealand, to familiarise himself with the task.[64] His departure from Ballarat was marked by a farewell at which his three brothers-in-law—Captain Johann and Lieutenants Jack and Ferdinand—entertained in vocal and instrumental trios, on cornet, violin and concertina. Emotional speeches were made, and "Mrs. McKenzie and her three Officer brothers rendered impressively the famous song, 'I Cannot Leave the Dear Old Flag'."[65]

McKenzie's three years in New Zealand[66] are among the least documented of his working life. As editor of *The War Cry*, his articles appeared frequently, but they were spiritual and devotional in nature, revealing little of his personal life, and the news stories he wrote were of others' work. However, several events stand out. He brought his usual energy to the task of editing, the Australian edition noting with affectionate humour that "Our genial friend, the Major, now presiding over the literary destiny of the New Zealand *War Cry*, has passed safely through the throes of a 'first' issue, and his satisfaction was no doubt unbounded. Perhaps this self-same satisfaction is responsible for the following lines:

Waihi-Walhigh-Waiho!
Take a dozen, and off you go.
Strike out for the bush, with a bike and some push—
You'll sell them; I'm sure this is so."[67]

A desk job was not McKenzie's ideal and a colleague of the time remembered that "He'd knock the eight pages together in a couple of days and be off," eager for more field work. However, his editorship was sufficiently accomplished to increase circulation.[68]

The second event of note was of a tragic nature. In December, 1906, his treasured daughter Jean died of diphtheria at the age of two and a half. The impact can be easily imagined on one of such warm affection and emotional disposition as McKenzie. It affected the whole family, to the extent that Donald later named his eldest daughter Jean in memory of "little Jean," as she was referred to in the family. At first this was misreported in the Australian *War Cry* as one of the sons who had died, but this was corrected in a later issue.[69]

Thirdly, almost exactly two years later, the McKenzies welcomed another girl into the family. As the baby of the family, Mavis was perhaps McKenzie's favourite,[70] receiving extra attention after the loss of her sister. She was the only child to follow her parents into Officership in The Army. During their time in New Zealand, one would imagine that McKenzie also caught up with his aunts Jane and Jean and their families, who had moved to New Zealand in the 1870s—but there is no record of such a meeting.

In February, 1909, McKenzie was transferred to the editorship of the Australian *War Cry*, an appointment that was "popularly received"[71] and that he held for just longer than a year. A sample of his writing themes demonstrate a concern for social justice and for spirituality, commenting on new Victorian legislature to protect working girls, the social and material malaise of contemporary society that lived on impulse not principle, the foundation of societal wellbeing, including harmonious employment relationships, elimination of poverty, respect for women, Sabbath-rest and the prohibition of child labour, and the provision of "a healing, warm and moral atmosphere" for children. In another editorial, he suggested that if polar explorers could endure hardship for the sake of science, "how much more freely should we be prepared to face contumely [insult], self-denial and hard work for saving the lost." Another editorial, based on Matthew 4:4, listed common substitutes for the Bread of Life: "The Bread of Custom and Fashion; The Bread of Frivolity; The Bread of Sport; The Bread of Mammon."[72]

Typical of The Salvation Army—and especially of McKenzie—was the emphasis on practical religion. There was little of the theological or academic in his presentation of religion. And again, typically, he took time off whenever possible to hold public meetings, conducting a notable series over the Easter break, with drunks again a feature of his redemptive work.[73] His motto was exemplified in a poem from this period, which has been preserved in his own handwriting:

> Not myself, but the truth that in life I have spoken;
> Not myself, but the seed that in life I have sown,
> Shall pass on to ages—all about me forgotten,
> Save the truths I have spoken, the things I have done.
> Signed William McKenzie.[74]

His influence in the Editorial Office was also great. George Carpenter—later the first Australian to become Salvation Army General—saw him early one morning praying with a boy bringing proofs from the printing office, "rising from his knees, his face wet with tears, his hands clasping those of the boy, and he was saying, 'Joe, my boy, go straight.'"[75] He also became a leading spirit on

Headquarters staff. They generally lunched together and McKenzie formed the Saveloy Club "from his hospitable habit of forking out a string of saveloy [sausages] from a bubbling tin kettle and slashing off a couple on each plate."[76]

In March, 1910, McKenzie was made Provincial Commander of Tasmania, being promoted to Brigadier at the end of the year, then he was shifted to the Provincial Command of Bendigo in 1911. There, he was noted for leading the tiny Corps Band in a Victorian country town, consisting of just a handful of instruments. "The Brigadier, as he then was, marched eight or ten yards ahead of; a tall, upstanding, virile figure, blowing away on an old brass cornet, and pausing anon to sing heartily—

Pull down the devil's kingdom,
Where'er he holds dominion;
Storm the forts of darkness,
Bring them down."[77]

It was here that he cut another comic musical caper. Always keen on the bagpipes, which he once toyed with learning, he decided that the two expert concertina players on his staff could combine with him on a kazoo, making a creditable imitation of a bagpipe. The concertinas would be the drone and the kazoo the chant. Naturally, his performance on the kazoo was powerful and—with masterly understatement—it was suggested that the further away, the better it sounded. It always attracted a crowd but perhaps more because of the ludicrous spectacle rather than the musical accomplishment of the group. The giant McKenzie led the parade blowing on his tiny kazoo, followed by the concertinas: the bean-pole deputy with the short, plump figure of the Divisional Secretary bringing up the rear. McKenzie put an end to the routine when a solid female spectator fell off her bench laughing at a march in Inglewood. He joined her in uncontrolled mirth.[78]

Amazingly, he was left in the post at Bendigo for four years, the longest he had spent in any one post. In January, 1914, he was chosen as a delegate to The Salvation Army's International Congress held in London. Travelling with him were two close friends, Arthur Arnott[79] and William Blaskett,[80] a noted Army journalist. In a sign that The Salvation Army had made great strides in social acceptability in the previous decade, the Australian delegates in London were addressed by the rotund figure of former Prime Minister, now Australian High Commissioner in the United Kingdom, Sir George Reid in Westminster Hall. Among the various events was a "March of the Ten Thousand," a huge parade through London's streets, attracting an estimated 250,000 to a meeting in Hyde Park, with speakers on 12 platforms.[81] McKenzie thoroughly enjoyed the conference and was invited to address one public meeting. He also took the time for some tourism, visiting places in England and Scotland, and interesting himself in their history.[82]

After the Conference, the trio made their way home. Stopping in at Gibraltar, they heard the news of the declaration of war by Britain on Germany. McKenzie felt it would be a long conflict and immediately wrote to Salvation Army Territorial Commander of Australia, James Hay, asking to be recommended to the Australian Army as a chaplain, posting the letter as soon as he arrived in Perth.

He had been away for five months in total for the Salvation Army Congress and his growing family, with the older ones now well in their teens, was delighted to see him again. But they had him for a mere four days, before he conducted a tour of his Bendigo Division, returning on September 25, where he received the news of his appointment as a Chaplain in the Australian forces being raised for overseas service.

1. *War Cry*, March 13, 1926, page 10.
2. Adelaide Ah Kow, *William McKenzie M.C., O.B.E., O.F. Anzac Padre* (London: Salvationist Publishing and Supplies, 1949), pages 15–16.

3. "Stirring Moments Mark the Memorial Service in Congress Hall," *War Cry*, August 16, 1947, page 5.
4. *War Cry*, February 11, 1933, page 8.
5. Ah Kow, page 12.
6. Letter of Acceptance for Officer Training, June 4, 1889, Archive Box R15, Salvation Army Heritage Archives, Melbourne.
7. Ah Kow, pages 12–13.
8. William McKenzie, "Australia is my first love," *Melbourne Herald*, June 24, 1930, page 271.
9. Ah Kow, page 13.
10. Frank Duracher, "'Fighting Mac' one of God's heroes," *Pipeline*, April, 2012, page 20. Variations of this story exist. Ah Kow, pages 14–15, says it was a publican who objected, while Col Stringer has McKenzie dumping the publican in the horse trough. Stringer's embroidered version seems highly unlikely, given McKenzie's post-conversion restraint from using violence in self-defence: *'Fighting McKenzie' Anzac Chaplain: Tribute to a Hero* (Robina, Qld: Col Stringer Ministries, 2003), page 36.
11. Some references incorrectly call it the "Royal Australian Guard's Band" (see *War Cry*, February 18, 1933).
12. "Troubadour for Christ," *The Musician*, September, 1947, page 8.
13. McKenzie, "Australia is my first love."
14. Letter to William McKenzie from J Birkenshaw, Staff Captain, March 4, 1891, Archive Box R15, Salvation Army Heritage Archives, Melbourne.
15. "Told at Tighe's Hill," *War Cry*, March 6, 1937.
16. "Told at Tighe's Hill," *War Cry*, March 6, 1937; Ah Kow, page 14.
17. Personal Report on Captain McKenzie, File J139653, Salvation Army Heritage Archives, Melbourne.
18. *War Cry*, August 6, 1947.
19. Ah Kow, pages 21–22.
20. Ah Kow, page 15.
21. *War Cry*, August 6, 1947.
22. Unfortunately, the journal appears not to have survived, although Ah Kow used it as a source.
23. Ah Kow, page 19.
24. Ah Kow, page 15.
25. "Pioneers on Parade. Number eight: William McKenzie," *War Cry*, March 1, 1980.
26. "The Commissioner revives memories of the 'Toowoomba Tearaways,'" *War Cry*, March 4, 1933.
27. Ah Kow, page 18.
28. *War Cry*, February 24, 1894, page 6.
29. Charters Towers charge sheet, Archive Box R15, Salvation Army Heritage Archives, Melbourne.
30. "Pioneers on Parade," *War Cry*, March 1, 1980; *Sydney Morning Herald*, February 7, 1933, page 8.

31. *War Cry*, March 17, 1894, page 6.
32. Ah Kow, page 17.
33. Ah Kow, page 16.
34. Ah Kow, page 16.
35. Ivan Hoe, "A long time ago," *The Young Soldier*, February 5, 1949, page 5.
36. Major Johann, Brigadier Carl and Brigadier Ferdinand, along with Annie, gave a total of more than 200 years' service to The Salvation Army: "Featuring the Hoepper family of Toowoomba, Qld," *War Cry*, May 16, 1959.
37. Ah Kow, pages 23–24; *War Cry*, March 18, 1939, page 9.
38. *War Cry*, August 27, 1898, page 8. Pen names were common among *War Cry* writers. Names such as "Northern Nectar," "White Wings" and "Ivan Hoe" appear in *The War Cry* and other Salvation Army publications.
39. "Australia . . . China," *War Cry*, February 6, 1937, page 7.
40. Personal Report on Captain McKenzie, File J139653.
41. McKenzie, "Australia is my first love."
42. Letter from Julius Horskins, Field Secretary Melbourne, to William McKenzie, December 21, 1897, Archive Box R15, Salvation Army Heritage Archives, Melbourne.
43. *War Cry*, August 13, 1898, page 8.
44. *War Cry*, July 15, 1899, page 6. The columnist writes under the name of "Fil Fiddle". Adjutant Carpenter, a close friend of McKenzie, would become the fifth General of The Salvation Army in 1939, succeeding Evangeline Booth, daughter of founder William Booth.
45. Service Record, William McKenzie, Archive Box R15, Salvation Army Heritage Archives, Melbourne. Note that these ranks are now long abolished.
46. *War Cry*, February 11, 1899, page 11; February 25, 1899, page 7; January 12, 1900; January 12, 1901, page 1; November 1, 1902, page 3.
47. Which duke is uncertain. There were no royal dukes at the time with birthdays in October.
48. *War Cry*, June 22, 1901, pages 3.
49. *War Cry*, November 1, 1902, page 3.
50. *War Cry*, June 6, 1902, page 11.
51. *War Cry*, June 2, 1900, page 7.
52. Ann Zubrick, Interview, October 28, 2013.
53. Ah Kow, pages 24–27.
54. Ah Kow, pages 20, 26.
55. "A Fighting Man's Farewell," *War Cry*, October 16, 1926, page 10; "Praising God for Self-denial," *War Cry*, October 23, 1926, page 11; Ann Zubrick, Interview, October 28, 2013.
56. McKenzie letters, PR 84/150, Australian War Memorial; Ah Kow, page 25–27.
57. Ah Kow, page 24–27.
58. Ah Kow, page 21; *War Cry*, May 6, 1905, page 2.
59. "Adelaide 'Register' Pars," *War Cry*, August 2, 1930, page 10; Ah Kow, page 21.
60. "Troubadour for Christ," *The Musician*, September, 1947, page 8.

61. *War Cry*, January 10, 1903, page 9.
62. "Major 'Mac' at Warrack-Nabeal," *War Cry*, March 4, 1905, page 16.
63. The *Warrimoo*, pride of the Australia and New Zealand Company, had made maritime history on the last day of 1899. It was close to the International Date Line at the Equator on a voyage from Vancouver to Sydney. By judicious navigation, the captain crossed the Date Line at the Equator at exactly midnight, meaning that the "ship was straddling two hemispheres, two seasons, two years and two centuries at the same moment"—Michelle Arrow, "The 'Warrimoo'," <www.abc.net.au/tv/rewind/txt/s1166966.htm>, broadcast August 1, 2004, accessed September 3, 2013.
64. *War Cry*, December 16, 1905, page 9.
65. *War Cry*, December 2, 1905, page 11.
66. Reviewing his career, McKenzie occasionally spoke of four years in New Zealand. The dates of his appointment were from November 17, 1905, to February 18, 1909, a total of 3 years and 3 months, though spanning the dates of four years.
67. *War Cry*, January 27, 1906, page 6.
68. Ah Kow, page 19.
69. *War Cry*, December 22, 1906, page 9; January 5, 1907, page 9.
70. Ah Kow, page 27.
71. *War Cry*, February 27, 1909, page 9.
72. *War Cry*, March 13, 1909, page 8; May 15, 1909, page 8; June 19, 1909, page 8; August 14, 1909, page 8; April 17, 1909, page 8; May 1, 1909, page 2.
73. *War Cry*, April 24, 1909, page 5.
74. *War Cry*, June 12, 1965.
75. *War Cry*, August 16, 1947.
76. *War Cry*, August 13, 1948.
77. "Troubadour for Christ," *The Musician*, September, 1947, page 8.
78. Ah Kow, page 22.
79. Son and brother of the famous Arnott's biscuits manufacturers. It is said that the popular SAO biscuit is named in Arthur's honour, an acronym for "Salvation Army Officer."
80. And father of showbiz personality ventriloquist Ron Blaskett.
81. *War Cry*, August 1, 1914, page 6.
82. William McKenzie minute book diary, Archive Box R15, Salvation Army Heritage Centre, Melbourne.

CHAPTER 3

MAKING HIS MARK

SYDNEY TO EGYPT, 1914–1915

On August 4, 1914, Australia found itself at war against Germany. While self-governing, Australia's foreign policy was still directed from Westminster, thus automatically committing the nation once Britain declared war. However, it was popularly received by the youthful country, which still saw itself as a transplant of Britain, though uncertain if it embodied the best of British due to its new start or the worst due to its convict stain. Many looked forward to the coming conflict as a crucible in which Australia would make its mark on the world, demonstrate the fitness of its men to stand alongside the pantheon of British military heroes, and provide a unifying national story more potent than the political machinations that led to federation in January, 1901, only 13 years earlier.

The Australian government quickly offered Britain a force of 20,000 men—the first instalment of what would become the Australian Imperial Force (AIF) of five infantry divisions and five brigades of

Light Horse—and authorities were initially overwhelmed with the number of volunteers. There was virtually no infrastructure for this new army, and men slept in the open on the bleachers at racecourses and sports grounds hastily commandeered to accommodate them.

The 1st Australian Division was recruited regionally, with the 1st Brigade drawn from the most populous state, New South Wales. Commanded by Colonel Henry Norman MacLaurin, the Brigade, was composed of four battalions, each of about 1000 men. The 4th Battalion—with the highly experienced 49-year-old Lieutenant-Colonel Astley John Onslow Thompson in charge—was recruited around Sydney and the south-western regions of the state, setting up camp first at Randwick Racecourse, then at the adjoining Kensington Racecourse (now the campus of the University of New South Wales), then at other locations in each of those suburbs. The Battalion "2iC"—second in command—was the 35-year-old Major Charles Macnaghten, a lively militia officer with a reputation for dealing successfully with difficult men. The battalion acquired the nickname "the Macs and the Micks" for its high proportion of men from Scottish and Irish backgrounds, and Macnaghten organised a pipe band for the battalion, the only one in the entire division.

Contrary to current popular belief, the British influence ran strongly through the AIF, particularly in its early days. While a majority of the division were Australian-born, Colonel MacLaurin noted that 60 per cent of the first recruits to his brigade were British-born. With a sprinkling of other nationalities—mainly from Europe, New Zealand, the Americas and South Africa—the Australian-born in the 1st Brigade at first struggled to outnumber those born overseas. While many of the British-born had lived in Australia long enough to have acquired distinctive Australian attitudes, like McKenzie, they often retained their affection and loyalty for their homeland, as well as shading an acquired Australian twang with a diversity of British pronunciations. So the accents of the British Isles were common within the AIF, especially among its officers, who were largely drawn from the upper strata of Australian society.

However, the early rush to enlist had also attracted an unfortunately high number of "wastrels," men of a criminal background who sought refuge from the police or a further outlet for their activities in the Army. Other men signed up to escape unhappy marriages or dodge family responsibilities, using false names to evade detection. Officers were under instruction to weed out men of doubtful commitment, a process that continued overseas, and about one in five of the initial recruits deserted or was mustered out of the force on these grounds.[1]

The newly raised AIF followed the long British tradition of attaching chaplains to its forces. There were differences, however. In Britain, the Anglican Church—as the official religion—supplied most of the chaplains, while Catholic and Non-Conformist chaplains were appointed in only small numbers. Australia had no state religion, so the Army's new Chaplain's Department, founded just the year before, created four Chaplain-General positions as a compromise to avoid the inter-faith rivalries of the major denominations: Anglican, Catholic, Presbyterian and Methodist. It was decided to appoint a mix of chaplains to represent the major religious groupings in Australia, according to the ratios of the previous census of 1911. Each brigade was allocated four chaplains: two Anglican, one Roman Catholic, and one Presbyterian or Methodist.[2]

However, one of the Anglicans could be replaced by a representative of what was eventually termed the "Other Protestant Denominations" (OPD), the various smaller sects such as Baptists, Churches of Christ, Congregationalists, The Salvation Army, and Brethren. In theory, chaplains looked after their own co-religionists across the entire brigade but, for administrative purposes, each chaplain was attached to a battalion and became closely associated with it. When the brigade was out of the line, church parades could be held where men would attend services of their choice, but active service anywhere near the front often meant that the various battalions were separated, and the chaplain had to serve the spiritual needs of his entire battalion, regardless of religious affiliations.

The evolving role of a chaplain had never been formally defined in the British army and therefore by default the Australian army, but included official roles such as running church services on Sundays at compulsory—and therefore, usually unpopular—parades. They also offered a range of voluntary religious services, including Holy Communion, formal worship services, Bible study and Confirmation classes, and informal meetings such as a "sing song" of popular and patriotic songs, some hymns and a prayer or two, with perhaps a short homily. Of course, they also conducted burial services for the dead, after which they usually wrote to the next-of-kin, although battalion officers might also carry part of that responsibility. In addition to leading these services, chaplains were expected to provide general spiritual guidance and to act as counsellors to the soldiers.

The chaplains' unofficial duties included the maintenance of morale and the commitment to the cause for which the army was fighting. They were often asked to organise wholesome recreation and diversions for the soldiers, through sports and recreation, concerts, popular lectures, cinemas and canteens. It was common for the chaplain to be appointed entertainment officer and elected president of the officers' mess, in charge of the kitty from which mess expenses—such as the costs of meals, drinks and entertainments—were paid. Many chaplains were concerned that the unofficial role would get in the way of the official, but others felt that the unofficial was the key to gaining the trust of the men.[3]

Chaplains were also expected to be optimistic, especially to men discouraged by the traumas and casualties of war. "Oh yes, to be cheerful, to be divinely cheerful, is an essential part of the duties of a Chaplain," wrote one British chaplain.[4]

Battalion commanding officers could add other tasks as needed. One of the most common of these in the AIF was censoring the men's letters home, which was unpopular with some chaplains, who felt they were prying into the private lives of the soldiers, but generally accepted by the men themselves, who preferred a chaplain reading their mail over an officer responsible for discipline. In describing the role of military chaplain in 1914, *The War Cry* shrewdly observed that, "Just where the work in detail will begin and end is difficult to say, but it is certain what may be called the *compulsory duties* are fairly onerous, and the *optional duties* have no limit."[5]

However, the vagueness of the role, the lack of experience of many officers and the absence of training for chaplains new to the culture of the Army meant that the position of chaplain was fraught, depending to a large extent on the goodwill of the brigade and battalion commanders, and the co-operation of their adjutants and company commanders. A number of officers saw the role of chaplains preaching peace, love and goodwill as incompatible with an army designed to kill their fellow men—and some chaplains also noted the incongruity. Some officers were actively anti-religious and made life difficult for their chaplain by ensuring other activities were scheduled when the chaplain wished to run services.

The popularity of chaplains with the ordinary soldiers was undermined by three other inherent disadvantages. First, they were officers and therefore disliked on principle. Second, they were noncombatants, staying behind the lines when the men went into action. One almost-universal phenomenon of combat is the remarkable bond created between men who risk their lives together that transcends most other barriers and accounts for the fidelity of the life-long friendships between veterans. Typically, chaplains were outsiders to this and were resented as intruders who did not really belong. Third, chaplains represented religion, whose moral prohibitions and strictures were often seen as unmanly.[6]

A further level of suspicion was raised with the appointment of chaplains from the smaller denominations. Most men tolerated the idea of Anglican and Catholic chaplains, representing religions well integrated and comfortable in society. Presbyterians and Methodists could arouse suspicion on the grounds of their well-known strict standards, while The Salvation Army publicly stood against almost everything the ordinary soldier did for light relief: drinking, gambling, smoking, swearing and womanising. A wowser was the last person many men wanted critiquing their behaviour every Sunday. A study of British chaplains concluded that an individual chaplain well attuned to the men might be liked but the institution of Chaplaincy was unpopular. Even popular chaplains rarely changed men's attitudes to institutional religion.[7] However, Michael

Gladwin's recent study of Australian chaplaincy speaks of the "positive relationship between chaplains and the AIF," demonstrating "a substantial body of evidence for the AIF's appreciation of their chaplains' pastoral and social concern."[8]

So the AIF was not all bad news for chaplains. While the Anzac story in Australia is almost always told in secular terms and, after reading the diaries and letters of about 1000 soldiers, noted historian Bill Gammage "concluded that the Australian soldier was indifferent to religion,"[9] the record actually points to perhaps about 10 per cent of men being active Christians—roughly reflecting the national average—and it is far from unusual to find statements of religious commitment in letters and diaries, even in Gammage's own book.[10]

Initially shocked at the profanities and blasphemies of the soldiers, one chaplain soon reported that on matters of religion, "the Australian soldier is a 'hypocrite' or perhaps to put it more mildly, a 'camouflage artist,'" arguing that the average soldier was more religious than he let on.[11] Not all Anzacs were hard-living men; one former soldier reported after the war that about half his unit neither smoked nor drank, and had high standards of behaviour and honesty. He was offended by the expectation in Australia that he would smoke and drink simply because he was a returned serviceman.[12]

In any case, the level of overt religiosity among British and American servicemen in World War I is strikingly similar to that of the AIF,[13] so there was nothing comparatively secular about the Australians. Unsurprisingly, the AIF represented the spectrum of religious diversity found in Australian society at large, from the aggressively atheistic to the aggressively evangelistic. The majority of men were largely indifferent nominal Christians, although open to faith if it was attractively presented. And there was a leavening of devout men, who usually saw a strong connection between their beliefs and their commitment to fight. But Gladwin notes that "there is evidence for the chaplains' effectiveness among even the most unruly elements of the AIF."[14]

In this context, McKenzie was appointed to the 1st Brigade as the

"OPD" Chaplain 4th Class (Captain) in mid-September, 1914, after representations from The Salvation Army to have its Officers included among the chaplains. He wished to "help the cause of Jesus Christ . . . to do what in me lay to help and bless those who were going forth to fight against the foes of the Empire," supporting "those principles of righteousness on which the whole foundation and superstructure of our civilisation is built."[15] This blend of religious and patriotic impulse was perfectly conventional, reflecting McKenzie's adherence to the values of his society, and was characteristic of many chaplains, indeed of most men of faith, for whom Christ and British Crown stood indissolubly united.[16] McKenzie was no reflective theologian or philosopher; brisk action based on unquestioned beliefs was his hallmark. He appears never to have questioned the philosophical basis of the war, nor the philosophical basis of the British Empire, accepting as a given the righteousness of the cause of the Empire and demonstrating a firm belief in the superiority of the British race, especially in its Caledonian manifestations. His was an essentially conservative social outlook.

His fellow chaplains were the Reverend James Green, a Methodist with the rank of 1st Class (Colonel) due to his chaplaincy experience since the Boer War, attached to the 1st Battalion; Father Edmund McAuliffe, Roman Catholic Chaplain 4th Class attached to the 2nd Battalion; and the Reverend Albert Edward Talbot, Dean of the Anglican Archdiocese of Sydney, as Chaplain 1st Class (Colonel) attached to the 3rd Battalion, who had been a chaplain in the peace-time Australian Army.

McKenzie's temperament and experience fitted him particularly well to military chaplaincy. While he had no prior involvement in the army, he was accustomed to the quasi-military organisation of The Salvation Army, with its pledges and oaths of allegiance to its flag, its top-down organisational structure and the self-sacrificing commitment expected of its members. Furthermore, he was experienced in the art of mixing with the most irreligious types. His blend of transparent sincerity, commitment, humour and humility, along with his charisma, robust physique, social inventiveness and unflagging vitality meant that, compared to most clergymen of the established denominations, whose congregations often consisted largely of respectable middle-class women, he was particularly attuned to the attitudes and experiences of the kind of men he would rub shoulders with. His phenomenal memory and his capacity to talk in an informed manner on a host of topics endeared him to thousands of men whose names he knew, and he could talk intelligently to them about their peace-time professions.

Almost all his life experiences to date, in combination with his natural gifts and dedicated application, had prepared him ideally for his role over the next four years. He was to regard the war years as the pinnacle of his ministry, where he did his best work. *The War Cry* opined:

> All will agree that the selection made is a wise one. The Brigadier [McKenzie's Salvation Army rank] is distinctly a soldier of God, and a man's man, and he has had a good training for the present post. . . . He has a wide outlook, is musical, can tell a good story and apply a pointed moral, has conspicuous ability on the platform, and has read extensively. Withal, he has a kind heart and a good knowledge of human nature. His splendid physique, too, should stand him in good stead in time of need.[17]

However, the appointment came as a shock to his family. He had kept the news to himself, in order to give them one last time of "happy rollicking fun."[18] McKenzie recounted the incident this way:

> Well, when I came home from Melbourne, it was in the evening, so I resolved to say nothing to my wife till after tea. So we had just a happy time with the children and then, about quarter past nine, I told them that next day I would be leaving to go away with the "boys" to the front. And I shall never forget my wife saying, "Well, dear, if it's God's will, let it be done." And with that, we started to get my things ready. Right through the night, while the children slept, we worked, and then on the

> morrow I left them. Poor wee Jean [sic] and the boys felt it greatly.[19]

McKenzie was in such a hurry to take up his new appointment in Sydney that he travelled in his Salvation Army uniform, not having had the time to acquire the appropriate military one. Writing to his wife from The Salvation Army's People's Palace in Sydney on September 19, he noted, "I am glad of this. It will make me out quite distinct from the others." He also wrote that he had been quizzed by fellow Salvationists about how the family had reacted to his sudden departure, but he had said that Annie "acted and spoke like the good Salvationist she is, and is thoroughly ready to fulfil the clause of her marriage contract 'not to hinder the other doing or giving anything within his power to do or give'." He was proud of the example of self-sacrifice she set, and said that it impressed his Sydney audience.

He added, "I trust you with the children are OK. I was sorry that I had such a rush at the train. I am sure that you and they will be all right and so will I, God will take care of us all. We will act and trust like good soldiers of Jesus. Work all you can for the Corps and Home League. These things will keep you cheerful. I will write to the boys tonight after the night meeting. Meanwhile I will again bid you adieu!" signing off with "hugs, love and kisses to all."[20]

The letter is revealing, capturing his impetuosity and his commitment. While there is no doubt of Annie's own commitment, the letter suggests that she felt the separation strongly, needing encouragement to view it in a positive light. In fact, when McKenzie told her of his decision, she had tried to dissuade him, aware that her growing boys needed a father's steadying influence at home. McKenzie was undeterred, thinking that he would be absent for six months—nine at most. That night, Annie retired alone and prayed for assurance, and found comfort in the text, "Be careful for nothing" (Philippians 4:6).[21]

But there is also an impression that McKenzie failed to fully grasp the emotional impact of his decision on his family. During the three-and-a-half years he was away, his boys passed through their adolescence and Annie struggled to cope with the challenges this posed. During the next few weeks, as the wheels of military preparation ground on slowly, he came to regret his hasty departure, finding that he had time on his hands that he would have preferred to have spent with his family at home.[22]

He was formally inducted into the army on September 25, his enlistment papers weighing in the 44-year-old at 17 stone 2 pounds (108.8 kilograms) and 6'1" (1.85 metres), with a chest measurement of 42 inches (106.6 centimetres). They list his wife's name as "Dorothy," her actual first name—technically it was Dorothea—rather than "Annie,"[23] by which she was otherwise universally known, but then details in enlistment papers could be inaccurate at times. For example, they were notorious in recording matters of religious affiliation, which deeply upset many Non-Conformists who could be lumped under the catch-all "C of E"—Church of England—by an unsympathetic recruiting sergeant indifferent to shades of Protestantism, and it created havoc for chaplains trying to identify their own "flock." Each man's religion as recorded on his papers was stamped on his identity disc and could have an effect on who conducted his burial service in the case of his death. In an era of fierce denominationalism and sectarian rivalry between Christian groups, such carelessness was distressing to the small numbers of devout Christians misidentified.

At first, McKenzie was allocated to the transport ship *Euripides*, along with the Anglican chaplain, Dean Talbot, of whom he was initially suspicious. He wrote, "I have got a hard row to hoe, as he is senior chaplain. However, he and I may get along all right. I hope so, but I'll have a very trying job, but I'll win out, without a fear."[24] Indeed, he had nothing to fear, not because of his own winning ways but because Talbot proved to be a willing colleague, impressed with the work of The Salvation Army and ecumenical in spirit, with none of the reserve or condescension often evident at that time in the dealings of Anglican clergy with other faiths. He had a reputation as a powerful and popular preacher. McKenzie soon came to consider him "a very fine fellow," becoming "close cobbers" working "hand and glove," but whose worst sin was that he was "an inveterate smoker."[25]

In the meantime, McKenzie busied himself, acquiring the correct uniform for his post, as well as additional heavy clothing on the advice of the eminently practical Salvation Army Commissioner for Australia, James Hay. He also obtained lantern and slides to illustrate some of his talks, and a weighty collection of games, hymnals and Bibles for the troops. He also updated his will. He was given an impressive farewell by The Salvation Army in Sydney on September 30, with Commissioner Hay dedicating him to his task, and Mrs Commissioner Hay presenting the Army colours and giving him his charge.

While in Sydney, McKenzie took the time to catch up with his in-laws—the Hoeppers. His delayed departure allowed Annie and five-year-old Mavis the welcome opportunity to come from Bendigo to see him for a few days, and he was "powerfully glad to see them again."[26]

He also started a war service diary, recording events in his big bold loopy hand with urgent pen strokes that often rushed to the next word without lifting off the page, leaving the reader to guess if a letter finished one word or began its successor. In his writing is a snapshot of his personality: sprawling, bursting with energy, untidy, with extravagant flourishes of penmanship yet carefully chronicling things of import. He asked Annie several times to keep all his letters, feeling the need to be able to reference the events that with foresight he saw would permanently change his post-war career.[27]

McKenzie soon found himself caught in a merry-go-round, as the AIF shuffled him from one posting to another. He was shifted to the Imperial Reserve and appointed as a training camp chaplain, but then allocated to the transport *Miltiades* and finally sent back to the *Euripides*, on which he embarked on October 19. In the meantime, his heavy luggage had been shifted several times from the hold of one ship to another, which McKenzie considered must have led to some swearing from the soldiers assigned to the work.[28] To add to the confusion, his official Army papers state he left on the *Suffolk*, while he himself wrote to Hay that he was on the *Liverpool*! At the same time, in writing to Annie, he spelt *Euripides* phonetically so that she would pronounce it correctly, but also wrote to Colin from Albany addressing the letter from *Miltiades*.[29] It seems that even McKenzie was confused by all the changes.

In later years, McKenzie would explain how he came to be assigned once again to the *Euripides*, claiming he was moved to the Reserve because the quota of Salvationists was too low to justify his place in the AIF. When the soldiers heard from McKenzie about this, they took matters into their own hands, officially changing their religion to The Salvation Army, so that the next day he discovered he had been credited with 3000 conversions and reassigned to the 1st Brigade.

This charming story comes with caveats from Envoy George Hazell, a respected Salvationist educator, who—as an eight or nine-year-old in the late 1930s—personally heard McKenzie tell the story. Hazell admitted that his memory may be faulty, leading to a garbled version of the original tale. On the other hand, McKenzie knew the value of a good story and was entirely capable of delivering a tall one, provided he felt his audience knew he was stretching the truth—a nuance that might have escaped an impressionable eight-year-old listener.

While contemporary evidence supports the notion that McKenzie was not originally listed to go with the 1st Brigade, Hazell acknowledged that the idea of several thousand soldiers changing their religion to get McKenzie appointed does not square with the rest of the evidence.[30] It is clear from other accounts that McKenzie was a virtual stranger to the 4th Battalion when he first came on board, so was hardly likely to have been the subject of a popular campaign to force the authorities to appoint him. What is certain from all of this is that McKenzie was not initially designated to go with the 1st Brigade but, through one means or another, ended up attached to the 4th Battalion.

It was not well received at first. Various stories indicate that the Australian Army was unsure what to do with its Salvationist namesake. One officer reportedly said, “I know very little about The Salvation Army,” to which McKenzie replied that he was equally ignorant of the ways of the King's Army but that they could learn together. Other soldiers swore, asking what they had done to deserve getting a Salvationist. Reputedly, when he tried to start his first sing-song with the troops, they counted him out[31]—a ritual whereby the men counted out loud to 10, by which time the offender must have left or risk forcible removal. It was the ultimate social sanction, the analogy drawn from a referee's count over a knocked-down boxer.

One soldier—bitterly antagonistic to The Salvation Army—baited, insulted and disrupted him throughout the voyage but never received anything from McKenzie except smiles and serenity. This equanimity in the face of such abuse finally broke the offender and he became a warm admirer.[32]

Other much later and less reliable accounts talk of practical jokes, such as a dead fish under his pillow or rude notes attached to his wall,[33] but none of these specific incidents can be supported from contemporary documents. Certainly, the record shows that he "was not very welcome at first, for he was a padre and that cramped their style somewhat."[34] His earliest AIF nicknames were "The Bloody Parson," "God Almighty," "Salvation Joe" and "Holy Joe." It took time to change to the more respectful "Old Mac" and "Padre Mac" before eventually becoming the reverential "Fighting Mac."[35]

Unsurprisingly, McKenzie recorded none of these difficulties in his diary or letters, focusing instead on the positives. He claimed that the men on the *Miltiades* were sad to see him go and noted that the officers on board the *Euripides* "treat me with extreme kindness, some of them are just 'ripping'," welcoming the strong Scottish flavour running through the officers of the battalion, brigade and even ship's crew. He was a little less effusive about the men, writing that "the men are most respectful to me and are taking to me OK. They give me a great cheer at the concerts when I preside."[36]

But one would expect sunny cheerfulness from McKenzie because he believed in seeing everything as rosily as possible. He was unlikely to reflect negative feelings in his letters, either to his wife, who was feeling his absence, or to Hay, his spiritual leader. Knowing his letters would frequently be printed in *The War Cry* also ensured a certain level of self-censorship to produce material suitable for his domestic church audience. In any case, McKenzie was a veteran in responding to such attitudes of hostility from his years of service as a Salvation Army Officer, and his unfailingly cheerful ways soon won the men over.

Ah Kow recounts that a week or two later, the men counted him in, rightly noting that this was a rare honour.[37] In 1937, then-Brigadier-General Iven Mackay "told of how the Commissioner came as a stranger to the 1st Battalion [sic: it should read "1st Brigade"] on the troopship, but before the boat arrived at Alexandria he was the best-known man on the boat; this was because of his personality, his simple sincerity, and his unbounded energy."[38] While Mackay was not on that troopship, having been hospitalised after a riding accident just before embarkation, as a 4th Battalion officer in Egypt and Gallipoli, and later as 4th Battalion commander, he was well placed to know of McKenzie's impact.

The *Euripides* embarked the 3rd and 4th Battalions, as well as the 1st Field Ambulance and Brigade Headquarters staff, on October 19. Along with the ship's crew, it made a total of about 2500 on board, all men with the exception of a handful of nursing staff. That evening, the ship moved down the harbour to Athol Bay, anchoring just under the land then under development for Sydney's new Taronga Zoo. The next morning, it set sail for Melbourne, then across the Great Australian Bight in company with other troopships to Albany, where the fleet of Australian and New Zealand transports and escorting warships gathered. McKenzie went ashore, but only just regained his place, finding himself swinging over the side by a rope as the *Euripides* cast off before he was properly on board. After several bone-bruising encounters with the hull, he hauled himself up.

The convoy of 38 transports and seven escorts steamed out of Albany on November 1 in three great columns, providing an awe-inspiring spectacle to those on shore as well as at sea. It was the last sight of Australia that many of the men ever had, and the last for McKenzie until February, 1918. Conditions aboard the *Euripides* were spartan, especially for the men, as the ship was fitted to carry only about 1000 passengers in civilian life. McKenzie was pleased with the size and comfort of his cabin, a travelling style he was unaccustomed to. But, while officers had cabins on the upper decks, the men were squeezed below with less than eight centimetres between hammocks. Poor ventilation made the air fetid, especially as the ship steamed through the tropics, and the "atrocious" food added to the misery. Many men fell ill.[39]

It was a situation in which McKenzie's talent for creative diversions could shine. He quickly worked out a busy schedule of religious meetings and popular entertainments, in cooperation with Chaplain Talbot, the Brigade commander Colonel MacLaurin, and the ship's captain. McKenzie and Talbot ran six meetings on the first Sunday on board, beginning at 6.30 am. The Dean conducted communion at 7.45—as a Salvationist, McKenzie did not practice the administration of the Sacraments, though of course he did not oppose them—followed by the official Church Parade at 11 am. A voluntary Bible class at 3 pm attracted 25, with a prediction of 60 the next Sunday. The ship's hospital hosted a half-hour meeting at 5.45 pm, then McKenzie held a "stirring free meeting on the foredeck at night 8 pm to 8.50 pm." In the meantime, a choir was planned for the religious meetings.

The weekly program included prayers each morning and a short meeting each evening featuring family prayers, two or three songs, a short reading, and a group recital of a well-known passage such as the Lord's Prayer. Perhaps more important to the bored and stifled men were the entertainments organised for each evening, including concerts, games and dancing, or band practices to help enliven the monotonous life on board. He was particularly pleased with how the men sang "most heartily," which also greatly moved the ship's Scottish captain.[40]

McKenzie loved a hearty "sing song" and was a master at organising them. He would use popular secular and patriotic songs, adding a few better-known hymns at the end. He also wrote a few songs himself, having a gift for topical lyrics and parodies of well-known songs. Some of his compositions have survived, having been printed in a special 4th Battalion diary—which he had initiated before his departure—in 1918.

The lyrics for his earliest recorded song, in 1914, are as follows:

We'll be There
Air: original

There's a land away across the rolling sea
It's the land of good things promised yet to be
If you're going to the Pole, you can stop and get
 your coal
And you'll find Australians rollicking and free
The Union Jack floats proudly in the breeze
And we mean to keep it flying, if you please
To do this we must determine
To outwit each wily German
And that is why we cross the rolling sea

Chorus
We'll be there, there, there!
You will find Australia there
In the smoke and din of battle
When the cannons roar and rattle
We will keep things moving there
We'll be there, there, there!
We're the boys to do and dare
And when Australia's wanted
She'll be there, there, there![41]

In sentiment, it is similar to a song made hugely popular in music halls during the war, but it precedes noted songwriter Walter "Skipper" Francis' "Australia Will Be There" by a year. It is possible that Francis was influenced by versions of McKenzie's memorable song brought home by repatriated wounded soldiers. In 1933, one soldier reminisced: "I can still hear the bellow that went up to high heaven as the lads, still untried soldiers, declared in song that 'when the cannons roar and rattle, Australia would be there! There!! THERE!!!'"[42]

McKenzie's speciality was leading the singing with gusto, his deep voice booming clearly over the roar of the men. Like other chaplains, he was encouraged by the way the men sang religious songs, feeling that this represented a level of spiritual engagement. And, like other chaplains, he was happily deceived in this matter, for the phenomenon of hymn-singing was widespread in most armies and bore no essential relationship to personal spiritual commitment.

Schweitzer's study of religion among British and American servicemen in the Great War notes the common feature of hymn singing and that "serious moments were best captured by religious hymns such as 'Abide with Me'," but did not necessarily indicate a religious sentiment. Singing hymns was a "communal activity," often drawing men's thoughts nostalgically to home, offering a level of familiar comfort, and contributing to the esprit de corps of a body of soldiers, regardless of their personal beliefs.[43] Martin Crotty's work on Australian masculinity notes the common association of communal singing with manly sports and the development of moral purpose in pre-war schools, which not only took the place of religion as the key shaper of character but also acted as a "powerful symbol of conformity and unity."[44]

Nevertheless, reports of rousing hymn-singing made for excellent domestic consumption in chaplains' letters published in Australian church journals, helping maintain the support for chaplaincy and for the war effort among Christian groups in Australia. On the other hand, not all chaplains succeeded in getting men to sing—in particular McKenzie's colleague Dean Talbot[45]—so it was a mark of McKenzie's capacity to motivate the common soldier that he almost always evoked enthusiastic singing from his often-unwilling congregations.

Apart from running the various meetings, McKenzie busied himself with getting to know the men. He was a little frustrated by the crowded nature of ship-board life, which restricted his capacity to have men speak confidentially with him. He was fortunate to have the strong support of Colonel MacLaurin for his work. McKenzie soon tracked down a number of Salvationists on board, including some "backsliders," while also making friends with as many men as possible from all walks of life. He reported to Hay that the services being run on board the ship were "producing striking results," citing the singing as evidence of spiritual interest, but he missed the weekly *War Cry*, which had kept him in touch with his church network.[46]

The monotony of the voyage was only occasionally relieved by external events. The evening they left Albany, news was radioed through that the Empire was now at war with Turkey—an announcement whose impact would be felt by all on board in the coming months. The first real diversion was on November 9, when news reached the great convoy that *HMAS Sydney* had sunk the German cruiser *Emden* off Cocos Island. Enthusiastic celebrations marked the end of the threat, and McKenzie penned a song for the occasion that was sung heartily that night, no doubt helped by the extra pint of beer allowed for each man.

"Crossing the line" ceremonies produced four hours of merriment as hundreds of novices to the northern hemisphere were ritually "ducked" but the horseplay became rough as men took out their grievances on the sergeants, and the festivities were hastily curtailed.[47] McKenzie contributed to the "ungodly noise" on the big bass brass—the tuba—in the all-officer band specially assembled for the occasion. He was one of only two officers who could actually play in the intentionally incompetent band, which was enthusiastically over-conducted by Dean Talbot, happily leading in the merriment.[48] A brief stopover in Colombo provided another break, but undisciplined behaviour ashore by some Australians led to lectures from Colonel MacLaurin on the need to instil implicit obedience.

In late November, the disappointing news arrived that the convoy was diverted to Egypt, as British training grounds lacked the capacity to hold them. The passage through the Red Sea and Suez Canal fascinated the men as they had glimpses of exotic places they had only previously heard about. On December 3, the ship docked at Alexandria and, during the following weeks, the men were taken in instalments by overnight train up the Nile to their camp at Mena, outside Cairo. Like many others, McKenzie wrote a description of the trip, capturing the novel sights, sounds and even smells as they journeyed through a "quaint, picturesque and interesting" landscape that seemed more or less unchanged since biblical times, dotted with mud-brick villages and farmers leading small flocks of sheep or riding donkeys. He was struck by the dramatic difference between the lush fields beside the Nile and the desert sand that abutted them, and by the size of the fruit and vegetables in the gardens. The camp itself was just a kilometre or so from the famous pyramids, whose tops formed a backdrop above the sand dunes behind the rows of the soldiers' pyramid-shaped bell tents.[49]

The 1st Australian Division's new camp facilities were inadequate at first and, with the rest of the soldiers, McKenzie slept in the open air, suffering from the cold nights and drenching dews. He slept badly for the first three nights. Not even his coat and two blankets could keep out the cold. By day, it was scorching sun and endless sand, and occasionally the dreaded sirocco winds blew sand and dust into even the finest of gaps.[50]

Authorities had not foreseen the extent of services needed for such a large body of troops and inexperienced officers were at a loss to keep their men gainfully employed. However, the 4th Battalion's commanding officer Lieutenant-Colonel Thompson was not among them, quickly setting up a training routine that challenged even the fittest men, taking them on gruelling marches in full kit in the desert, which saw up to half of them dropping out through exhaustion.

Like other administrative officers, chaplains were not required to attend such exercises. Many chose to rest in camp or seize the opportunity for some religious tourism, visiting various churches and mosques, as well as sites of biblical significance in and around Cairo. This leisurely attitude contributed to the nickname that unforgiving troops eventually gave to the chaplains: "Cook's tourists," named after the well-known travel agency, for their tendency to serve for short commissions, be seen to work only one day a week, and avoid the greater hardships and risks endured by the ordinary soldier.[51]

McKenzie was one of the exceptions to this, although he managed to squeeze in some welcome sight-seeing as well. He was an observant and interested spectator of people and places, and his diary contains extended fascinated commentary on the cultural, historic and archaeological wonders all around. But he also thrived on the rigorous training routine, relishing the iron-hard marches with the men and throwing himself into all their activities. His diary and letters are replete with multiple examples of joining route marches, digging trenches, target practice, where he shot four out of six bulls-eyes, and even leading sham charges and attacks to encourage the men. His standing in the men's eyes was also enhanced by his horsemanship on parade when his nervy jet-black charger shied and rolled over. McKenzie leapt from the saddle while still firmly holding the horse, preventing serious injury to himself and others. Such practicality was much admired by ordinary soldiers.[52]

He admitted to Hay that "I'm discovering that I possess the fighting instincts in some measure, and quickly grasp the significant facts of the various situations that arise."[53] His current situation was as close as he could come to his boyhood dream of being a soldier, and it was clear that the dream was not entirely dead. On one occasion, he recorded setting a pace on a desert march that no-one else could sustain, a remarkable feat given that he was twice the age of many of the men. On other marches, he carried the packs of those too exhausted to continue.

"Don't they think I'm a tartar for work," he proudly wrote. "This gives me a great hold on the boys. . . . You can hardly imagine how popular I am with the men and this helps me so much."[54] He claimed to be the only padre to go on route marches, accusing the others of slackness.[55] The bragging tone, which often creeps into his diary and letters in Egypt, was not quite accurate in this case. A few other chaplains—including Walter Dexter, the Anglican chaplain of 5th Battalion in the 2nd Brigade, Frederick Miles, Baptist, 6th

Battalion, and Andrew Gillison, Presbyterian, 14th Battalion—also accompanied the men on training exercises and so gained the respect of the men they served. But McKenzie was enjoying his role tremendously, feeling totally in his element. To both Annie and Hay he wrote, "The longer I am at this work, the better I enjoy it. I'm happy indeed, among the men and have no hankerings to leave them for smoother and less exciting scenes."[56] He described himself to Hay in his characteristically colourful language as feeling "full of snap, vim and elastic vitality."[57]

But, while things were progressing swimmingly in Egypt, all was not well at home. Annie was struggling with several pressing matters and longed for him to be in "smoother and less exciting scenes" with her at home. Feeling isolated and unsupported, her letters protested his lack of correspondence. He had of course written long letters at least twice a week, with separate ones to the children, but Annie's accusations led him to wonder if military censorship had removed his newsy epistles for saying too much.

The tone of Annie's letters was quite negative. In particular, she fretted over their eldest son Donald, who was approaching his 15th birthday and whose performance at school was of concern. The family having moved from Bendigo to Melbourne, Donald had just begun at the prestigious Anglican Camberwell Grammar School. Furthermore, she naturally worried over the safety of her impulsive husband, eager for action in a war zone.

To Annie, McKenzie wrote as much encouragement as possible, although the wording may not seem particularly helpful to a modern reader. He told her that his military service "will lend me considerable prestige in coming days and you my dear must seize with me this opportunity." He reassured her that he had an "inner conviction" that he would be kept safe and asked her to "banish such thoughts."[58] His reply appears to lack a true understanding of her emotional needs, being framed more in terms of his own career.

However, to his mentor and friend Hay, McKenzie wrote asking for his personal intervention to support Annie. He felt that Donald, having reached a "critical age," needed a "firm hand" with "understanding kindness and advice," while McKenzie had "no fear whatsoever for his ultimate triumph and spiritual victory." He felt that Annie did not understand him well and that Donald did not respond as well to her as he did to McKenzie. "I'm afraid she scolds at him a little too much at times," he added, noting that Donald's "surplus energy must have an outlet as a safety valve." He described Annie as suffering from "extreme self-consciousness and numbing nervousness."[59] The letter reveals insight into how to handle Donald and demonstrates his capacity to think flexibly to accommodate teenage restlessness.

However, this letter also shows a manifest absence of empathy. His attitude to Annie seems to be drawn from the inflexible Calvinism of his upbringing, where weakness was not to be tolerated and a fall from grace was unacceptable. His evaluation of her had not progressed from his assessment of her when they first met, when he thought she needed pushing in order to succeed. McKenzie was probably not well placed to evaluate Annie's merits, having a tendency to measure those close to him by his unrealistic and unreasonable expectations both of himself and others.

Annie was a strong personality and a natural leader in her own right but might have felt overwhelmed by him. It would appear that Donald felt this way as well, commenting at McKenzie's funeral decades later that it was "a great honour to be his son, and, incidentally, a very great responsibility. He set a standard which is extremely hard to maintain."[60] Donald was not as easy to direct as McKenzie imagined, for he had his father's strength of will if not his single-mindedness. He wished to emerge in his own right from his father's giant shadow and found the burden of fatherly expectations intolerable at times.

Two other matters added to Annie's misery. Faulty administrative paperwork meant she was not receiving the authorised allocations from McKenzie's army pay, leaving her "penniless" for a time. Telegrams between Cairo and Sydney eventually resolved the problem but it took until at least March, 1915.[61]

The other matter was not so easy to fix. Anti-German sentiment sprang to life in Australia with the declaration of war, whipped up by the press and fostered to an extreme by the Australian government, particularly once Billy Hughes became Prime Minister in October, 1915. Hughes increasingly relied on hysterical paranoia to maintain support for the war effort, and he relentlessly fed the German xenophobia in an attempt to boost voluntary enlistment. Rumours of German spies were a media staple throughout the war,[62] and the German communities in Australia were persecuted and suppressed. Many German citizens were interned in camps, even sometimes Australian-born British citizens of German descent. All it could take to trigger it was a denunciation by a disgruntled "loyalist" eager to settle a grudge.

Of Alsatian–German descent, Annie was terrified that she and her children would be rounded up and incarcerated, from which there was no real avenue of appeal. Her chief shield was that McKenzie was an active serviceman, but there were cases of family members of serving Anzacs being interned. With McKenzie on the other side of the world, Annie felt extremely vulnerable. It does not appear that she communicated her fears to him but she certainly drummed into her children the imperative of representing themselves as exclusively of Scottish descent.[63]

McKenzie's letters in reply to Annie show that his affectionate concern was unabated, if somewhat unperceptive due to his total immersion in his own work in Egypt. Her letters and messages from the children meant the world to him, as did the first copies of *The War Cry* to reach him since his departure, which he "devoured with rare avidity."[64] His letters to his children over several years reveal the depth of his interest in their affairs, following with tender regard their progress at school, in musical and sporting achievements, and in their games, toys, pets and hobbies. He periodically sent them small presents according to their interests, and always tried to add details in his letters that would appeal to them, such as reports of the animals he saw.

McKenzie may have misjudged the needs at home, but he was correct in gauging his "great hold on the boys" in Egypt. A tribute published in the soldier's journal *Reveille* in 1933 had this to say: "In camp at Mena, 'Mac' was in his element. He was indefatigable attending to the material as well as the spiritual welfare of his boys. Nothing was a trouble to him." Soldiers and officers, it continued, "had the greatest respect for him—a respect that was to deepen to something greater later on when he proved himself in the front line at Gallipoli."[65]

His popularity was striking, enhanced by the wonderful entertainments he organised. He held a "monster" Christmas church parade on Christmas Day, then organised a New Year's Eve "Great Scotch dinner" for officers, including 18 invitees from other battalions, including several brigadiers, followed by a Scotch concert that earned him extravagant praise from Thompson. His prankish sense of humour emerged when he ended the dinner with a raid on the 2nd Battalion's lines.[66]

McKenzie became an accomplished promoter of public lectures on topics of popular interest, which were well attended. His concerts became legendary, attracting men from the other brigades in Egypt, and beginning the process of making his name a byword in the whole AIF. His newest song, "Goodbye Cairo," proved to be another enduring hit, with topical verses added as the war progressed. In its earliest incarnation, it ran partly as follows:

Goodbye Cairo
Air: original

They took me out to Pharaoh's land
To train me for a soldier
I got fed up with mummy sand
Whilst training for a soldier
I marched through deserts day and night
'Twas said 'twould fit me for the fight
My feelings felt it was not right
And so my feet grew colder

Chorus
Good-bye Pharaoh, Pharaoh, good-bye Pharaoh,
Pharaoh
Good-bye Pharaoh, good-bye
My heart is aching, aching
My back is breaking, breaking
Good-bye Pharaoh, good-bye

They pay me each alternate week
One twenty-five piastres
I straightway into Cairo go
To get some stomach plasters

One day I thought I'd gammon sick
Whilst training for a soldier
The doctor guessed my little trick
And dosed this scrimshank soldier
Although I tried to look so ill
And schemed to baffle all his skill
He simply said, "Smith give a pill,"
And cured this shirking soldier

Chorus
Good-bye Doctor, Doctor, etc.

I'm longing now to meet the Turk
And prove myself a soldier
No longer will I duty shirk
I want to be a soldier
I'll shoulder arms and take the track
To Port Said, Suez or Belzac
When wanted most, I will not lack
The grit that makes a soldier.

Chorus
Good-bye Cairo, Cairo, etc.

Serving in the 1st Field Ambulance, the well-known pre-war dual Rugby Union international, Tom Richards,[67] recorded the debut of the song at a McKenzie concert, along with the now-established "We'll Be There":

> At night Captain McKenzie had arranged a concert, by his energy and bustle. He is an old Salvation Army man and follows the First Brigade everywhere while the other chaplains are never to be found. The concert was a great success, some of the items being really good and some of them humorous and accidental. . . . At the conclusion the Captain sang a self-composed song "Goodbye Cairo" midst great enthusiasm; closing with "There, there, there" and cheers. God Save the King.[68]

A month later, Richards commented, "A grand concert was given in the Y.M.C.A. tonight." He wrote that soldiers who couldn't get into the crowded hall had pulled the mats off walls to see through the windows. He continued:

> The concert was a huge success. . . . The Salvation Army Captain McKenzie was in his crude element and handled the fellows splendidly. This captain is a rough, ill-educated, adventurous type of man. I don't got a rap on the strength of his religion but he is the man for the boys all right and worth a dozen of the other and better Chaplains that we have here. He follows the route marches if the men are camping out and organises concerts etc.[69]

It got to the point where no-one else dared chair a concert if McKenzie was available. His status with the men was confirmed when "a Methody parson"—Chaplain Green—was "howled and clapped . . . down" by a rowdy crowd in the concert hall. McKenzie proudly recounted that he "jumped up immediately, blew a whistle and there was instant quiet. I did a quiet chuckle to myself as the Methody was a Colonel."[70] His diary records that some of his concerts entertained crowds as large as 3000.

McKenzie's games and sports events were equally popular,

and he admitted to Hay, "I must confess that I enjoy some of the recreations myself when I see the men enjoying them so. I guess we are like overgrown children at times."[71] There are stories that McKenzie participated in the boxing contests he organised, and that he triumphed over some of the best fighters in the AIF.[72] His diary contains an ambiguous comment about a boxing match, at which there were "half a dozen willing foes, a half got the knockout blow"[73] but whether this refers to his own bouts or to the collective occasion is unclear.

There is no evidence from soldiers' diaries that he participated in boxing. Despite some extended comments on boxing tournaments run on board the *Euripides* and in Egypt, none mentions McKenzie. One would imagine that so singular a character as McKenzie would be noted somewhere if he did indeed win matches, so the silence appears telling. However, his participation is in character,[74] and his statements to Hay and in his diary are as close as he comes to saying that he actually boxed. Perhaps he was shy to admit it as he was not proud of his own pre-conversion pugilistic past, and he might have felt that his wife and his church might have disapproved.

But boxing itself was considered a noble sport. One champion amateur boxer—the "fighting parson" Reverend Hulton Sams—was one of a number of clergymen who enlisted as combat soldiers and was eulogised for his "muscular Christianity."[75] In any case, prowess at sports was widely promoted in Australian schools as the mark of the real man[76] and McKenzie's organisation of, and successful participation in, sports certainly helped shift the men's perception of him from that of the stereotypical clergyman—master of the gentle Sunday school picnic—to that of a more red-blooded man.

His popularity compared to his fellow 1st Brigade chaplains can be measured by the size of his church parades. Sunday morning church parade was compulsory and, with the Brigade in one place, each of the four chaplains ran a service and the men could attend the service of their choice. At first, there was a comic merry-go-round. The 3rd Battalion historian notes:

> It was rather humorous how quickly the men change their religion. On one occasion the Church Parade under Dean Talbot had a wonderful attendance—there were thousands there. The Brigadier and his staff were also in attendance, and in their honour everybody had to stand throughout the service. The news soon got around that at the service conducted by Padre Mackenzie [sic]—known as "Fighting Mac", now Commissioner Salvation Army for all Australia—the men were allowed to sit down and smoke. The following Sunday all hands had become Salvationists and turned out in thousands for the service conducted by Mackenzie [sic]. Just as the service was about to commence who should put in an appearance but the Brigadier. Again everyone had to stand. There was nothing left for it now but to turn Roman Catholic, and the following Sunday was noted for the magnitude of the Roman Catholic Parade. But alas! There was no R.C. service that day. In its place an extra large fatigue party was required, and the unhappy converts to the R.C. religion spent the morning cursing as they never cursed before. Such was the religion of the 3rd Battalion.[77]

However, a trend soon became clear. Talbot was a powerful preacher in Anglican circles and he retained a following in the AIF, particularly among committed Anglicans.[78] But, by January, 1915, his numbers, as well as those of James Green, were withering away, while even some of the Catholics crossed the great religious divide to attend McKenzie's parades.[79] His lively services were better attuned to soldier psychology, particularly those of secular habits, even if they were notably short of theological rigour.[80] He usually allowed the men to sit during his service and he also adapted to circumstances. A giant sandstorm on March 21 forced his sermon to be "cut short in righteousness" as everyone took cover.[81]

McKenzie recorded the numbers he attracted: 1600 on December 28, 1914; 1400 in mid-January; and more than 2000 by early March, representing more than half the entire 1st Brigade, leaving the rest divided between the other three chaplains. Twice he wrote that men were changing their religion to attend his services. He defended himself for his bragging by saying that Hay needed to know the good impression he was making for The Salvation Army. "So far as the 1st Brigade is concerned I've got the parsons snowed under. . . . It's quite laughable to watch the shuffling of the cards in this direction," he added.[82]

Yet it wasn't because McKenzie's messages were easier to digest. He preached very strongly worded sermons against "swearing, stealing and whoremongering with good effect. On another occasion, he suggested the substitution of "hokey pokey" for any stronger language. A tent near McKenzie's soon bore a large banner proclaiming "the Hokey Pokey Push," a joke that McKenzie appreciated.[83]

But, as with his impressions of hymn singing, he may have been optimistic in his assessment of his impact on swearing. A study of the Canadians in the Great War found that Army swearing went far beyond the norm for civilians,[84] and one cannot imagine the Australians taking a back seat to anyone in that department. In fact, Australians were noted for deliberately using extreme profanity to distinguish themselves from English troops.[85]

McKenzie's evenings were largely filled with concerts, games or evangelistic meetings, often run in the various Brigade YMCA Halls or other similarly large venues. By day, when not on training exercises, he moved among the men, tracking down those whose families requested news, encouraging them to write home, and finding Salvationists among the various units. He was constantly on the move across the Australian camp, which encompassed not just the tens of thousands of soldiers but also the hospitals scattered around Cairo where the men who fell ill were treated.

McKenzie's reputation allowed him to do what no other chaplain achieved or even attempted in Egypt. Almost all the Australians—McKenzie included—were appalled by the sights that surrounded them daily in Egypt, in what was for many their first experience of a foreign culture and one that was in stark contrast to their own.

The filth, corruption and moral degradation struck many of them as the lowest on earth, even among those who sampled its "earthly pleasures." The Australians were contemptuous of the local people and many letters and diaries describe them and their country in crude and racist terms. The conditions in Egypt confirmed the widespread racial prejudices of the Australians, "proving" that white civilisation, particularly in its British form, was the pinnacle of human evolution, and justified the casual violence that so many Australians meted out to the Egyptians.[86]

Nevertheless, many men took advantage of the seedy side of Cairo, especially in the early stages when the army had little in place to distract or divert them. McKenzie was predictably shocked by the moral state of Cairo, having a diatribe against the Egyptians and their willingness to fight, riot, lie and murder, all for a piastre or two.[87] He was also deeply disturbed by the number of soldiers patronising the notorious brothel district of Haret el Wassa, also known as the Wazzir, Wasser or Wozzer, as well as being upset by the failure of the authorities to provide more wholesome leisure facilities. Part of his motivation for staging sporting events and concerts was to counter the evil attractions of Cairo.

All the chaplains preached against these vices from a distance and some of their diaries noted, with prurient disgust, the extent of the prostitution industry.[88] Some even passed through the red-light district: one chaplain was pressed by some officers to enter the brothels and "see things with your own eyes, Padre" but was ashamed of what he saw while merely in the street.[89]

But, with his Salvationist tradition of direct confrontation of evil, McKenzie went further than that. His appeals to the authorities to take action against the brothels fell on deaf ears or, more accurately, on administrative paralysis. Unafraid of being tainted, he repeatedly entered the district to chase out the soldiers, asking them how their mothers, sisters and nation would feel about their behaviour. His diary notes one night in December, 1914, when he "dragged and ordered well on for 100 men (troops) some in a deplorable state. I had them taken into a well-lit street and sent off to camp."[90]

After the drunken Christmas celebrations, he wrote to Hay,

> I have done some mighty plain talking on this point and also gone into the brothels and steel holes to drag the men out. I shouldn't be surprised if I get a stab one of these nights for this as the Brothel keepers are mad with me for emptying their places and ordering the men home. Still I can't avoid it when my blood gets stirred with this giant foe.[91]

Such was his reputation for fighting evil that when Anzac soldiers rioted in Wassa on Good Friday, April 2, burning down some of the brothels, McKenzie was credited in some circles with having inspired the attack. The story grew over time into an account of how he personally led the attack, chopping up the fire engines' hoses to ensure the fires were truly destructive. Noted Canadian journalist F A McKenzie—no relation to William—began the legend by writing in 1918, "It would be too terrible to suggest that a Chaplain had any hand in such lawless proceeding! But when I have talked with the boys over that night, and have asked how it came about, I have heard more than once, 'Well you see, Bill McKenzie got talking to us, . . . and . . . [sic]'."[92]

A soldier's tribute published in the *War Cry* in 1937 added, "We recalled your efforts for the abolition of the dens, and being unsuccessful with the authorities, owing to the peculiar conditions of Cairo administration, we remembered your burning words to the boys, and the Aussies rising in a body wiping out many of these hells."[93]

In 1947, C E W Bean, war correspondent and author of the imposing official Australian war history, said in his radio eulogy for McKenzie, "But it was at Mena that he fought his greatest fight, and none who saw it, or knew his work later, will ever forget him."[94] These allusions were given a major makeover in a series of newspaper articles between 1959 and 1981, and expanded on in a hagiography in 2003.[95]

But such lawless behaviour was alien to McKenzie. He may have unintentionally inspired the riot, for in exasperation he had once wished that "the whole block were burnt to the ground" and some soldiers later claimed that they decided "that the padre should have his wish." Ah Kow adds, "He learned . . . to his great amusement . . . that not a few troops thought he inspired the eventual riot which resulted in the wholesale demolition of these hell-houses. He disclaimed the honour but grimly expressed his satisfaction with the result."[96]

Bean's statement was not a reference to the Wassa riots at all but a tribute to the huge work he had done to keep the men from corrupting their British manhood by hauling them out of the brothels and providing engaging wholesome alternatives. The riot itself was the subject of an official investigation at the time and has since been the subject of numerous historical accounts. Yet no other account has connected McKenzie with the riot at all.

Further evidence of McKenzie's non-involvement in the Wassa riots is his diary and a letter to Hay. He makes no reference to the riots at all—an unusual omission if he had been there. Instead he records a devotional time of mystical intensity, where he realised:

> the nearness of [Jesus'] presence and something of the sweetness and power of His great salvation. I confess that I cried myself to sleep last night or in the early hours of this morning after long meditation over the sacrifices and death of the Christ of God. That is, I got a new and clearer view of Calvary, the Garden with its agony, the trial with its travesty, the mockings, the scourgings, the journey with the Cross and the dying groans of Jesus—all for sins that I had done to bring me peace and redemption throu' His blood.[97]

McKenzie then delivered an early morning Easter sermon with particular power to a congregation of 2000, then spent the rest of the day organising his affairs for their freshly announced departure from Egypt.

Another story circulating about McKenzie at this time is that, "incensed that the venereal diseases camp had taken on the appearance of a prison, he helped the men to pull down the barbed-wire fence."[98] Historian Michael McKernan accurately notes that this was unlikely, for McKenzie's diary records his desire for VD cases to be isolated in a "Lepers' Camp" and their pay stopped, for they "should be made to suffer for their sin" as they had been "deliberately and wilfully bad," not heeding the warning and entreaties they had been given.[99] Despite such attitudes and actions, he retained his popularity with the men. Indeed, such behaviour probably enhanced it.

An even greater testimony to McKenzie's impact was the sheer numbers turning up at his many voluntary services during the week, which were fervently evangelistic in focus. Every meeting ended in a direct appeal to come to the Penitent Bench, usually with some result. One mid-week meeting with the Victorians of the 2nd Brigade attracted 600 men, while another meeting for the 3rd Brigade—recruited from the four smaller states—drew 1000 listeners. They were given a 45-minute sermon, with many "greatly moved and quite a few in tears."

McKenzie found the Victorians of the 2nd Brigade more receptive to The Salvation Army than the New South Welshmen of the 1st, attributing this to the positive influence of The Salvation Army in the Victorian training camp at Broadmeadows.[100] His evangelistic work with other brigades meant that his name and character were well known across the division, even at this early stage of the war. A sermon on the ship anchored off Lemnos before the Gallipoli landings had the ship's Scottish chief engineer proclaiming, "Man, isn't it gran tae hear such strong fine manly sermons. I wad gang a lang wey tae listen tae they sermons."[101]

An obviously thrilled McKenzie kept records of the numbers of conversions at each meeting, sometimes one or two, often four or five, occasionally up to 14 and once 28. Other men came to visit in his tent, to be counselled, prayed with and to receive Christ there.

He also recorded many of the comments he received from officers and men. He was repeatedly affirmed in the warmest language by Colonel MacLaurin, who said, "I cannot find words to express my appreciation for all you are doing among the men." Officers complimented him on another sermon in which he spent 20 minutes expounding on "Save your soul at all costs," saying the men gave "perfect attention and evidently like it." According to another officer the men "drank in like new milk" a sermon on Samson, with humorous touches, which he used to make his moral punchlines easier to swallow. Overheard comments were that "he's the best Chaplain of the whole bloomin' bunch of them," while another man told him, "You're the most popular man in the regiment, everybody likes you, even the R.C.s think and say that you are a 'Ding Donger'."[102]

While McKenzie's moral stance was always unwavering, he respected those who didn't agree with him and men felt he never forced his standards on them. And he had the humour to accommodate their reactions. After he imposed a one-shilling fine for swearing in the mess, an officer gave McKenzie a shilling in advance, then said, "There you are Mac. There's your bob. Now I'm going to tell you what bloody fools these men are."[103]

These are the kinds of stories McKenzie loved to recount. He was perceptive enough to understand that another man who said, "It's the bloody Salvation Army for me every time," was actually saying a prayer of commitment in the most earnest way he knew. McKenzie was seeing beyond the surface words to the heart behind them. He was also wise enough when visiting men in the camps or trenches to forewarn them of his arrival by singing as he approached, so they could hide their cards, cigarettes and alcohol, and modify their language so they would not be embarrassed by his sudden appearance.[104]

It would have taken humility far more saintly than McKenzie's not to be flattered by the overwhelming reception. He had a strongly competitive streak, exacerbated perhaps by the perceived or actual snobbery of some other chaplains of higher social class and respectability but who were less popular with the men. Twice he talked of the jealousy of other chaplains,[105] which is also unsurprising, their having been trumped by him so conclusively.

No doubt the extent of the praise was a novelty. He had probably never received so much positive response in his life, and it is understandable that his delight overflowed in his diary and letters. Perhaps most flattering was a request from the Brigade Major that McKenzie accept a commission as a company commander, as he "was too good and valuable a man to be a *Padre* [sic]." The major also said that The Salvation Army "had gone up a thousand per cent in both the Colonel's and his own opinion since they had known him." McKenzie was pleased that the impact of his work was to the benefit of his church and not just to him alone.[106]

Yet his success did not turn his head. As delighted as he was with his manifest public triumph, his conversion experience and commitment to God reminded him that he should never overvalue his own importance. His beliefs made him too conscious of his own faults and need of repentance, too aware of the sole merits of Christ in attaining salvation, to let him dwell on popularity. He enjoyed being popular—of this there is no doubt—but he valued far more being true. His pre-war career in The Salvation Army already demonstrated that he was willing to risk every shred of his popularity to fulfil his spiritual calling.

One observer later wrote, "in public he is modest and unassuming above most men I have met. He has humility without servility; he is firm without being hard; genial in disposition; incorruptible in character, transparently honest and sincere; he is of that type which commands not only full confidence but profound esteem."[107] Such a testimonial was not lightly conferred by the irreverent Anzacs, whose Australian sensibilities were finely tuned to the detection of spiritual pride, humbuggery and hypocrisy. Any lesser behaviour would have been quickly found out by the men with whom he lived daily. That he held their lifelong respect is a testament to the genuine humility of his character, despite his competitive and even combative nature.

But the battalion's time in Egypt was rapidly drawing to a close. In his letters home on Good Friday, he already signalled that they were on the move and that his future correspondence might be less frequent. The battalion entrained for Alexandria and there took the *Lake Michigan* through rough seas to the harbour at Mudros on Lemnos, one of the islands off the Gallipoli peninsula that acted as the staging base for the invasion. Another island base was Imbros, from which the Gallipoli coast was clearly visible. The men were kept more or less idle for more than a week until landing exercises began on April 14.

The region was rich in biblical and classical history: the apostle Paul had twice sailed through these waters on his missionary voyages to Macedonia and Greece; and just over the eastern horizon from where they were anchored was Troy, the setting for Homer's epic. Like most of the other chaplains in these waters, McKenzie could not resist preaching a sermon based on Paul's time in this location, attracting a huge audience to a voluntary evening service, after which the soldiers stayed for an hour, singing their favourite hymns: "Tell Me the Old, Old Story", "Where is My Wandering Boy", "Sun of My Soul", "Jesus, Lover of My Soul", "Shall We Gather at the River", "Abide with Me", "Nearer My God to Thee", "Lead Kindly Light", "God Be with You", "The 100 Psalm" and "The Glory Song".

Earlier on the same day, Sunday—April 18—his official church parade was also largely attended, including about 115 of the 140 Catholics on board, as well as some of the Jews. A devout Anglican soldier affectionately diarised, "Old McKenzie held a church parade, gave fine sermon." McKenzie couldn't resist noting with a hint of triumph that a visiting Catholic priest had a congregation of just 35 the week before. In deeply sectarian Australia, he had achieved the rare status of being regarded as "an 'everybody's man' and not a mere Protestant."[108] He had transcended that great divide, so rigid in civilian life but deeply hated by soldiers, of what one soldier termed "the fragile superfluous barriers [of] denominationalism."[109]

The men's attention to spiritual things was probably lifted by the sobering possibility of being killed in the landings that the men knew were imminent. Such was his popularity that the men "reckon[ed] to put [him] in parliament" as "the highest honour they could confer."[110]

On Friday evening, April 23, McKenzie ran one final concert, about which Private Charles Bosward wrote, "Had a glorious concert on board for the last night led by Salvation Army Chaplain Capt. W. McKenzie who is a champion." Another wrote, "Perhaps it was the most enjoyable we have ever had and everyone was in very good spirits."[111]

On April 24, the 4th Battalion was on board the *Lake Michigan*, which sailed that night for the coast of Gallipoli. Orders were opened and officers at various levels of command were briefed, and the men given a rousing talk by the Brigadier, Colonel MacLaurin, responding with cheers for their battalion commanders. The men were ordered to land while wearing their service caps and not their distinctive slouch hats. Reveille was ordered for 3 am on Sunday, April 25, and the men were given one last hot meal as they waited for the dawn.[112]

1. Ronald J Austin, *The Fighting Fourth: A history of Sydney's 4th Battalion, 1914–1919* (McCrae, Vic: Slouch Hat, 2007), pages 15–17; Robert C Stevenson, *The 1st Australian Division in the Great War, 1914–18* (Melbourne & Cambridge: Cambridge University Press, 2013), pages 20–21.
2. Michael Gladwin, *Captains of the Soul: A history of Australian Army chaplains* (Newport, NSW: Big Sky, 2013), page 34.
3. Gladwin, page 84.
4. Edward Madigan, *Faith Under Fire: Anglican Army Chaplains and the Great War*, (London: Palgrave Macmillan, 2011), pages 99–114, 116–117.
5. *War Cry*, October 3, 1914, page 9.
6. Martin Crotty, *Making the Australian Male: Middle-class masculinity 1870–1920* (Melbourne: MUP, 2001), page 6; see Madigan, pages 127–134 for a more detailed account of factors affecting the popularity of chaplains.
7. Madigan, pages 151–152.
8. Gladwin, page 75.
9. Bill Gammage, *The Broken Years: Australian soldiers in the Great War* (Canberra: Australian National University, 1974), page xiv; Michael McKernan, *Australian Churches at War: Attitudes and activities of the major churches 1914–1918* (Sydney & Canberra: Catholic Theology Faculty and Australian War Memorial, 1980), page 134.
10. See Gammage, pages 108, 119, 150, 156, 157, 187, 211, 220; and also Robert D Linder, *The Long Tragedy: Australian Evangelical Christians and the Great War, 1914-1918* (Adelaide: Open Book, 2000), page 14, and note 15 on page 17.
11. Chaplain Donald B Blackwood, "Experiences of Revd Donald B Blackwood, M.C., M.A., Th Schol, as a chaplain with the AIF, October 1915 to February 1919, and impressions gained as a chaplain," 1 DRL 619, Australian War Memorial (AWM).

12. Sapper Henry William Dadswell, MM, quoted in Patsy Adam-Smith, *The Anzacs,* (Melbourne: Penguin, 1991), page 461.
13. See Richard Schweitzer, *The Cross and the Trenches: Religious faith and doubt among British and American Great War soldiers* (Westport, CT & London: Praeger, 2003); and Madigan, pages 195–196.
14. Gladwin, page 76.
15. Gladwin, pages 34–35.
16. Gladwin, page 79.
17. *War Cry*, October 3, 1914, page 9.
18. Adelaide Ah Kow, *William McKenzie M.C., O.B.E., O.F. Anzac Padre* (London: Salvationist Publishing and Supplies, 1949), page 28.
19. *War Cry*, October 10, 1914, page 9: "Jean" should read "Mavis" as Jean had died in 1906. The mistake may have been McKenzie's or the writer of the article.
20. Letter to Annie, September 19, 1914, "McKenzie, Chaplain William, Salvation Army," PR 84/150, AWM.
21. *War Cry*, March 16, 1918, page 3.
22. Letter to Annie, October 3, 1914, PR 84/150, AWM.
23. National Australia Archives (NAA): B2455 McKenzie, W.
24. Letter to Annie, September 19, 1914, PR 84/150, AWM.
25. Letter to Annie, October 26, 1914, PR 84/150, AWM.
26. McKenzie, Diary, undated entries during early October, 1914, PR84/150, AWM.
27. Letter to Annie, undated, circa mid-1916, PR84/150, AWM.
28. Letter to Annie, October 18, 1914, PR 84/150, AWM.
29. Letters to Annie, October 3, October 18, October 26, 1914, PR 84/150, AWM; NAA B2455 McKenzie W; Letter to Hay, October 21, 1914, PR 85/815, AWM; Letter to Colin, January 10, 1915, PR84/150, AWM.
30. Hazell to the author, conversation at Sydney Heritage Room, Bexley North, December 17, 2007.
31. Ah Kow, pages 28–29; Peter Stanley, *Bad Characters: Sex, crime, mutiny and murder and the Australian Imperial Force* (Sydney: Murdoch/Pier 9, 2010), pages 99–100.
32. Ah Kow, page 43.
33. *Daily Mirror*, April 25, 1959, page 5; *Sun*, April 24, 1972, page 12; *Daily Mirror,* August 28, 1981, page 60.
34. *White over Green: The 2/4th Battalion and reference to the 4th Battalion*, Unit History Editorial Committee (editors) (Sydney: Angus and Robertson for 2/4th Australian Infantry Battalion Association, 1963), page 22.
35. Ivan G Chapman, *Iven G. Mackay Citizen and Soldier* (Melbourne: Melway, 1975), page 96.
36. Letter to Annie, October 26, 1914, PR 84/150, AWM.
37. Ah Kow, page 29.
38. *War Cry*, May 1, 1937.
39. Austin, page 24.
40. Letter to Hay, October 26, 1914, PR 85/815, AWM.
41. 4th Battalion Soldiers Diary 1918, among the papers of Warrant Officer John

Green, 3DRL/6046, AWM.

42. *Reveille*, March 1, 1933, page 8 (A2).
43. Schweitzer, pages 18–21.
44. Crotty, page 55.
45. Diary of Thomas Richards, September 6, 1914; February 21, 1915; March 21, 1915, AIF AWM-2DRL/0786.
46. Letter to Hay, dated "The High Seas," November, 1914, PR 85/815, AWM.
47. Diary, undated, PR84/150, AWM.
48. Ralph Ingram Moore, Letter, November, 1914, MLMSS 288, Mitchell Library, State Library of New South Wales.
49. *War Cry*, February 6, 1915, pages 3, 6.
50. *War Cry*, February 6, 1915, page 6; *War Cry*, February 27, 1915.
51. McKernan, *Australian Churches at War*, pages 135–136.
52. Letter to Hay, March 5, 1915, PR85/815, AWM.
53. *War Cry*, February 27, 1915, page 10.
54. Letter to Annie, March 11, 1915, PR84/150, AWM.
55. Letter to Hay, December 17, 1914, PR85/815, AWM.
56. Letter to Hay, March 11, 1915, PR85/815, AWM; Letter to Annie, March 11, 1915, PR/84/150, AWM.
57. Letter to Hay, published in *War Cry*, February 27, 1915, pages 9–10.
58. Letter to Annie, January 8, 1915, PR84/150, AWM.
59. Letter to Hay, January 9, 1915, PR85/815, AWM.
60. Ann Zubrick, Interview, October 28, 2013; *War Cry*, August 16, 1947.
61. NAA, B2455 McKenzie, W.
62. Daniel Reynaud, *Celluloid Anzacs: The Great War through Australian cinema* (Melbourne: Australian Scholarly Publishing, 2007), page 15.
63. Ann Zubrick, Interview, October 28, 2013.
64. Letter to Hay, January 8, 1915, PR85/815, AWM.
65. *Reveille*, March 1, 1933, page 8 (A2).
66. F W Taylor and T A Cusack (compilators), *Nullis Secundus: A history of the Second Battalion, A.I.F. 1914–1919* (Swanbourne, WA: John Burridge Military Antiques, 1992), page 52.
67. The Rugby Union trophy contested between the Wallabies and the British Lions is named after Tom Richards, as the only man ever to represent both teams, and he came close to representing the Springboks as well. He was a member of the Australian team that won the Rugby Union Gold medal at the 1908 Olympics. His detailed war diaries reveal a complex man with loyalties as conflicted as his rugby allegiances: mixed feelings about religion, disliking the formality of his father's faith but hating the intellectual poverty of Non-Conformism; a volunteer who questioned the justice of the British side in the war; a stretcher-bearer who felt guilty about not fighting; and eventually a distinguished combat officer, despite his prejudices against officers. Upwardly mobile from a working class background, he hated the lazy exploitation by the rich, but sometimes indulged in it himself when he could get away with it.

68. Thomas Richards, Diary, February 15, 1915, 2DRL/0786, AWM.
69. Richards, Diary, March 29, 1915, 2DRL/0786, AWM.
70. Letter to Annie, April 2, 1915, PR84/150, AWM.
71. *War Cry*, February 27, 1915, pages 9–10.
72. See, for example, McKernan, *Australian Dictionary of Biography*, <http://adb.anu.edu.au/biography/mckenzie-william-7391>. There are no contemporary records of him boxing. The earliest reference is in a factually unreliable *Daily Mirror* article, April 25, 1959.
73. Diary, January 9, 1915, PR84/150, AWM.
74. Two of his grandchildren had never heard of this, but considered it to be something he might very well do. Interviews with Ann Zubrick, October 28, 2013, and Jean Newall, October 30, 2013.
75. *Sun*, August 7, 1915, page 25; August 15, 1915, page 11.
76. Crotty, pages 32–73.
77. Eric Wren, MSS0720, AWM.
78. Alfred Prichard Kington Morris, Diary, February 7, 1915, MLMSS 2886, Mitchell Library, State Library of New South Wales; Harrie Joseph Cave, Letter No 9, January 23, 1916, MLMSS 1224, Mitchell Library, State Library of New South Wales; Howard John McKern, Diary, March 7, 1915, 3DRL3906, AWM.
79. Talbot had a lot of coaching from the men around him. Major Bennett tutored him to loosen up, while his officer mess-mates got him down to 10-minute sermons under threat of shouting a round at the mess if he exceeded that time by a second. Nevertheless, Talbot was a champion of the working-class soldier and defended them once back in Australia against attacks from the upper-class, largely Anglican hierarchy, while Green eventually became a respected chaplain: J W Bean, "The Fighting Third," *Reveille*, April 1, 1934, page 26; Herbert G Carter, Letters, 1 DRL 0192, AWM, December 25, 1914, January 3, 1915; McKenzie, Letter to Annie, January 31, 1916, PR 84 150, AWM; Dexter, October 25, 1914; Standard, December 15, 1948; Michael McKernan, *Padre: Australian chaplains in Gallipoli and France* (Sydney: Allen & Unwin, 1986), pages 42–43.
80. Harold Begbie, "Captain Mac: A famous Australian Salvationist," *War Cry*, March 3, 1917, page 3; Richards, Diary, March 29, 1915, 2DRL/0786, AWM.
81. Letter to Hay, March 25, 1915, PR85/815, AWM.
82. Letters to Hay, January 4, 1915, March 5, 1915, March 16, 1915, PR85/815, AWM.
83. Diary, February 7, 1915; Letter to Annie, February 15, 1915, PR84/150, AWM; Letter to Hay, February 10, 1915, PR85/815, AWM.
84. Tim Cook, "Fighting Words: Canadian soldiers' slang and swearing in the Great War," *War in History*, Vol 20 No 3, July, 2013, page 335.
85. Graham Seal, *Inventing Anzac: The digger and national mythology* (St Lucia, Qld: University of Queensland Press, 2004), page 27; Sidney Charles Dewey, Letter, July 12, 1915, PR85/412, AWM.
86. Suzanne Brugger, *Australians and Egypt, 1914-1919* (Melbourne: Melbourne University Press, 1990), pages 33–36.

87. Letter to Hay, March 16, 1915, PR85/815, AWM.
88. T P Bennett, Diary, May 14, 1915, PRMF 0015, AWM. Bennett's data on the number of prostitutes and their prices is almost certainly exaggerated, but was commonly accepted as true.
89. "War Reminiscences of an Australian Padre," MSS 1342, AWM, proof sheet 8, page 34.
90. Diary, no date, December, 1914, PR84/150, AWM.
91. Letter to Hay, December 27, 1914, PR85/815, AWM.
92. F A McKenzie, *Serving the King's Men: How the Salvation Army is helping the nation* (London: Hodder & Stoughton, 1918), page 57.
93. *War Cry*, February 20, 1937.
94. C E W Bean, "Eulogy for William McKenzie," transcript of radio broadcast, *News Digest*, early August, 1947, PR 84/150, AWM.
95. *Daily Mirror*, April 25, 1959, page 5; *Sun*, April 24, 1972, pages 11–13; *Daily Mirror*, August 28, 1981, page 60; Col Stringer, *'Fighting McKenzie', Anzac Chaplain* (Robina Qld: Col Stringer Ministries, 2003), page 55. The purpose of Stringer's work is evangelistic rather than historical, accounting for the lack of rigour in his use of evidence. See "Do you think I'm now afraid to die with you?" in Graham Wilson, *Bully Beef and Balderdash: Some myths of the AIF examined and debunked* (Newport, NSW: Big Sky Publishing, 2012).
96. Ah Kow, page 34.
97. Letter to Hay, April 2, 1915, PR85/815, AWM.
98. McKernan, "McKenzie," ADB.
99. Diary, December 29, 1914, PR84/150, AWM.
100. Letter to Annie, March 3, 1915, PR84/150, AWM.
101. Letter to Hay, January 4, 1915, PR85/815, AWM; Letter to Annie, April 21, 1915, PR84/150, AWM.
102. Letter to Hay, January 4, 1915, PR85/815, AWM; January 27, 1915; Letter to Annie, January 31, 1915, PR84/150, AWM.
103. Ah Kow, page 42. Her book replaced the Great Australian Swear Word with "blanky blanky".
104. Ah Kow, pages 42–3. Again, Ah Kow used the word "blanky".
105. Letters to Hay, December 27, 1914, March 16, 1915, PR85/815, AWM.
106. Letter to Hay, January 27, 1915, PR85/815, AWM.
107. *War Cry*, August 6, 1947, page 5.
108. McKern, Diary, April 18, 1915, 3DRL3906, AWM; Letter to Annie, April 21, 1915 , PR84/150, AWM.
109. Leo T Pearce, "A religious service on the eve of battle," *Spectator*, June 25, 1915, page 918.
110. Letter to Annie, April 21, 1915 , PR84/150, AWM.
111. Charles F Bosward, Diary, April 23, 1915, 3DRL/4104, No 958, AWM; McKern, Diary, April 24, 1915, 3DRL3906, AWM.
112. Austin, page 34.

CHAPTER 4

THE LEGEND IS BORN

GALLIPOLI, 1915

The first troops to land at what is now known as Anzac Cove in the pre-dawn light of April 25, 1915, were those of the 3rd Brigade, whose task it was to secure the beaches for the 2nd Brigade, followed by the 1st Brigade, which was to push through to the ambitious objectives laid down for the first day. As part of the third wave, the first groups of the 4th Battalion began boarding the boats that would take them ashore at around 6.45 am, arriving an hour or so later. By midday, the entire battalion had disembarked, but it was held in reserve by the 1st Division commander Major-General William Bridges, while its fellow 1st Brigade battalions were moved to critical points in the confused fighting taking place in the scrub-covered gullies and crests of the rugged Gallipoli landscape.

By 4.45 pm, Bridges had released the 4th Battalion to plug a gap in the Australian line to the south of the Anzac positions. The Battalion dug in at dusk, just in time to help repel a Turkish counter-attack against the thinly held Australian line in front of the 8th Battalion positions. By the end of the first day, the 4th Battalion had seen action but had suffered only a handful of casualties, remaining the only intact Australian battalion by the end of the day.

The next day changed this picture. Ordered to improve the location of their lines in front of what would soon become known as Lonesome Pine on 400 Plateau,[1] Battalion commander Lieutenant-Colonel Thompson and his second-in-command Major Macnaghten rallied the men around them and impulsively advanced. The move was heroic but misguided. They had failed to issue proper orders and other units around them were ignorant of what they were trying to do. The disorganised advance soon turned into chaotic retreat and the gallant Thompson was killed, Macnaghten grievously wounded and several other officers also became casualties. Various groups of the 4th were left isolated in exposed positions, unaware that the rest had retired. It was only after dark that all groups pulled back to consolidate their line.

Worse was to follow. The following day the Brigadier, Colonel MacLaurin, was shot dead while observing the enemy positions. Strung out over a great distance and without a Brigade or Battalion commander or deputy, the 4th Battalion still managed to defeat a Turkish counter-attack that day from the safety of their hastily-dug trenches. Despite efforts to recover it, it was too dangerous to move Thompson's body, which had to be left in No-Man's-Land. By the end of the first week, the 4th Battalion had lost about 50 killed, more than 90 wounded and another 67 missing, some of whom would later be accounted for on hospital ships.[2]

During all this action, McKenzie was still on board the *Lake Michigan*. Chaplains had been strictly forbidden from joining the troops in the landings, remaining instead on their ships and helping the doctors with the wounded streaming back, often with sickening injuries, from the shore in the returning boats. Only one chaplain had evaded the order: Father John Fahey, the Roman Catholic chaplain of 11th Battalion from Western Australia. Fahey was as tough and practical as McKenzie, with considerable experience roughing it in the timber settlements and mining towns of the West. He claimed not to have received the order for chaplains to remain on their ships, so joined his men in the first wave of the landings at 4.30 am.

Fahey's battalion landed on the northern end of the beach, above Ari Burnu, into the heaviest fire and probably suffered the severest casualties of all the battalions in the first wave. Fahey himself saw the men on either side of him killed on the beach. His coat, haversack, waterproof sheet and tobacco tin were riddled with shrapnel and bullets in a series of separate incidents, a book was shot out of his hands, a tin of jam perforated as he ate from it, and he was half buried by shells twice—all in the first three weeks.[3] It was the kind of adventure McKenzie would have thrived on and he must have been envious when he found out.

McKenzie's diary reported the landings in some detail, composed from what he could see and from the accounts of men returning to the ship. It is written with great immediacy and, from the diary, it is possible to think McKenzie landed with the men. Indeed, the 4th Battalion history—written in 2007—mistakenly implies he was there.[4]

Of his first experience under shell fire, he reported, "It is remarkable to relate that . . . I first felt in a most gleeful happy mood all fear vanished and I revelled in it and longed to get at them."[5] But the shelling happened whenever the *Lake Michigan* moved closer to the shore and was subjected to bombardment, as his diary records, noting that "we withdrew to Imbros and anchored for the afternoon and night."

McKenzie's work on board consisted of tending to the wounded, leading services and "special duties," which involved the heart-breaking task of making inventories of the possessions of the dead and wounded in the battalion. He managed to get ashore several times, but only briefly, probably each time to help bring out the wounded, although on one occasion he passed on a message from a restless Iven Mackay stuck on board ship to Colonel Bennett, who had assumed command of the 4th Battalion.[6]

Witnessing for the first time the terrible injuries inflicted by shrapnel came as a shock to many, especially those like the chaplains who spent a disproportionate amount of their time with those horribly mangled bodies. McKenzie was deeply affected by the agony of the wounded and, writing to Salvation Army Commissioner Hay, he requested that people in Australia give pastoral support to the bereaved through letters and visits.

To both Hay and his wife Annie, he wrote that the men "are longing for me to be with them in the trenches and have sent messages to say that they miss me sorely and want me to be with them," which could hardly have reassured the anxious Annie, knowing how likely it was that her impulsive husband would thrust himself into danger. Showing a better sympathy for Annie's plight at home, he added to her, "I am continually thinking and praying for you all and ask that God may specially strengthen you to carry the heavy burden that is now on you in managing the children in my lengthy absence."[7]

His thoughts often returned to home during the following months and he lapped up news received by letter or through *The War Cry*, relishing the vicarious involvement in domestic matters. He continued to encourage Annie, affirming her talents and tracking Donald's academic progress, which slowly improved. He also urged Annie to take a holiday to revive and refresh, and sent her money for the break.

McKenzie had hoped to go ashore permanently on May 6 but it was May 10 before he was released, landing days after other chaplains Walter Dexter and Andrew Gillison were ashore. He was soon engaged in burial services as "the bullets whistle round us by tens of thousands while the field guns drop shells each day by the thousand."

Among the first burials was that of Lieutenant-Colonel Thompson, whose body had finally been recovered by troops digging a sap—a trench dug toward the enemy line—into No-Man's-Land on May 11. In a hasty whispered night service right on the front line, McKenzie "had to kneel and keep head and body in a crouching posture while reading the service" with bullets passing just overhead as Thompson's body was buried in the side wall of the trench, although another soldier remembers that the Turkish fire seemed to slacken during the service "almost as if the Turks were paying their respects to a gallant enemy."[8]

In just 10 days, McKenzie buried about 170 men. These acts of burial were of great importance to almost all soldiers. No matter how irreligious the Anzacs might have been, "there was never indifference to the burial of the dead" and the funeral services conducted by chaplains were often as well attended as battlefield conditions permitted. Through these services, the chaplains won the deep and enduring respect of soldiers and families at home.[9]

McKenzie had a number of narrow escapes during this early period. A bullet grazed his scalp, leaving a permanent scar—remarkably, it was to remain his only war wound. Another buzzed past his right ear and he was showered with earth by a near miss from an artillery shell.[10] So busy was he that he didn't have time to change his clothes for the first two weeks.

On May 19, the Turks launched a massive assault to drive the invaders back into the sea. At Lone Pine, where the 4th Battalion was, the attack began at 10.30 pm the previous evening, then resumed at 3 am. Wave after wave of Turks came from Wire Gully and moved across the Australian front line, presenting easy targets. Journalist and historian C E W Bean likened it to a kangaroo shoot, with soldiers competing for space on the parapet.

One 4th Battalion soldier, Corporal Alfred Mower, reported firing his rifle as fast as he could. Each time the magazine was empty he was handed another loaded one—by McKenzie, who was offering as much practical support as he could in keeping with his status as a chaplain.[11] As usual, he was irresistibly drawn to where the action was the hottest. The Turks were mown down, leaving thousands dead and dying in No-Man's-Land as the shattered survivors retreated to their trenches at about 5 am.

McKenzie wrote a detailed account of the battle, noting the Turks' heavy losses and those among his own men. About 185 men in the 1st Brigade were killed, with more than 400 wounded. The 4th Battalion lost 16. With a striking combination of elation and grief, he recorded, "Our boys were in great heart, they climbed up on the trench parapets and fired with accurate and determined aim. Many reckoning it the best sport they ever had. It put them in great heart, and they long for such another go. The noise and racket of the firing of big guns and rifles was terrific, and no sleep was possible. I had a very trying duty the next day, burying our own dead. I thought so much of the many sad hearts in Australia, when they know of their losses. We laid 28 in one grave all in a row."[12] Missing from his account is any mention of his passing loaded rifles to the men.

Over the following days, the hot sun caused the Turkish corpses to swell and burst, adding to the already sickening smell of the unrecovered Australian dead, while the pitiful appeals of the wounded slowly faded into death. A truce was brokered, as the air was intolerably toxic for both sides. At 8.30 am on May 24—British Empire Day—McKenzie joined Australians and Turks in No-Man's-Land for seven wearying hours, identifying the bodies, taking their identity discs from around their rotting necks and, from their pockets, personal effects wet with putrefaction, burying friend and foe side by side.

The work was indescribably horrifying and the stench made him sick. McKenzie wrote, "I had a trying time gathering the discs off and other identification marks off them. I never had such a task and hope never shall again. War is indeed 'Hell' and no adequate description can picture it." He felt intimidated by the sight of the Turkish officers and their German advisers, but "I threw out my chest and marched past them with a touch of 'Rule Britannia swagger' seeing it was our 'Empire Day'."[13] It may have helped ease his distress just a little to receive—the next day—his first mail from home in five weeks, including pictures from the children.

For the first few weeks on Gallipoli, McKenzie was unable to hold any large meetings. The situation was too perilous to permit any gathering that would have become the target for artillery. The Allied position occupied only a shallow foothold and was under constant observation by the Turks on the hills above. Almost every place was vulnerable to artillery fire, and many even to direct rifle and machine gun fire. But after the failure of the Turkish May Offensive, the front eventually settled into something resembling a routine, punctuated by skirmishes, raids, sniping, bombardments, tunnelling and mining.

The day before the truce, he had conducted his first Sunday services ashore, spending four hours in the front line reading to the men in small groups and running a song service in the evening. An observer wrote of this service, "Sunday after the bombing and noise it was very quiet about sunset and it was a wonderful sight. I watched it from a lookout and at the same time a Salvation Army Padre from Sydney was having a sort of small church behind the trenches on the side of a hill. It was great to hear the singing in the quiet of the evening with such a beautiful and peaceful sunset."[14] On the following Sunday, despite an artillery duel, he held two evening services, which he considered "cheery, bright and helpful."[15]

McKenzie occupied himself by visiting the wounded in the beach hospitals, then moving about the trenches by day. He would meet with the men singly or in small groups in whatever confines the rapidly expanding and deepening maze of trenches permitted, or hold meetings in the modest shelter of gullies behind the front lines. He distributed letter-writing materials, reading matter and soldier comforts, chased up those who hadn't written home and wrote hundreds of letters himself, usually to the families of men in his unit, especially those killed or wounded.

At night, when it was marginally safer, he conducted burials. As the only chaplain from his brigade ashore, his work was overwhelming in scope. Soldiers rotated between hauling up supplies under sporadic artillery and sniper fire, and the relative safety of the trenches. But McKenzie was constantly on the move, tramping the long hike from the beach up the steep slopes of the hillsides, often through positions covered by Turkish artillery, snipers or machine guns, visiting the scattered units of the entire brigade, as well as dealing with the administrative work involved, mostly regarding the massive mails. Late in the campaign, he was sorting through 7000 letters and parcels per post,[16] and was answering hundreds of letters personally.

It was only in mid-June that Chaplains Talbot and McAuliffe arrived on Gallipoli, having previously been engaged in the hospitals on ships and at Lemnos.

McKenzie made his name by his sacrificial work on behalf of the soldiers on Gallipoli. At one point, his dugout "adjoined the biggest wire entanglement system opposite the enemy; it could not be farther advanced in the front line." Putting himself at the forefront impressed the soldiers with his courage.[17] A soldier reported, "He spares no labour or weariness of body, mind or spirit to make the dear fellows happy and comfortable as circumstances will permit."[18] Decades later, others recalled, "Your endurance was simply astounding, and your courage and consecrated audacity amazed the bravest of the boys."[19]

His normal routine was arduous enough, given that he worked all day, then often conducted burials for several hours at night. A typical day's work was usually around 18 hours.[20] Sometimes, he got no sleep because the funerals lasted till dawn. For a man of 45— even for one as robust as McKenzie—it was taxing physical work. Yet he extended himself over and over again. Wherever he could, he lent a helping hand, carrying one end of a stretcher, lugging the awkward but precious water tins tainted with the taste of their former contents of kerosene or petrol up to the trenches, or bringing other supplies on his way to the front.

Noticing that a "treacherous" section of steep hillside was problematic for the men carrying the huge tins of water or wounded men on stretchers, McKenzie spent one free night cutting steps into the track. "Wasn't that just like him," wrote a fellow Salvation Army chaplain, "but they could never get him to say who did the work. No wonder they all love him! He is undoubtedly a servant of all."[21] Later, as a burial party ascended those steps, a soldier was overheard to say to his mate, "Another digger gone up old Mac's steps."[22] Soldiers also fondly remembered that when he overheard a wish for eggs or for chocolates, he went scrounging all over the peninsula, appearing later "bearing on [his] massive shoulder a crate of eggs for the hungry 'Diggers' up the line" or boxes of chocolates for them.[23]

From June onwards, the chaplains were able to run more frequent services, gathering the men in more sheltered parts of the line, though still vulnerable to random shell fire. McKenzie scheduled his main Sunday services around 4 pm, as the Turks had their principal meal at that hour and tended to be quiet for a time afterward. Several of these services have been captured in the diaries of other soldiers, as well as in his own.

Lieutenant-Colonel Le Maistre of 5th Battalion recalled on Gallipoli, "On Sunday afternoons, a little after four, you would see the Padre [McKenzie] coming down Shrapnel Valley, singing 'Jesus, Lover of My Soul' and the lads coming out of the dug-outs like rabbits out of burrows and following him. When he got them into a comparatively sheltered corner he proceeded to lead them in a short Sunday afternoon service."[24]

Brigadier General John Forsyth of the 2nd Brigade recalled being drawn from his dugout:

> [Amid] the fierce crackle of musketry and roar of guns—along the distant trenches a battle was in progress—he heard the sound of singing. It was one of the Church's grand old hymns. At last he left his dug-out to see where the singing was, and he beheld some thousands of men grouped along the hillside in front of Chaplain 'Mac,' who stood below them, and under his direction the grand old hymn swelled above the roar of battle. It seemed to him that the roar of the guns went in majestic but terrible harmony with the sound of that grand old hymn.[25]

McKenzie wrote of several services where the atmosphere—despite the battle setting or sometimes partly because of it—was particularly moving. One letter records, "Our Sunday night meeting was a most helpful occasion, held on the hillside. It is a welcome break and the singing is good to listen to. The war is having a very sobering effect on the spirits and natures of the men."

Another letter noted,

> It is Sunday night and I have just conducted the evening

> meeting behind the trenches on the hillside under the usual conditions, big bombs and shells flying about and the crack of the rifles. However, nothing untoward happened. Indeed, we had a precious season of blessing, a fine crowd, helpful attention, good singing and a very devotional spirit manifest.[26]

A week later, just before the awful attack on Lone Pine, McKenzie wrote of his "tremendous sense of solemn responsibility" when preaching, "looking into the faces . . . of men, some of whom will have been killed or wounded ere the next Sunday comes around." He was "obsessed with the idea and yearned with unutterable longing to lead them to the blessed Saviour." He continued, "One is very near to the eternal here, indeed all subterfuges are rudely torn aside and one is ever treading on the threshold of the Eternal World and marching in step with the sinister shadow of death."

He concluded with a description of his service, which captures something of its surreal, mystical atmosphere:

> [As] we sang the familiar Hymn "Jesus, Lover of my soul, let me to Thy bosom fly" the strains of the grand helpful prayer wafted down and around the valley and was taken up by men on all sides, who were engaged on duty. The sentries standing on guard at the mouths of the trenches nearby with bayonets fixed likewise joined in the refrain and while we were singing "Plenteous grace with Thee is found" a platoon of armed warriors marched right past us to take up their position in the support trenches and they too marched on singing "let the healing stream abound, make and keep me pure within." Men realise as never before that the most manly thing to do is to worship and glorify God.[27]

McKenzie's passion to see men saved was driven by his evangelical conviction that, without his brand of personal salvation, men were destined to an eternal oblivion. Hence, there was a kind of desperation in his efforts to make sure the men were saved.

His admiration and love for the men shone in all his correspondence.

Their bravery and daring, fortitude under great suffering and calmness evoked his praise. He considered it an honour to be there, describing himself to Annie as "delighted to share the discomfort including dirt, lice, sore bones, damp ground and cold nights, loss of sleep, lack of water and the rifle and shell fire with its dangers of instant and lingering death for the privileges of their association and telling them of Jesus the mighty to save."[28] One 1st Battalion soldier recorded seeing him: "My first introduction to Padre McKenzie (Fighting Mac) was behind the cookhouse, where he was stripped to his pants, chatting [delousing] his shirt and he called out his score at 47 lice for the morning's catch."[29]

After the war, McKenzie regaled an audience with his account of conditions on Gallipoli:

> I have learned the art of shaving, washing my face and hands, and having a sponge bath over my whole body with only a pint of water. (Laughter.) The sponge was pretty dry when it reached my number tens. (Increased laughter.) The Anzacs discarded their shirts because of disputes with other lodgers. (Roars of laughter.) Plenty of "recruits" joined up there, and men were always being "brought up to scratch." (Sides aching.)[30]

Occasionally, his intolerance of weakness showed itself, but those moments were rare. One soldier recalled, "He had no time for shirkers or milksops. He considered a man should be made of stern stuff and capable of hard work."[31] It was a standard that most of the men came up to, and one by which he rigorously measured himself.

His letters to Annie during June and July reflected the harshness of the conditions and his longing to be home. One included a pound note for her birthday, quite a generous present for McKenzie to offer. He insisted he was in "fine form—body, soul and spirit" and added that he had a good appetite for hard biscuits, bully beef and rough conditions.[32]

But, by late June, McKenzie was suffering from dysentery, an affliction that decimated the Allied forces on the peninsula, brought about by hot weather, the plague of huge and aggressive flies that bred in unburied corpses, poor sanitation, little water, and a diet low in fresh vegetables and fruit. His teeth were also suffering from his attempts to eat the rock-like biscuits. In the official OPD report, Chaplain Frederick Miles wrote, "Mr McKenzie suffered from [dysentery] very badly: he was so weak he could scarcely walk, yet he persisted in 'carrying on'. The present writer cannot adequately praise the fine spirit that was manifest by this chaplain and his special grit at this time."[33]

In late June, McKenzie was rotated out of Gallipoli to the hospitals on Lemnos. It was not merely his turn, but also a chance for him to take some badly needed rest and recuperation. But McKenzie had no time for such "milksop" behaviour. Instead, he ran a multitude of meetings and concerts, with daytime visitations to wounded soldiers, while keeping up his busy correspondence. He also bought £65 of supplies for the men of the brigade, including those small "luxuries" like eggs, chocolate and a "barrel of sweet lollie biscuits were just the 'juicy joy'," that made such an impression on the soldiers—one man writing with evident pleasure of the stock of special foods he purchased off McKenzie on his arrival.

McKenzie returned to Gallipoli on July 19, still weak with frequent bouts of "Di'o're'a," as he wrote it in his diary.[34] The great August offensive was looming. Many of the men of the brigade were in no better shape than he was and he would not have missed the battle for anything.

The high command had been thinking about how to break the stalemate that had settled over Gallipoli since late May. The plan was a series of coordinated attacks to take the Sari Bair range combined with new British landings at Suvla Bay, north of the positions held. The New Zealanders would take Chunuk Bair, the highest point on the peninsula with support from Australian and Indian troops, while the Australian Light Horse would attack at The Nek to draw off Turkish reserves. At Lone Pine, to the south of the beachhead, the 1st Brigade would attack strong Turkish positions as a diversion before the main attacks.

Preparations for the attack at Lone Pine had begun as far back as

June. Saps were dug into No-Man's-Land toward the enemy, then a tunnel dug parallel to the front lines. This allowed the first wave of attackers to advance unseen and nearly halve the distance they had to run to the first Turkish trench to less than 75 metres. Others were set to making bombs—as hand grenades were then called. The Turks had a handy bomb about the size of a cricket ball, but the Australians had to improvise them out of jam tins stuffed with bits of metal and stones, with a detonator and an unpredictable wick that could be troublesome to light.[35]

Now under the command of Lieutenant-Colonel Macnaghten, newly promoted though barely recovered from his wounds, the 4th Battalion was to attack on the left—or northerly—side of Lone Pine, while the 3rd Battalion attacked in the centre and the 2nd Battalion on the right. The 1st Battalion formed the reserve. Reconnaissance confirmed that the Turks had covered the first trenches with pine logs, sleepers and earth, and were doing the same to the reserve trenches. Barbed wire in front of the trenches also provided an obstacle to the Australians.

The diversionary attack on Lone Pine was set for 5.30 pm on Sunday, August 6, with the attacks on the principal targets to commence later that night and continue the following day. The 4th Battalion was withdrawn from the front line for the first time since the April landings, and given a day or two of rest in a position now known as 4th Battalion Parade Ground.

On the morning of the battle, the battalion stacked its packs under the watchful eye of a corporal who would prevent their contents being looted by light-fingered opportunists from other battalions. The men threaded their way south from the position behind Wire Gully to the trenches up the steep slope on the western side of 400 Plateau, arriving at Brown's Dip behind The Pimple in the early afternoon.[36]

As they moved into the front-line trenches, the British bombardment pounded the log-covered trenches of the Turks, smashing some holes in them and creating gaps in the barbed wire. Waiting for the grim moment to attack, the men had fallen silent, as the Turkish artillery replied. While the 1st Division diary claimed a "sangfroid and steadiness" among the reserves for the battle, a soldier recorded that the joking had been replaced by sober fear and "drawn faces."[37]

The attack went in at 5.30 pm and, within half an hour, the Australians had captured the forward trench system and had begun blocking them off from the maze that led to either side and to the rear of the Turkish positions. The battle was savage. Soldiers fired in on the Turks through gaps torn out of the overhead logs or they raced to the uncovered trenches at the rear, then fought their way forward with rifles, bayonets, bombs and any other weapon that came to hand.

In the darkness of half-covered trenches, especially as evening fell, the bodies of the dead and wounded lying three or four deep clogged the trenches. The men had to walk over them, horrified at the quivering of the bodies underfoot, but desperate to ensure their own survival in the fierce trench fighting.[38]

But capturing the trenches was one thing, holding them was another. The Turks rallied reinforcements and, during the next few days, made repeated efforts to retake Lone Pine, attacking with artillery, bullets and particularly bombs the barricades that the Australians had mounted. Casualties grew until, by the evening of August 9, having retaken some outposts, the Turks conceded the loss of their main positions and the fighting died down.

The cost had been horrendous: nearly half of the 4th Battalion officers were dead, as were a third of its men. Fewer than half the battalion escaped being wounded. Chaplain Talbot was shocked at the appearance of the survivors: "I shall never forget as long as I live, seeing the 4th Battalion coming out of the trenches. The men looked like a thin line of spectres."[39]

Other battalions involved in the fight also suffered heavy casualties. A mark of the intensity of the battle was that it resulted in seven Victoria Crosses—Britain's highest decoration for gallantry—being awarded, though none was for a 4th Battalion soldier. But the success of the battle was doubly ironic: instead of distracting

Turkish reinforcements from the main attack, it drew them north into the main fight and Lone Pine was the only real success in the string of battles in the August Offensive, which petered out later that month.

McKenzie's proper place during such an attack was normally at the Regimental Aid Post, which had been established at Brown's Dip, working with the Battalion Medical Officer, Captain Walter Stack. But McKenzie was too excited to be confined to one place. Three times in the lead-up to the battle, he ran messages from Lieutenant Colonel Macnaghten in the reserve trench to the Brigade-Major, Major Dennis King, in the fire trenches, who was directing the men to their positions. In his diary he recorded that "many trembled from head to foot, yet despite it all I felt strangely elated and somewhat excited over the prospects."[40] He was eager to join in the attack. Whenever battle was imminent, he had to fight his impulse to leap out of the trenches with the men.[41]

His exact role in the battle that followed has been the subject of various mythic makeovers, the first being admiring stories by influential Australian journalist Keith Murdoch, popular author and journalist Harold Begbie and leading British Salvationist Colonel Isaac Unsworth, while *The Scottish Australasian* featured his story in 1918.[42] Canadian war correspondent F A McKenzie, former editor of the weekly edition of *The Times* and neither a relation to William nor a Salvationist, included several McKenzie stories in his tribute to the Salvation Army's assistance to the British Army during the war.[43] All authors were able to write from first-hand experience: Murdoch met McKenzie in France and possibly at Gallipoli, Unsworth in Egypt and London, and Begbie and F A McKenzie also in London in 1916.

Murdoch wrote, "He is a wonderful man is Fighting Mac. At times he has been more than a padre, as when he led a group of men with an entrenching tool at Lone Pine. But that story has been told."[44] Where it had been told, Murdoch left unstated, apparently assuming it to be common knowledge, but it has yet to come to light in modern research. But others take up the story, with minor variations.

F A McKenzie records, "I first heard of William McKenzie in the days when the Australian troops returned to London from Gallipoli." He continued:

> "We had a Salvation Army Chaplain with us," one hard-bitten Australian trooper told me. "My! He was a big, burly fellow, and without a bit of nonsense in him! Some of the stunts he did would make your hair stand on your head. One day at Gallipoli we had to storm the stiffest part of the Turkish trenches; it was the worst bit of the whole show, and 'Mac' declared he was going with us. 'Boys,' he said, 'I've preached to you and I've prayed with you, and do you think I'm afraid to die with you? I'd be ashamed of myself to funk it when you are up against it here.' And he came along with us right in the front line. He had nothing but a little stick with him, and he came out of the fight without a scratch. He had a bandanna handkerchief on his head to keep the sun off. The handkerchief was riddled with shrapnel and he hadn't a scratch. He was a man!"

The story concludes with another soldier repeating a joke that William McKenzie reportedly told: that the men followed him closely in the action only because he had their pay in his pocket and they were afraid of losing it.[45]

A number of sources refer to his astonishing deeds in the heat of battle, but without going into detail. While Murdoch brushes off stories of McKenzie's heroics on the presumption that they were already known, Harold Begbie's article disingenuously suggests the heroics, while disclaiming specific knowledge: "He was with the dying, but he was also with the fighting. Once, when the Turks came thrusting up to the trenches, he seized a . . . But I really do not know the rest of the story."[46]

A Salvation Army writer after the war credits McKenzie's Military Cross award to his rallying leaderless retreating men and heading a counter-attack against the Turks with an entrenching tool—again—which took the enemy line.[47] Salvation Army Lieutenant-Colonel

Percival Dale's eulogy at McKenzie's funeral separates the stick and entrenching stories into two separate events. The stick is associated with the "I've preached to you . . ." speech, while the other story is couched as a rhetorical question, as if unsure of the tale: "Was it another occasion when the Turks advancing almost into the trench in which he crouched, he seized a trenching tool and led the counter attack[—]the Officers in that Sector having been killed."[48]

Later writers have also echoed the contemporary sources. Prolific Salvationist author Adelaide Ah Kow's 1949 biography of McKenzie made passing reference to McKenzie's speech, while stories in a number of Murdoch tabloid newspapers on McKenzie from the late 1950s to the 1980s featured the spade in their accounts. Australian evangelist Col Stringer expanded on it with imaginative detail in his book.[49]

However, the famous inter-war author and AIF veteran Ion Idriess abandoned a partially written biography of McKenzie when he discovered that he had never taken part in any personal fighting. While noble, his story lacked the dash, conflict, bloody scenes and terror required for the Idriess treatment.[50] The battalion history labels the stories as "tales [that] may have been apocryphal, but are worth repeating."[51]

A recent study also refutes any suggestion of McKenzie charging the enemy carrying a spade or a stick. Graham Wilson dismisses the various inventions that have accrued around the story, demonstrating that the only battle that the various stories could possibly refer to is Lone Pine—the 4th Battalion was involved in no other offensives—and insisting that McKenzie served at the Regimental Aid Post where he was meant to be.

"I cannot believe and will not believe that William McKenzie was such a poor priest and such a poor soldier that he would have [taken part in an armed assault]," Wilson concludes, adding for emphasis a few pages later, "To think that a man . . . who was ever mindful of his duty to both God and the army as a military chaplain would do something so naive, so crass and shallow, so totally out of character as to lead a charge on the Turkish trenches armed with a shovel is totally ridiculous and is an insult to the memory of a great and wonderful man."[52]

Wilson dismisses the literal possibility of McKenzie's statement that the men followed him because he had their pay on the grounds that the men at Gallipoli were never paid in cash, although soldiers' diaries record getting paid and purchasing items, and McKenzie was among those who sold items such as matches and chocolates when supplies came in.[53] However, he does not consider the likelihood of McKenzie telling a deliberate tall story for humorous effect, for which he was renowned. Wilson bases his conclusions on an examination of the evidence in the tales, his own experience of service in the army and on many years of historical research as an employee in the Department of Defence.[54]

He is far from the first to dismiss exaggerated stories about chaplains at Gallipoli. Chaplain Walter Dexter, a man whose war record perhaps surpasses that of McKenzie's, wrote of the "stories told about myself and a couple of other chaplains leading charges on the first day here, which of course is piffle," especially as only Father John Fahey went ashore on April 25.[55] First Battalion Methodist chaplain Colonel Green noted in a letter, "The men greatly appreciate the work of the chaplain, and are over generous in their estimates. If you carry a fellow's rifle to help, or some such thing as that you 'have led a charge'."[56] In a letter home, a soldier discounted a newspaper story of Chaplain McAuliffe hunting a Turkish chaplain who was seen bearing arms.[57] So one must be cautious of giving too much credibility to such stories, especially with the passage of time. Like fishermen's tales, they had a tendency to grow in the retelling, not so much big-noting themselves but the achievements of others whom they admired.[58]

Yet, the accumulation of evidence seems to suggest that McKenzie did not spend his time at the Regimental Aid Post throughout the battle. First, Macnaghten remembered McKenzie as being fully determined to accompany the men, duty or no duty at an Aid Post. He wrote to McKenzie in 1916, "I will never forget you when we were waiting to go over at Lone Pine—when I found you up with us, and you stated quite simply you were coming over with the boys, and I refused to allow you to come without a rifle and bayonet."[59] This is no rebuke, for the lead-up to this statement congratulates him on winning the Military Cross, but considers that it should have been the Distinguished Service Order, if not the Victoria Cross for his heroic work. Clearly Macnaghten did not think poorly of McKenzie for not being at the Aid Post.

Second, later reinforcements who joined the 1st Brigade took as truth the stories that McKenzie had led the charge, one noting that leading his church parade in February, 1916, was "the parson . . . that led the charge at Lone Pine." A 1st Battalion soldier wrote home, "[4th Battalion survivors] who took part in that terrible 'Lone Pine' charge speak of 'Mac' with great pride and reverence, for his daring and fearlessness in taking a lead to the enemy with entrenching-tool-handle in one hand and Bible in the other, I have heard the tale recounted so often by different lads that there is hardly any cause to misbelieve it."[60]

The lovely touch of the handle in one hand and Bible in the other suggests a mythic element to this much-repeated account, neatly capturing McKenzie's temporal and spiritual engagement. It seems to have formed part of the folklore of the 1st Brigade, despite the writer's faith in the strict factuality of the account. However, it adds weight to the idea that McKenzie actually took part in the battle in some way, and shows that the story had a very early currency within the brigade and was not merely invented for journalistic ears. In a 1937 *War Cry* article, soldiers remembered, "That day we stormed the stiffest part of the Turkish trenches, you insisted on going with us."[61]

Finally, David Cameron's recent account of the Battle of Lone Pine notes Chaplains Talbot and McAuliffe working together in ecumenical harmony behind the lines in the Brown's Dip Aid Post, but McKenzie is not mentioned.[62]

However, McKenzie was in the captured trenches no later than Saturday, August 7—the second day of the battle, while it was still raging hotly. On that day, an exhausted Lieutenant Lecky of the 2nd Battalion, passing through a communication sap,

> felt tempted to sneak down a little way and have a rest. However, an undaunted chaplain was there administering to the wounded and dying. He looked at me. One look was enough and I went round to the new position with the survivors, without any more inclination to quit the job. That Chaplain was "Fighting Mac" the Salvationist.[63]

Cameron accepts that McKenzie charged across No-Man's-Land with his "flock," then quotes extensively from McKenzie's letter to Annie, a passage almost identical to his own diary entry for August 6. "I was there in it all, the trenches were the most awful sight I have ever witnessed," he wrote to Annie. "Hundreds of dead Turks and these intermingled with Australia's sons lay in tiers deep in some trenches. The dead on top of the wounded and what a terrible struggle to get the wounded out."[64] His diary recorded, "My experiences of getting the wounded out of the trenches over the dead and wounded underneath the dead was sickening. The burials in the tunnels within the trenches too was nerve wracking, as also was the recovery of the dead in the open as the Turkish guns were very busy by day and sometimes by night."[65]

While Wilson is undoubtedly correct in debunking the idea that McKenzie led a charge, it is not difficult to imagine him going across to the recently captured trenches, carrying a stick or a shovel, which he would need for the burials he conducted. It seems likely that a restless McKenzie went across some time either late on Sunday, August 6, or on Monday, August 7, probably joining groups of men who were fed into the battle as it progressed. He would not have had a formal leadership role, but he was unlikely to have been at the back of the pack and his moral leadership would have been felt. In any case, he was observed in the captured trenches less than 24 hours after the start of the fight, while the shells and bullets were still flying thick across No-Man's-Land.

McKenzie was not alone among designated carers to take such initiative: the 2nd Battalion Medical Officer, Captain Alexander "Doc" Fullerton, followed the last platoon of his battalion on the night of the attack and worked on the wounded in the trenches as the others fought around him. Neither Fullerton nor McKenzie was negligent in his behaviour. On the contrary, both were recommended for decorations for their commitment to their duty.[66] A recent history of the Australian Chaplaincy Corps identifies multiple examples of chaplains attending to the wounded in No-Man's Land in the Great War, making McKenzie's behaviour not particularly exceptional.[67]

Leading an attack may have been out of character; but staying as close as possible to the action to attend to the wounded was entirely in character—as he had already demonstrated—and was also compatible with his role as a chaplain. A 4th Battalion soldier specifically lists McKenzie by name as one of the five surviving officers at the muster on August 10, when the battalion was relieved from the trenches.[68] To list him at this point implies strongly that he was active in the danger zone over the previous four days.

McKenzie's work during and immediately after the battle was of a draining intensity. He wrote:

> When this work was done, I buried in all something like 450 men killed in this and [illegible] consequent days. These burials cover a period of three weeks, when the smell of the bodies after the first four days was overpowering, and frequently I had to leave the graves to retch from the effects of the smell. The burials in Brown's Dip by day were frequently performed under shell fire. Several occasions men were hit and some killed.[69]

McKenzie said he found four dead Australians on their knees. They had been gravely wounded and knelt to pray as they died.[70]

One example of his tragic work was the story of burying Private James McGregor, a 3rd Battalion soldier who had sought him out before the battle through his mother's urging. McGregor was "labouring under great emotion and possessing all the religious reticence of the typical Scot, he was reluctant to reveal his true religious feelings." With tears in his eyes, he eventually asked McKenzie, "I want to be on the side of Jesus but I don't know how to get there." McKenzie prayed with him and he accepted Christ, telling McKenzie how happy he was and how happy his mother would be about the news. McKenzie found his body at Lone Pine and buried him. A letter in his pocket to his mother told of his conversion, which McKenzie forwarded to her as a partial consolation in her grief. McKenzie also made the effort to meet her on a later visit to Scotland.[71]

The tail end of this battle also entered McKenzie mythology. Several accounts have him, with some credibility, working without rest for three days and nights in the immediate aftermath of Lone Pine, surviving on a handful of biscuits and a few pannikins of water or "poisonous tea."[72] Later versions up the ante considerably, claiming he buried 647 men in that time, on the same diet. A recent Salvation Army newsletter improved even on this by having McKenzie dig and fill many of the graves while he was at it.[73]

But the sheer logistics of so many funerals in so short a time, let alone digging and filling even a small proportion of this figure, beggars belief. Both on Gallipoli and in France, McKenzie often dug and filled graves but there is no need to go past his more tempered, yet still overwhelming, account of 450 burials in three weeks, which by his own admission, left him utterly exhausted both physically and emotionally.

"My experiences of the [first] week are beyond telling," he wrote. "I was worked to a frazzle for days and nights. I was in great pain from neuritis—all my reserved strength was used up and I could hardly crawl around except in pain and with sheer force of will and the aid of a stout stick. The officers urged me to go away, but I was determined to 'stick it' and see it through until the regiment was relieved."

McKenzie was reported as having not only brought in the wounded but also to have collected two sand bags full of pay books and identity discs off the dead.[74] He was awed by the courage of soldiers: "I felt honoured in staying with them and I felt I needed them and they needed me, particularly as I was the only Protestant Chaplain in the brigade."

He was left alone in this role because, on August 12, Talbot had moved with the wounded to Lemnos. Talbot himself had a close shave when a Turkish bullet deflected off his belt buckle at 4 am on August 7. It left a slight wound, which he regarded with pride, but an unimpressed McKenzie dismissed it as a mere graze.[75] Meanwhile, McKenzie's own shrapnel-shredded cap was souvenired by Salvationist Colonel Unsworth, who presented it to General Bramwell Booth, his denominational chief. Booth was moved to write to McKenzie, begging him—on the evidence it provided—not to risk his life unnecessarily.[76]

McKenzie spoke of the battle in a letter designed for public consumption published in *The War Cry*. Its sanitised tone is in stark contrast to his private letters and diary. However, he could not restrain himself from noting that "War may be magnificent, but I think it the most damnable insensate folly of which mankind could be guilty." He also wrote in admiring but regretful terms of the death of Presbyterian Chaplain Andrew Gillison, who was fatally wounded on August 22 when attempting the rescue of a wounded man in No-Man's-Land.[77]

But as the fighting died down, McKenzie failed to recover. He had lost 32 kilograms—nearly one-third of his weight—mainly as a result of dysentery. To Annie, he confided that he suffered from a bad back, and his energy was at a "low ebb and I've got to apply 'the whip' occasionally." Years later, he confessed that he was so low after his labours for the dead and dying that he wished he could also die.

He was dealing with the correspondence of the entire brigade, including censoring all letters, and for the first time he admitted that he needed a rest. He felt that he had done more than any other chaplain, "but it does not do to boast in any way. . . . No other chaplain does these duties mentioned. I'm now the 'Daddy' of the regiment. The respect shown me is wonderful, officers especially." He warned Annie to keep quiet about this as it could make others jealous.[78]

The breadth of McKenzie's work at this time can be seen in a letter he wrote to the parents of Willie Dunstan soon after the battle. Dunstan was one of those awarded the Victoria Cross for heroism in defending a barricade at Lone Pine during the Turkish counterattacks. McKenzie assured the parents that Dunstan's wounds were not life-threatening and that he would make a full recovery. He also spoke in glowing terms of William's heroics, and was aware of the details of his actions and the severity of his wounds.[79]

Yet Dunstan was not one of McKenzie's men: he was a Methodist not a Salvationist, and served in the 7th Battalion of the 2nd Brigade—not even in McKenzie's own brigade, let alone battalion—and McKenzie had only met him once or twice. Apart from everything else that he had to do during those appalling few weeks after the battle, he had tracked Dunstan's condition and found time to write reassuringly to his family. And McKenzie's letter made it clear that this was no one-off event: he had spoken to Dunstan when he arrived on Gallipoli as a reinforcement days before the battle, urging the young man to write to his parents.

In early September, the 2nd Division arrived at Gallipoli and, on September 12, they took over the position at Lone Pine from the pitiful remnants of the 1st Brigade, now only about 1600 strong and many of them crippled with dysentery. The 4th Battalion numbered fewer than 300. With the Turks still shelling Lone Pine, McKenzie visited the 2nd Division in the trenches. "'Many good lives were lost in taking this position, boys! Hang on,' he exhorted."[80]

Down at the beach, the 4th Battalion men were angry when the promised transports to Lemnos failed to arrive. Memories of it were still strong in 1937:

> We were ordered away to Lemnos for rest, refitting and reinforcement. The ship was overloaded, and two hundred and twenty had to remain behind. The boys were ugly and rebellious when informed they must return and wait another twenty-four hours. All "Mac's" kit was on board, and he had orders to go, yet he volunteered to remain.
>
> The General placed the Padre in charge, and he led the men back from the ship, up the hillside, as he had done

> into Lone Pine. Bringing us to a spot sheltered from the shells, he gave us a two-hours' concert, and finished up with the boys repeating after him, as they had done at their mother's knee, "Our Father, which art in Heaven," and the Shepherd's Psalm. The boys all reckoned it was a better "go" than they could have had on the ship.
>
> And yet how much this must have cost him, for that night there was stolen from the boat his kit containing all the precious records he had so jealously guarded, with particulars of wounds, deaths, burial places of the thousands of men he had buried, and which he was anxious to send to loved ones.[81]

McKenzie was devastated to lose his records, as well as his hoard of war trophies and winter clothing. He railed at the Greek sailors, calling them the biggest robbers he'd eyer met—quite an epithet for a man with experience of Cairo's touts.[82] Despite his phenomenal memory, these papers were vital in helping provide clear official records as well as informing grieving relatives of the fate of their loved ones.

Their loss may have contributed to the confusion over the death of James McGregor, whom McKenzie had identified and buried on August 7. Unfortunately, the 3rd Battalion administrators did not get that information and he was listed as "Missing in Action" in the battalion records until a Court of Inquiry on June 5, 1916, determined he was dead. Having already written to the family, McKenzie must not have known that the battalion records were not up to date. After the war, McKenzie's version of the story was confirmed when McGregor's body was exhumed from the Brown's Dip cemetery, identified and reinterred at the Lone Pine cemetery.[83]

Soon McKenzie was taken to Lemnos on board *HMTS Simla*. But, on landing on the island, he resumed his hectic schedule with the mails and with concerts, and distributing 1000 copies of the New Testament. He ministered to all the men on the island, including a group of devout Tasmanian gunners, who appreciated his services and Bible studies.[84]

Brigadier General Smyth, 1st Brigade commander, decided to send him on one month's leave at the urging of the Chaplain General, who insisted that McKenzie needed rest. On September 19, he departed for Egypt—his official service records say Malta!—away from the temptation to throw himself into working for the men. But despite getting a luxury berth on the P&O liner, the voyage from Lemnos to Alexandria was not an easy one. The ship had a large contingent of British Medical Corps staff and 70 nurses. McKenzie noticed that "the men sat in a large group on the well deck forward, looking miserable, swearing, grumbling and ill at ease, fearful lest the ship might be torpedoed." He seized the moment to begin an impromptu concert to lift their spirits.

"All were terrified and under great mental strain," a soldier recalled. He continued:

> When Chaplain McKenzie came on board, his presence changed the whole atmosphere of the ship. He appeared to be a kind of superman, with power to perform miracles. His sublime courage, his magnetic personality, and efforts for the nurses and men, had the effect of stilling the tempest of fear. He was a comrade Coeur de lion.
>
> At his memorable Church Parade on the Sunday morning, he seemed to be inspired. A hush fell over the crowd . . . [sic] It seemed as though an Unseen Presence walked over the waves. Nurses and men were so greatly moved that they fell on their knees in rows, and the man who was both saint and soldier offered prayer.[85]

McKenzie found his time in Cairo refreshing. He was able to rest and enjoy some sight-seeing. He was also able to have some dentistry done on troublesome teeth that had suffered from trying to eat the rock-hard biscuits on Gallipoli, alongside four serious cavities, though the cost of £7-7-0 appalled him. He spent time with fellow Salvationist Officers and, of course, he soon was involved in running meetings, bringing men to tears in the religious ones and to laughter in the concerts. He was as instantly popular there with soldiers he barely knew as with his own battalion.

TOP MEET THE MCKENZIES: William's parents Donald and Agnes McKenzie (seated) with five of their sons and Agnes' brother. Back row (left to right): James (Jas), Jack Callen (Agnes' brother), Robert. Front row standing (left to right): Archie, Evan and Alexander. Photo circa 1892–93. William—the eldest son—had already left home. (Photo courtesy of Rhonda Symonds)

RIGHT WILLIAM DREAMING: McKenzie had wanted to join a Highland regiment since childhood. Here he poses dressed in the uniform of a sergeant of a Scottish regiment, probably that of The Queen's Own Cameron Highlanders or his favourite The Seaforth Highlanders.
(Photo: The Salvation Army Heritage Centre, Melbourne)

BOTTOM YOUNG MARRIED: William and Annie around the time of their wedding, 1899.
(Photo: The Salvation Army Heritage Centre, Melbourne)

TOP MCKENZIE THE MUSICIAN: William with a Corps band around 1905, probably that of the St Arnaud Corps. (Photo: The Salvation Army Heritage Centre, Melbourne)

BOTTOM THE ACCIDENTAL COMEDY TRIO: McKenzie as Provincial Commander of Bendigo (left) is pictured with his diminutive Divisional Secretary, Winter, and bean-pole Deputy Commander, Holdaway, in 1912. The three formed a band of kazoo (McKenzie) and concertinas (Winter and Holdaway) more famous for its comic appearance than for its musical accomplishment. (Photo: The Salvation Army Heritage Centre, Melbourne)

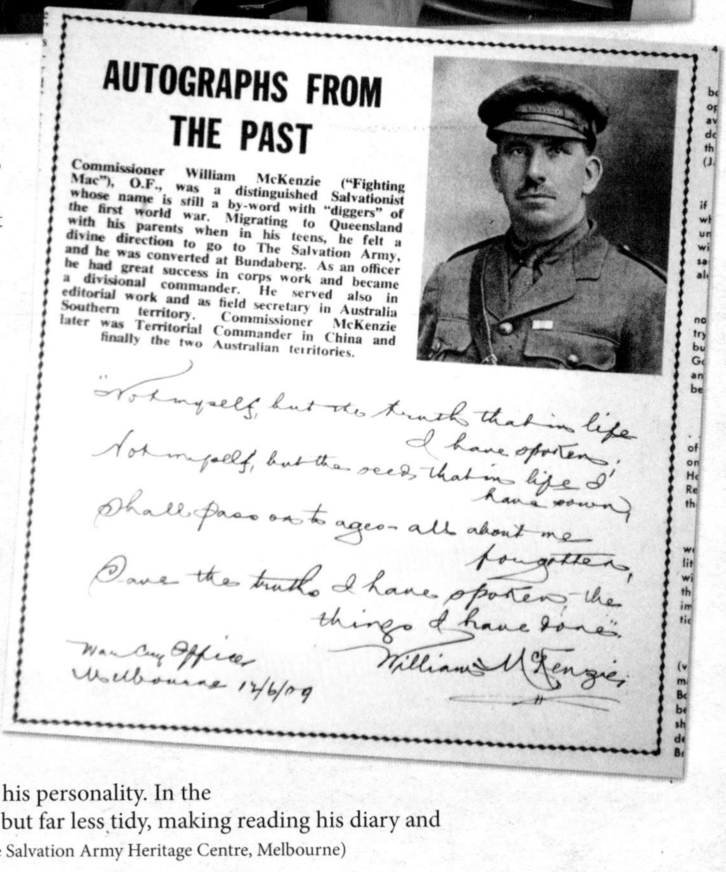

AUTOGRAPHS FROM THE PAST

Commissioner William McKenzie ("Fighting Mac"), O.F., was a distinguished Salvationist whose name is still a by-word with "diggers" of the first world war. Migrating to Queensland with his parents when in his teens, he felt a divine direction to go to The Salvation Army, and he was converted at Bundaberg. As an officer he had great success in corps work and became a divisional commander. He served also in editorial work and as field secretary in Australia Southern territory. Commissioner McKenzie later was Territorial Commander in China and finally the two Australian territories.

"Not myself, but the truth that in life
I have spoken;
Not myself, but the seeds that in life I
have sown,
Shall pass on to ages – all about me
forgotten,
Save the truths I have spoken, the
things I have done."

War Cry Office
Melbourne 12/6/09

William McKenzie

TOP THE SAVELOY CLUB: McKenzie's colleagues at the Administrative Headquarters of the Salvation Army in 1909 (left to right): John McMillan, Arthur S Arnott, scion of the famous biscuit manufacturer and after whom the SAO (Salvation Army Officer) biscuit is allegedly named, George L Carpenter, later 5th General of The Salvation Army (1939–46), Walter Suttor and William McKenzie. (Photo: The Salvation Army Heritage Centre, Melbourne)

BOTTOM MCKENZIE'S PLEDGE AS EDITOR OF *WAR CRY* IN JUNE, 1909: "Not myself, but the truth that in life I have spoken/ Not myself, but the seeds that in life I have sown/ Shall pass on to ages all about me forgotten/ Save the truth I have spoken, the things I have done." His large, flamboyant handwriting reflects his personality. In the trenches, his writing was urgent but far less tidy, making reading his diary and letters a real challenge. (Image: The Salvation Army Heritage Centre, Melbourne)

TOP PARADE GROUND AT CAIRO: McKenzie's 4th Battalion parades at the Mena Camp in January, 1915, with the pyramids as a backdrop. (Photo: Author's collection)

BOTTOM THE THREE MUSKETEERS: William McKenzie poses in front of the famous Sphinx and the Pyramid of Cheops, with Salvation Army colleagues Colonel Isaac Unsworth from the United Kingdom, and Chaplain Alfred Greene of the New Zealand Expeditionary Force. The three worked closely together in Egypt. (Photo: Author's collection)

TOP AT MENA CAMP: McKenzie with some of the men of the 4th Battalion at Mena in Egypt, early 1915. (Photo: Author's collection)

BOTTOM GALLIPOLI BURIAL: McKenzie (right) taking one of the hundreds of funeral services that he held on Gallipoli. (Photo: Australian War Memorial H15688)

TOP LEFT WIRE GULLY: McKenzie (2nd from left) close to the front lines between Johnston's Jolly and MacLaurins Hill, on the Gallipoli Peninsula. The 4th Battalion was stationed here during the Turkish counter-attack of May 18–19, 1915. (Photo: Australian War Memorial G01347)

BOTTOM LEFT AFTER LONE PINE: A studio photo of a slimmer McKenzie some time after the battle of Lone Pine in August, 1915. He had lost about one-third of his weight due to dysentery. (Photo: The Salvation Army Heritage Centre, Melbourne)

TOP CENTRE AND RIGHT THE FIGHTING MAN: McKenzie in full kit in France with his steel helmet and gas mask. (Photo: The Salvation Army Heritage Centre, Melbourne)

BOTTOM RIGHT: ROYAL TELEGRAM: The telegram calling McKenzie to Buckingham Palace for his investiture with the Military Cross. (Photo: The Salvation Army Heritage Centre, Melbourne)

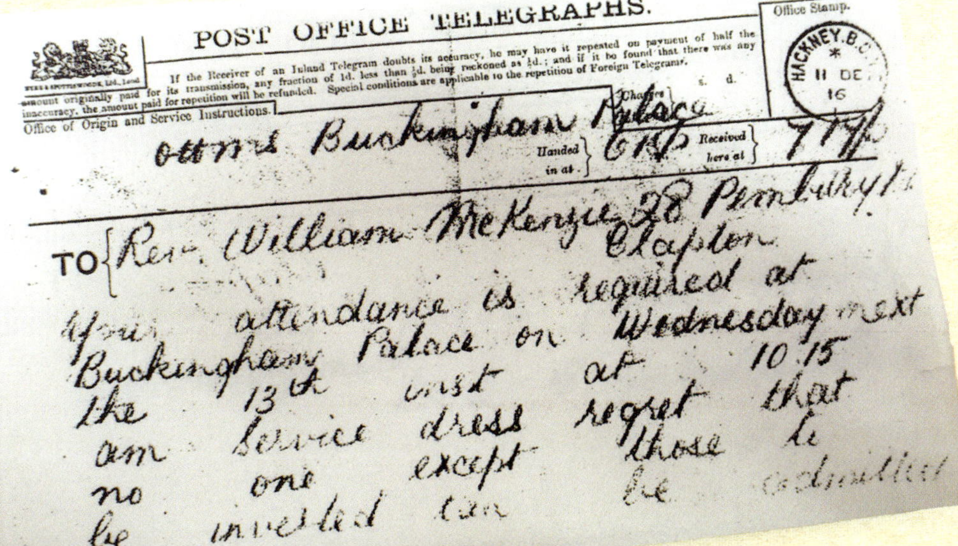

POST OFFICE TELEGRAPHS.

If the Receiver of an Inland Telegram doubts its accuracy, he may have it repeated on payment of half the amount originally paid for its transmission, any fraction of 1d. less than ½d. being reckoned as ½d.; and if it be found that there was any inaccuracy, the amount paid for repetition will be refunded. Special conditions are applicable to the repetition of Foreign Telegrams.

Office Stamp. HACKNEY. B.O. 11 DE 16

Charges s. d.

Office of Origin and Service Instructions. OHMS Buckingham Palace

Handed in at 6 R — Received here at 7 ...

TO { Rev. William McKenzie 28 Pembury Rd Clapton

Your attendance is required at Buckingham Palace on Wednesday next the 13th inst at 10.15 am Service dress regret that no one except those to be invested can be admitted

MAJOR MCKENZIE: A studio portrait of McKenzie around 1917. (Photo: The Salvation Army Heritage Centre, Melbourne)

TOP REVIEWING THE "TROOPS": William McKenzie "inspects" his children in early 1918, having just returned home after four years' absence—(left to right) Mavis, Donald, Colin and Gordon. Mavis is wearing the uniform of the Life Saving Guards, The Salvation Army equivalent of Girl Guides, while the boys appear to be wearing cadet uniforms. (Photo: The Salvation Army Heritage Centre, Melbourne)

BOTTOM THE MCKENZIE RECEPTION: A crowd of more than 6000 people gathers to hear McKenzie speak at the Melbourne Exhibition Hall in March, 1918. McKenzie can be seen standing, speech in hand, middle left, immediately behind the pipe band. (Photo: The Salvation Army Heritage Centre, Melbourne)

TOP **ANZAC DAY, 1920s:** McKenzie at a Sydney Anzac Day parade in the early 1920s, surrounded by men of the 4th Battalion. He wears his military medal ribbons on his Salvation Army uniform. (Photo: The Salvation Army Heritage Centre, Melbourne)

BOTTOM **THE SUNBEAMS:** Commissioner McKenzie reviewing a Salvation Army youth "Sunbeams" parade. (Photo: The Salvation Army Heritage Centre, Melbourne)

TOP MCKENZIE IN CHINA: A visiting Salvation Army official is welcomed to McKenzie's China headquarters. (Photo: The Salvation Army Heritage Centre, Melbourne)

BOTTOM PREACHING IN CHINA: McKenzie holds an audience in a Chinese village. His translator is probably Ensign Kuo. (Photo: The Salvation Army Heritage Centre, Melbourne)

TOP THE LIEUTENANT COMMISSIONER: A formal portrait of McKenzie during his time in command of the Southern Territory, circa 1930. (Photo: The Salvation Army Heritage Centre, Melbourne)

BOTTOM MIXING WITH THE INFLUENTIAL I: McKenzie addresses the powerful businessmen's group The Constitutional Club in Brisbane, 1933. The blackboard behind him announces the next distinguished guest—Prime Minister Joseph Lyons. (Photo: The Salvation Army Heritage Centre, Melbourne)

TOP MIXING WITH THE INFLUENTIAL II: A civic reception at Newcastle for McKenzie in March, 1933. The Lord Mayor of Newcastle, William Sheddon, and a bevy of distinguished clergymen and citizens pose with McKenzie. The tall clergyman immediately behind McKenzie, Reverend B C Wilson, served alongside him on Gallipoli. (Photo: The Salvation Army Heritage Centre, Melbourne)

BOTTOM MIXING WITH THE INFLUENTIAL III: McKenzie with Dame Mary Hughes, wife of wartime Prime Minister Billy Hughes at a Salvation Army function. (Photo: The Salvation Army Heritage Centre, Melbourne)

LET THE LITTLE CHILDREN COME TO ME: A childlike McKenzie at a children's home in 1931. The matron is trying to stop the children from "annoying" the great Salvation Army leader. (Photo: The Salvation Army Heritage Centre, Melbourne)

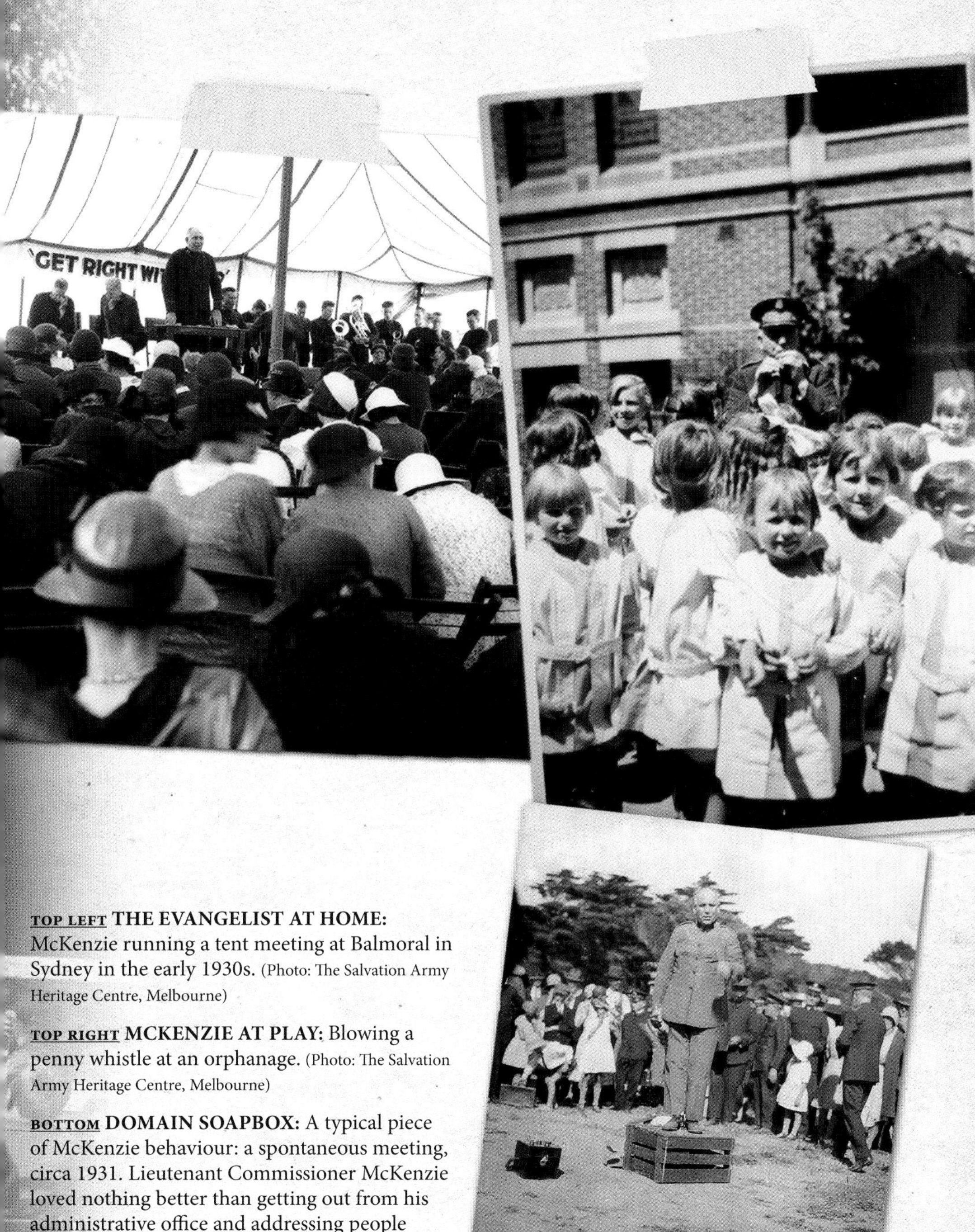

TOP LEFT THE EVANGELIST AT HOME: McKenzie running a tent meeting at Balmoral in Sydney in the early 1930s. (Photo: The Salvation Army Heritage Centre, Melbourne)

TOP RIGHT MCKENZIE AT PLAY: Blowing a penny whistle at an orphanage. (Photo: The Salvation Army Heritage Centre, Melbourne)

BOTTOM DOMAIN SOAPBOX: A typical piece of McKenzie behaviour: a spontaneous meeting, circa 1931. Lieutenant Commissioner McKenzie loved nothing better than getting out from his administrative office and addressing people directly. (Photo: The Salvation Army Heritage Centre, Melbourne)

TOP JUBILEE: McKenzie celebrates 50 years as a Salvation Army Officer in 1939. With him are Annie and Mavis, his daughter, who was finishing her medical training before taking up a missionary posting in Africa. (Photo: The Salvation Army Heritage Centre, Melbourne)

MIDDLE A SECOND WAR: McKenzie photographed in 1940 with the first Salvation Army chaplain of World War II, G W Sandells. He looks tired and distant, but it didn't stop him from trying to volunteer again. (Photo: The Salvation Army Heritage Centre, Melbourne)

BOTTOM THE MCKENZIE LADIES IN THE 1950s, AFTER MCKENZIE'S DEATH: Annie (seated) with daughter Mavis and granddaughter Anne. (Photo: The Salvation Army Heritage Centre, Melbourne)

On November 14, reporting himself to be "in the pink," he returned to Lemnos with renewed energy to match his undiminished zeal. "I still laugh when I think back of those impromptu concerts put on in the old marquee at Lemnos," one soldier remembered, claiming that McKenzie's work in entertaining the troops kept many from either "the clink" or the mental hospital, so boring was the island with nothing to do.[86]

The 4th Battalion had returned to Gallipoli on October 27 and McKenzie re-joined them gladly on November 22. McKenzie noted the periodic heavy bombardments, being nearly buried twice and slapped on the side of the head by a shell fragment.

The weather had changed from the baking heat of August. On November 27, it snowed. It was the first experience of snow for many of the men, but its magic did not last long. The bitter cold made trench life miserable, while accumulated ice on the shady side of the steep tracks made movement treacherous. Darkness set in so early that it was impossible to read in the dugouts after 2 pm, making for long, cold and boring nights. Church meetings had to be abandoned and morale plummeted as men suffered from frostbite.[87]

It was another situation that triggered McKenzie's resourcefulness. He was inspired to ask people in Australia to write "To a lonely soldier" as mail "is one of the chief events of their soldier life, and dearly they love to linger over the news from home." He had hoped to get 100 letters a week. But his request struck a chord and, within a couple of months, he was receiving more than 1000 letters, as well as papers and parcels, which he distributed to soldiers who had received no mail. It was a resounding and enduring success, which did much to lift the mood of the men. When the weather eased, he resumed his services, reporting:

> I have had a very good time today. I held four services each in different parts—two in the trenches, one known as "the Strand," from which shoot off Pitt Street, Lithgow street, etc, etc. It was a hearty, happy meeting, as indeed were all the others, including the two held in the valleys. I felt well pleased with the nature and volume of my

> work today, and I trust it was acceptable to God. I write this by the aid of a rushlight made of bacon fat and a piece of thick string for a wick, an empty biscuit tin for a seat, and a small box for a table, but I'm OK, and as happy as can be.[88]

The stalemate at Gallipoli led the generals and politicians to decide to evacuate the peninsula, and McKenzie left on December 15 for Mudros on the island of Lemnos with three other chaplains, a few days ahead of the rest of the battalion. In true Scottish fashion, he deplored the "unnecessary" destruction of stores at Gallipoli, which he felt should have been evacuated with the men.

In the camp at Sarpi, McKenzie joined other chaplains in distributing to the soldiers Christmas billies packed with treats by volunteers in Australia. He reported that "their joy was unbounded, the gratitude manifested was delightful to witness, and the original expressions and exclamations were side-splitting."[89] On December 24, he sailed for Alexandria on board the *Simla*, by now a familiar friend and on which he would sail again to France in 1916.[90]

McKenzie presided over the inevitable ship-board evening concert, attended by a host of men, including four Generals and other high-ranking officers. "The whole thing went along with vim and wholehearted enthusiasm," he wrote.[91] He was so busy that he forgot his own birthday, though he did not forget that of Mavis. To Annie, he again tried to humbly brag of his almost complete control over the men. A ship's officer said he couldn't remember any of the thousands of soldiers they had transported:

> "but we can never forget you. Why, we are continually singing your songs," and each wished to shake hands as if I was a really "Daddy Xmas" . . .
>
> I thought I preached a "ripping" sermon. I never feel a scrap nervous. In fact I just say "I'm the Boss here at this job so here goes and it helps one thus." The officers and men reckon I'm the "Daddy" Chaplain of the whole bunch and can completely lick the most at stirring preaching and none dare take the boards at a

> concert as chairman if I'm about. The men won't have anyone else. The applause is deafening as soon as I appear and they "mock" at my slightest sally and I can say anything to them and pull them up at will. The [Salvation] army stands mighty high as a consequence and will have many more friends as a result. This has been a hard trying job but I can humbly say:- "I've more than justified my appointment by incontestable results and certainly many thousands can never forget me and something of what I have said and stood for." This I know my darling will be a cheer to you and bring some satisfaction to your heart at this time of separation.[92]

His competitive nature also showed through his evident resentment over decorations awarded to other chaplains, like New Zealand Salvationist Chaplain Greene, "though not at the firing line. It is for efficient service etc."[93]

Christmas Day was spent on board, and they disembarked in Alexandria on December 29. After a short stay in a temporary camp, they moved to a permanent camp at Tèl el Kebir, northeast of Cairo, where the Egyptian fortifications from Lord Wolseley's famous victory in 1882 were still visible. McKenzie took care over setting up and furnishing his large tent, describing it as "a dinky swank affair . . . so I'm awfully comfy."

However, there was little else to do in the middle of the desert and McKenzie's skill as an organiser of entertainments again came to the fore. He also distributed more New Testaments, noting that "the men rushed these Testaments in 'wolves' and many were eager to get my autograph in their copy."[94] He may have been less impressed if he had realised that some men valued the Testaments for their fine paper, which was perfect for rolling cigarettes. Often conducted in the open air by moonlight, his voluntary religious meetings continued with great success and, on one memorable occasion, he attracted more than 200 men to the Penitent-form.[95]

McKenzie continued to attract the largest crowds to the compulsory church parades. Macnaghten's admiration for McKenzie knew no bounds, constantly showering him with praise for his preaching and declaring that the only religion he respected was that of his mother and of McKenzie. "I had a tremendously large parade yesterday morning," McKenzie wrote to Annie. "Only 6 officers and men left my Battalion to go to the C of E parade though there are hundreds designated as such. Then I had the [half] of the C of E Padre's Battalion and [one-third] of each of the 1st and 2nd Battalions. So judge the size of my congregation."[96]

However, some were not won over to his brand of religion, annoyed at the lack of theological depth. Former dual Rugby Union international Tom Richards twice attended McKenzie's official church parades, enjoying the singing but finding McKenzie "not particularly interesting" and "without an intelligent subject. . . . So I don't bother going now as there are horses that I can look after."[97]

McKenzie survived a bout of food poisoning and jaundice, refusing to be hospitalised. But he was forced to miss some events, noting how unpopular his replacements were compared to him. During this time, the battalion was split to provide an experienced core in the parallel 56th Battalion for the newly raised 5th Division, then brought up to strength with reinforcements. Other men were taken from the 4th to build artillery, pioneer and machine gun units. These former 4th Battalion soldiers helped spread McKenzie's reputation beyond the 1st Division. His standing was such that Brigadier General Smyth sought a private audience, then a dinner with him, and McKenzie was consulted on issues of morale by no less a figure than General Birdwood.[98]

McKenzie's energy, charisma and care for moral welfare had first brought him widespread attention in Egypt in the months before the Gallipoli landings, but it was on the peninsula that his reputation was secured and that legends accrued around his name. He had several qualities that won the undying love of the soldiers. His physical capacity for punishingly hard work on their behalf was a foundation stone, embodying the key mythic elements of physical prowess as the marker of manliness of pre-war Australian society. His unrelenting cheerfulness was also important. A study of British Anglican Great War chaplains observed that "What the army really appears to have valued was a chaplain who was infectiously cheerful and optimistic and who made the morale of the men his primary concern."[99]

The testimony of Archie Barwick of the 1st Battalion, among many, shows how true this was of McKenzie:

> No matter how hot the day was you would see Mac among the boys cheering and cracking jokes with them, and he would go down to the beach and help the boys carry up the rations, hard work it was too, he rarely had his coat on. That man was almost worshipped by the boys. He was attached to the 4th Battalion, and many and many a time he buried our chaps under fire. He was always merry and bright and never downhearted and I don't think he was off the peninsula the whole time; he's a man I would take off my hat to and there's not many I would do that to.[100]

Barwick's facts were not totally accurate—McKenzie spent more than two months off the peninsula—but the respect is clear, as is the cause of that respect. McKenzie's determination to be in the most dangerous spot as often as possible also made a huge difference:

> Significantly, it was the padres who were prepared to be present at times of most danger . . . that received the most praise. The evidence overwhelmingly suggests that . . . a personal willingness to expose himself to danger was the one attribute a chaplain had to possess in order to win the respect of the men to whom he was trying to minister.[101]

Again, the testimony of soldiers confirms this, and also the fact that his courage had a direct relationship with how seriously they took his religion. "That was the reason your church parades were so tremendously popular," recalled some old soldiers in 1937. "We were all ready to listen to the preacher who was not afraid to die with us."

"Up and down the hills, lumping stretchers, carrying water, doing anything and everything, always with a cheery smile, and a joke—or a kindly word of sympathy or advice—he did more for Christianity than a host of sermons," wrote another veteran.[102]

McKenzie was not the only chaplain to earn the admiration and respect of the soldiers: Dexter, Gillison, Fahey, T P Bennett and Father Michael Bergin, among others, were also loved for their dedication, practicality, spirituality and courage. Yet McKenzie's larger-than-life personality outshone them all. He was one of the exceptions to the rule that chaplains did not attract men to organised religion; post-war, many men testified that it was McKenzie who influenced them to support The Salvation Army. Lieutenant-Colonel Macnaghten enthusiastically championed McKenzie, while snidely denigrating Dean Talbot for his ineffectiveness.[103] It would appear that McKenzie did nothing to defend the reputation of his professional colleague, rather enjoying the flattering comparison. Both Macnaghten and his father Sir Melville, former chief of the Criminal Investigation Department of Scotland Yard, changed their wills to leave a substantial legacy to The Salvation Army.[104]

Chaplain Miles singled out McKenzie in his report on the work of "Other Protestant Denominations" chaplains, saying that what he wrote of his own work was true of other chaplains, "and more emphatically of Chaplain Wm McKenzie."[105] His particular blend of talents made him, as Barwick noted, one of "the two outstanding personalities" on the peninsula, alongside General Birdwood.[106]

1. A solitary pine tree led this position to be given the name of a popular contemporary song, later shortened to "Lone Pine." "400 Plateau" was named for its approximate altitude as shown on topographic maps.
2. Ronald J Austin, *The Fighting Fourth: A history of Sydney's 4th Battalion, 1914–19* (McRae, Vic: Slouch Hat Publications, 2007), pages 32–45.

3. Michael McKernan, *Padre: Australian Chaplains in Gallipoli and France* (Sydney: Allen & Unwin, 1986), pages 50–51.
4. Austin, page 39.
5. McKenzie, Diary, April 25, 1915, PR84/150, Australian War Memorial (AWM).
6. Ivan D Chapman, *Iven G Mackay Citizen and Soldier* (Melbourne: Melway, 1975), page 35.
7. Letter to Hay, May 5, 1915, PR85/815, AWM; Letter to Annie, May 5, 1915, PR84/150, AWM.
8. Chapman, page 37.
9. Michael Gladwin, *Captains of the Soul: A history of Australian Army chaplains* (Newport, NSW: Big Sky, 2013), page 81.
10. Diary, May 10, 1915, PR84/150, AWM; Adelaide Ah Kow, *William McKenzie M.C., O.B.E., O.F. Anzac Padre* (London: Salvationist Publishing and Supplies, 1949), page 36; *War Cry*, December 25, 1915. The bullet wound was never reported to authorities.
11. Austin, page 54; Chapman, page 38.
12. McKenzie, Diary, May 18, 1915, PR84/150, AWM.
13. McKenzie, Diary, May 24, 1915, PR84/150, AWM.
14. Robert Pearce Flockart, Letter to Mother, May 28, 1915, 1DRL/0296, AWM.
15. McKenzie, Diary, May 30, 1915, PR84/150, AWM.
16. Letter to Annie, September 5, 1915, PR84/150, AWM.
17. *War Cry*, March 6, 1937, page 3.
18. Ah Kow, page 39.
19. *War Cry*, February 20, 1937, page 3.
20. Other Protestant Denominations Senior Chaplain Report, August, 1914–October, 1917, AWM4 6/4/1.
21. *War Cry*, November 13, 1915; *War Cry,* February 19, 1916.
22. Ah Kow, page 39.
23. Ah Kow, page 39; *War Cry*, February 20, 1937, page 3.
24. Austin, page 90.
25. Lieut-Colonel Bond, *The Army that went with the Boys: A record of Salvation Army work with the Australian Imperial Force* (Melbourne: Salvation Army, 1919), page 112.
26. Letters to Hay, June 17, July 25, 1915, PR85/815, AWM.
27. Letter to Hay, August 2, 1915, PR85/815, AWM.
28. Letter to Annie, May 30, 1915; Diary, August 6, 1915, PR84/150, AWM.
29. Ben Champion, Diary, November 9, 1915, 2DRL/0512, AWM.
30. Bond, page 116.
31. Ah Kow, page 39.
32. Letters to Annie, June 3, June 17, 1915, PR84/150, AWM.
33. Other Protestant Denominations Senior Chaplain Report, August, 1914–October, 1917, AWM4 6/4/1.
34. Richard Asaph Edwards, Diary, July 19, 1915, PR91/192; Diary, June 29, PR84/150, AWM.

35. Austin, page 64.
36. Visiting Lone Pine today, the 4th Battalion attacked from the western or seaward side of what is the Lone Pine Cemetery, toward the monument. The western wall is approximately where The Pimple was, and the eastern wall is roughly over the forward Turkish trenches.
37. Chapman, page 53; Private Charles Ernest Scott, in Austin, page 69.
38. Austin, pages 75, 81; David W Cameron, *The Battle for Lone Pine: Four days of hell at the heart of Gallipoli* (Melbourne: Penguin Viking, 2012), page 227.
39. Austin, page 80.
40. Diary, August 6, 1915, PR84/150, AWM. Although dated August 6, this entry was written at least several days later. McKenzie was too busy to have written in his diary for several days and the account is written with the benefit of hindsight.
41. Ann Zubrick, Interview, October 28, 2013.
42. Keith Murdoch, "'Boy's Best Friend': What the Anzac thinks of his mother. A conversation between Chaplain-Major McKenzie and Keith Murdoch at the Anzac Headquarters," reprinted in *War Cry,* December 22, 1917, page 9; Harold Begbie, "Captain Mac: A famous Australian Salvationist," *War Cry*, March 3, 1917, page 3; Colonel Unsworth, "Captain Mac," undated clipping, probably from *War Cry,* early 1916, Archive Box R15, Salvation Army Heritage Room, Melbourne; *The Scottish Australasian: A monthly newspaper of Scots-Australian interest*, August 1918, pages 6415–6419.
43. F A McKenzie, *Serving the King's Men: How the Salvation Army is helping the nation* (London: Hodder & Stoughton, 1918).
44. *War Cry*, December 22, 1917, page 9.
45. F A McKenzie, pages 56–7.
46. Begbie, *War Cry*, March 3, 1917, page 3.
47. John Bond, "Fight it Through," *War Cry*, no date, Archive Box R15, Salvation Army Heritage Room, Melbourne.
48. Percival Dale, "Fighting Mac Answers New Reveille," Typescript of eulogy, August 5, 1947, Archive Box R15, Salvation Army Heritage Room, Melbourne, and quoted in *War Cry*, August 9, 1947, page 6.
49. Adelaide Ah Kow, page 41; *Daily Mirror*, April 25, 1959, page 5; *Sun*, April 24, 1972, page 13; *Daily Mirror*, August 28, 1981, page 60; Col Stringer, *'Fighting McKenzie', Anzac Chaplain* (Robina Qld: Col Stringer Ministries, 2003), pages 73–76.
50. Beverly Eley, *Ion Idriess* (Sydney: ETT, 1995), pages 171–172.
51. Austin, page 68.
52. Graham Wilson, *Bully Beef and Balderdash: Some myths of the AIF examined and debunked* (Newport NSW: Big Sky, 2012), pages 340, 343.
53. Lennox Douglas, Diary, November 24, 1915, MLMSS 5480, Mitchell Library, State Library of New South Wales; Leslie De Vine, Diary, June 6, 1915, 1DRL/0240, AWM; Francis Godlee, Diary, September 26, 1915, and pay book at end of diary, PR01507, AWM; Eric Burgess, Letter, October 18, 1915, 1DRL/0162, AWM.
54. Graham Wilson, emails to author, August 12, October 8, 2008.

55. McKernan, pages 49–50.
56. J Green, Letter dated August 22, 1915, published in *Methodist*, October 9, 1915, page 8.
57. Terence Ward Garling, Letter to parents, September 11, 1915, MLMSS 3432, Mitchell Library, State Library of New South Wales.
58. See Robin Gerster's *Big Noting: The heroic theme in Australian war writing* (Melbourne: Melbourne University Press, 1997), for an acclaimed study of the Australian tendency to big-note.
59. Letter from Macnaghten to McKenzie, August 7, 1916, Letters, programme and poem of Lt Col (Padre) WM McKenzie 4 Bn, PR 85/049, AWM.
60. George Thomasson Gill, Diary, February 19, 1916, MLMSS 2765, Mitchell Library, State Library of New South Wales; Harrie Joseph Cave, Letter 77, June 9, 1917, MLMSS 1224, Mitchell Library, State Library of New South Wales.
61. *War Cry*, February 20, 1937, page 3.
62. Cameron, pages 182–183.
63. Cameron, page 244.
64. Letter to Annie, undated, circa August, 1915, PR84/150, AWM.
65. Diary, August 6, 1915.
66. Cameron, pages 176, 335.
67. Gladwin, page 59.
68. De Vine, Diary, August 10, 1915, 1DRL/0240, AWM.
69. Diary, August 6, 1915, PR84/150, AWM.
70. Keith Murdock, "The Boy's Best Friend," *War Cry*, December 22, 1917, page 9.
71. *War Cry*, November 13, 1915, page 3; February 23, 1924, page 11.
72. *War Cry*, February 20, 1937; Ah Kow, page 40, repeated in *Daily Mirror*, April 25, 1959, page 5; *Sun*, April 24, 1972, page 13; and *Daily Mirror*, August 28, 1981, page 60.
73. Ah Kow, page 41; Richard Collier, *The General Next to God: The story of William Booth and the Salvation Army* (London: Fontana, 1969), page 229; Barry Gittins and Faye Michelson, "Wars and Rumours of Wars," *On Fire*, Vol 9 No 8, April 26, 2008, page 9.
74. Austin, page 81.
75. Diary, August 6, 1915, PR84/150, AWM.
76. Bramwell Booth, Letter to McKenzie, January 17, 1916, Archive Box R15, SA Heritage Room, Melbourne.
77. *War Cry*, October 23, 1915, pages 8, 19.
78. Letter to Annie, September 5, 1915, PR84/150, AWM; Ah Kow, page 40.
79. Stephen Snelling, *VCs of the First World War: Gallipoli 1915* (Gloucestershire: Sutton Publishing Limited, 1995), page 186.
80. Austin, pages 86–88; *Reveille*, March 1, 1933, page 8 (A2).
81. *War Cry*, February 20, 1937, page 3.
82. Diary, dateless, mid-September, 1915, PR84/150, AWM.
83. Actually James MacGregor. National Australia Archives (NAA): B2455 MACGREGOR J.

84. Albert Arthur Orchard, Diary, January 31, 1916, February 1, 1916; *Diary of an ANZAC: The front line diaries and stories of Albert Arthur 'Bert' Orchard M.C.: Gallipoli & the Western Front 1914 to 1918*, compiled by Arthur Orchard (Otago, Tas: A F Orchard, 2010).
85. Diary, undated, October, 1915, PR84/150, AWM; *War Cry*, February 20, 1937, page 3.
86. Letters to Hay, November 7, November 14, 1915, PR85/815, AWM; *Reveille*, March 1, 1933, page 8 (A2).
87. Dairy, November, 1915, PR84/150, AWM; see also Chaplain T P Bennett's diary, November 28, 1915, PRMF0015, AWM.
88. *War Cry*, February 5, 1916, page 3; Ah Kow, page 45.
89. Diary, November 15, 1915, PR84/150, AWM; *War Cry*, February 19, 1916, page 3.
90. NAA: B2455, MCKENZIE W.
91. *War Cry*, February 19, 1916, page 3.
92. Letter to Annie, undated, circa Christmas, 1915, PR84/150, AWM.
93. Letter to Annie, January 21, 1916, PR84/150, AWM.
94. Diary, undated, January, 1916, PR84/150, AWM.
95. Lt Percy Smythe, 3rd Battalion, Diary, March 5, 1916, March 12, 1916, PR01463, AWM; *War Cry*, March 18, 1939, page 9.
96. Letters to Annie, undated, early January, 1916, January 17, 1916, PR84/150, AWM.
97. Thomas Richards, Diary, January 16, 1916, February 13, 1916, 2DRL/0786, AWM.
98. *War Cry*, March 18, 1916, 3; *War Cry*, May 1, 1937, page 8; Ah Kow, page 52.
99. Edward Madigan, *Faith under Fire: Anglican Army Chaplains and the Great War* (London: Palgrave Macmillan, 2011), page 116.
100. Archie Barwick, Diary, September 12, 1915–March 28, 1916, 41–42, MLMSS 1493 Box 1/Item 2, Mitchell Library, State Library of New South Wales.
101. Madigan, page 139.
102. *War Cry*, February 20, 1937, page 3; *Reveille*, March 1, 1933, page 8.
103. Macnaghten's criticisms were somewhat unfair: Talbot had soldiers who appreciated his ministry and, on his return to Australia in 1916, Talbot became quite unpopular among elite circles for crossing the class conflict lines in his determined defence of striking Australian workers, from whom the bulk of the Anzacs were drawn.
104. Letter to Annie, January 31, 1916, PR84/150, AWM.
105. Other Protestant Denominations Senior Chaplain Report, August, 1914–October, 1917, AWM4 6/4/1.
106. Barwick, page 41.

Chapter 5

Consolidating the Legend

France, 1916–1917

After the end of the Gallipoli campaign, the next question for the command of the Australian Imperial Force was where best to use the Anzac divisions. A force was needed in Egypt and around the Suez Canal to defend against the Turks and, preferably, take the offensive, liberating Palestine from Turkish rule and ultimately bringing down the Ottoman Empire. However, this would always be a sideshow from where the war had to be fought and won—on the Western Front, at the Somme and in Flanders in northern France and Belgium. The infantry of the AIF—newly expanded from two to five divisions—was to be transferred to France once the reorganisation was sufficiently complete. Most of the Light Horse units were kept in Egypt, as there was little use for such troops in the trenches of France, while a highly mobile force would be invaluable in a campaign through the Sinai and Palestine.

The rumours of France soon became solid reality. The 4th Battalion was ordered to Serapeum on March 22. They moved out, led by the battalion pipe band playing "McKenzie's War March," which was most probably composed by him. After a gruelling march through deep soft sand carrying a full pack in the heat of the day, the soldiers then had a five-hour wait at the siding before entraining at 3 am, for a bone-chilling 480-kilometre night ride in open carriages to Alexandria. There, the battalion boarded *HTMS Simla* for the six-day voyage to Marseilles, the principal port on the Mediterranean coast of France.[1] As the soldiers left Egypt for the final time, "the words of 'Fighting Mac's' old song 'Good-bye Cairo-Cairo, Good-bye Cairo-Cairo' came into our minds as we sailed out over the blue Mediterranean—to new adventures."[2]

McKenzie ran his usual services and activities on board, slowly winning over his most resistant detractor, Tom Richards, who noted, "Rev John [sic] McKenzie's little after tea service was attentively listened to. McKenzie has done wonders with the 4th [Battalion]. I am still of the opinion that he is a big Salvation Army adventurer, yet I like him and nobody dare say a word against him, even among the roughest of the 4th [Battalion] men."[3] During the voyage, McKenzie sent Annie his new address so that her letters would reach him in France. He anticipated that the fighting would be awful, but optimistically expected it to be over by October, then "we'll start for 'home sweet home'."[4]

Marseilles to Flanders was a three-day train journey in the French railway carriages that always astonished first-time military users: they were marked "40 hommes, 8 chevaux," indicating their carrying capacity in men or horses. Nevertheless, like so many others, McKenzie enjoyed the "refreshing" landscapes, especially after the desert sands of Egypt. He found the countryside "fruitful" and its people impressed him with their "friendliness, cleanliness and cheerfulness." He considered it "a country well worth fighting for and a people worthy of much sacrifice to help and succour. We were charmed by the picturesque beauty of much of the journey."[5]

Finally, they arrived at Hazebrook in French Flanders, just a stone's throw from the Belgian border. The region was of mixed Flemish and French culture and language, the odd Flemish place names often being distorted to something easier for British tongues to pronounce. For example, nearby Ypres became "Wipers" and Ploegsteert became "Plugstreet."

The Australians were billeted 16 kilometres to the rear of a part of the line that saw little action, commonly referred to as a "nursery" sector. This gave time for training and an introduction to the routines and tactics of the Western Front, with their elaborate trench systems and massive artillery support. Through the cold and showery spring, with occasional snowfalls, the battalion blistered their feet over the uncomfortable cobblestone roads. They also rehearsed new tactics to use the mobile firepower of the four Lewis machine guns they had acquired just before leaving Egypt, which replaced the largely immobile Vickers guns they had given up to the freshly created Divisional Machine Gun Battalion.

McKenzie joined in the training exercise, using the new gas masks in a trench filled with real gas. A brief sniff of it left him with a headache all afternoon.[6] Later, the men were issued with the steel Brodie helmet, which was to dramatically reduce the incidence and severity of head injuries from shrapnel, although it provided little protection against rifle fire. McKenzie had himself photographed in his new accoutrements.

Within weeks of their arrival, they celebrated the first anniversary of the landings at Gallipoli, already termed "Anzac Day." McKenzie used regimental funds to buy about 200 kilograms of fruitcake in eight large cases from a canteen at Bailleul, about 14 kilometres away, distributing one piece to each man. "They liked it well," he recorded, though one soldier wrote that the meagre slice "caused much indignation and amusement among the men,"[7] who probably would have preferred a beer. But soon they moved into the support trenches. Even though this was a quiet sector, McKenzie found the daily shell fire heavy. He buried his first casualty on Anzac Day. On the night of May 4, the 4th Battalion moved into the forward trenches, spending 16 days there busily improving the trenches and dugouts, during which time 10 men were killed and 16 wounded.[8]

This was a vastly different proposition from what they had experienced on Gallipoli. The modern reader may have the impression that soldiers were mostly in the front line, actively fighting on an almost daily basis. But units in France spent relatively little time in the firing line, being rotated regularly between the front and support trenches, the reserve trenches and time away from the trenches altogether. Usually a battalion would spend eight to 10 days in the front trenches before shifting to the supports, reserves and the rear for the rest of the month. Even then, individual companies and platoons would only be in the very forward trenches for a few days before being relieved by other companies in the battalion. Regular periods away from the stress of the front were required to avoid the rapid deterioration of a battalion as a fighting unit.

Active combat could vary considerably, depending on whether it was an "active" sector or a "nursery" sector. However, attacks would happen surprisingly infrequently. There was small-scale fighting, such as the regular night patrols in No-Man's-Land by a handful of men, where enemy patrols were sometimes encountered, and as often as not studiously ignored or avoided. There were also trench raids of varying scale, complexity and frequency, usually ordered by higher command to seize prisoners and documents to identify enemy units for intelligence purposes, and to keep the men in fighting trim. Actual battles were relatively rare for any given unit: a full-blown attack would usually leave a battalion so decimated that it could take months to rebuild and retrain.

A soldier who avoided death, injury and disease might have been involved in a pitched battle only once or twice a year, though each battle may have extended across several days or even weeks. Most of the time in the line was spent in routine, boring work, such as repairing shell-damaged trench works, improving dugouts, digging new lines, and carting the enormous quantities of supplies—timber, barbed wire, pickets, corrugated iron, duckboards, sandbags, wire netting, telephone wire, food, water and ammunition—required to keep an army in the field.

However, even during these "quiet" times, there were regular casualties, mostly caused by shelling, with the occasional sniper casualty. These losses, and the even greater numbers of men succumbing to trench foot, trench fever, influenza, pneumonia and frostbite in the unsanitary conditions of often cold, wet and muddy trenches, were euphemistically referred to by the authorities as "wastage" and over time would accumulate to represent a significant impairment of a battalion's fighting strength.

The concentration of artillery was far greater than anything experienced at Gallipoli. While there were more targets and at a greater depth behind the line in France, a particular sector such as a key supply road junction or a recently captured position could be subjected to a storm of shelling that made anything experienced at Gallipoli seem utterly inconsequential in comparison. And shelling usually occurred on a daily basis, even if it was often ritualised and predictable in time and place.

The war front itself covered a deep area. While it varied from place to place, the march from the rear positions to the beginning of the trenches was usually several kilometres, then the elaborate trench system itself was composed of reserve trenches, support trenches and the actual firing line, all connected by a maze of communication trenches, forming a disorderly and confusing labyrinth that itself extended forward up to several kilometres. From the rear positions to the start of No-Man's-Land, this whole system was within shelling distance of enemy guns, which could play on targets of choice at random. And the predominantly flat landscapes of Flanders and the Somme were devoid of protection during the long exposed sections of the trip. What little cover that had existed—villages, crops and woods—had been mostly stripped away by the sustained shelling of the static lines. Thus, the area of risk ran for a great distance behind the lines.[9]

On the other hand, there were huge regions behind the front lines that were barely touched by war. Out of the line, the Battalion moved from billet to billet, sometimes on a daily basis for no apparent reason other than to keep the men active, fit and out of mischief. McKenzie had the habit of striding out in front of the battalion on the march, with the colonel beside him and the band immediately behind. The procession would often attract French villagers who would walk with them for some distance. The men were much amused when the giant genial figure of McKenzie, waving to the locals, was mistaken for the commanding officer.[10]

Once at their billets, the officers mostly slept in houses, while the men usually had to make do with barns. There was a semi-normal civilian life surrounding them, though it was noticeably deficient in fighting-aged Frenchmen. Estaminets—the French wine bars—provided wine or the weak local beer, and there were shops from which they could supplement their rations or buy souvenirs for family at home.

When the men were out of the line, McKenzie had fair access to them but, when in rotation through the trenches, it was much harder. First of all, with the front system so deep, it was no small journey to make from the battalion base to where the men actually were. Then there was the expectation that chaplains would not accompany men into danger. On Gallipoli, this was virtually impossible to enforce, since everywhere was subject to shell fire. But in France, the British had forbidden chaplains to go to the front and the Australian forces followed suit. It was thought to be bad for morale if a chaplain was seen to be killed and, in any case, a noncombatant was a positive liability in a trench if fighting broke out.

As the war progressed, this restriction was eased, encouraged by British Commander-in-Chief Douglas Haig, himself a devout Presbyterian who understood firsthand the value of the clergy at points of grave danger.[11] But it took time for such an attitude to filter down and McKenzie's superiors issued orders for him to be kept out of the trenches. Of course, such instructions had little effect. Reputedly, an officer claimed that short of arresting him, he could not be kept out, despite orders.

> You see (explains an old sergeant), a mile or two ahead of the main body, just behind the barbed wire entanglements, was what we called the Sacrifice Line. . . . Each battalion sent a platoon there. . . . No chaplain

> was supposed to go so far forward; but Major McKenzie was back and forth more than any of the men. . . . Sometimes he'd overtake a man going up with a pack of food on his back. He'd lift it on to his own back to give the man a spell. He was always doing that sort of thing.[12]

Whenever possible, McKenzie held services in the trenches before any attack by the battalion. On the occasion of one impending attack, McKenzie was deliberately sent to take a parade far from the front to keep him out of the trenches—but he saw through the ruse. He rode a borrowed bicycle, then walked through the maze of trenches to reach the men, who were overjoyed to see him. After talking and praying with them in small clusters along the trenches, he returned, arriving at his appointment exhausted but just in time.[13]

The punishing work schedule that McKenzie began in Egypt and Gallipoli was again the norm in France, but despite his rest over the year-end, he was not as robust as he had been. A letter to Annie in early May recorded that he was in the trenches but not feeling well:

> After doing ten services on Sunday entailing considerable walking and biking, which evidently was a bit too much for my nervous reserves, as I was trembling like a leaf at 8 pm. Consequently I got a high fever and had a terrible night of it, with all sorts of nightmares and had to get up and retch 4 times. . . . From 8.30 am to 7 pm with 1 hour for lunch is a long time to be singing and praying, talking and travelling. I certainly had some fine services and the men even most of the RCs also attend them. I could tell you some funny incidences re the jealousies of other Chaplains on this score and their efforts to counter.[14]

After spending nearly a month in the trenches, he was hoping for leave in England. He described the dugout he inherited as comfortable and relatively safe, adding in jest, "Why should we pay rent in future? Let us buy a half acre of ground and make a series of *lovely* dugouts and run a poultry farm on the spare lot. It would save you a lot of money, work and expenses. We'll have to leave all these fine places here but then we may get the Germans domiciles. Some of which are great places likewise."[15]

While McKenzie was absorbed in his work in France, matters at home were always on his mind. The news there was still troubling. Annie was continuing to struggle with the boys, particularly the independent-minded and strong-willed Donald. A string of issues emerges through the correspondence of 1916 and 1917. Don had failed again at school in 1916 and Annie was in great pain over it. It was also spoiling McKenzie's hope that the academically gifted boy would take out a bachelor's and eventually a master's degree at university. From the other side of the world, McKenzie empathised and counselled:

> Once more my darling I say without hesitation that I have no present fears for Don's ultimate well doing. He is a heavy cross for you, but I think you are inclined to worry just a bit too much over him and compare him with other boys who haven't half his brains or spirit. Let me only ask you my dear not to *nag* at him unduly. Take him aside quietly and talk to him as his mother. Treat him as a *man now* and this will break him quicker than anything I know. Don't say too much to him, but make him feel there is honour, manhood, truth and righteousness to stand for and he'll do better than you imagine. The Commissioner thinks Don's a marvel and a great credit to us.[16]

Then a letter, long-delayed in the post, arrived in August announcing the good news that Don had been converted. "I am glad to know that there is a great change in Don and he is now a different boy," said McKenzie, hoping that the new attitude would mean that he would "stick in" and pass his exam this time. But the next day he received two more letters dated from early July, saying that the improvement was short-lived. "He is at the cranky age and needs a lot of firm supervision," he replied to Annie. "They no doubt miss my presence considerably and thus increase your task by a great deal." He praised her for buying Donald a bicycle, suggesting she should present it a personal gift from herself in order to improve Don's attitude to his mother.

The gift made little difference. In November, 1916, McKenzie heard of Don's latest distressing escapade. He had obtained cash and clothes by false representation, and used the money to run away and try to enlist in the AIF. It took personal intervention from Commissioner Hay to return the lad to his mother. Upset though he was, particularly by the dishonesty, McKenzie must have seen something of his own rebellious youth in Don's behaviour, for his response was to recommend allowing him to have his own way: "Really I don't think it would have done him any great harm to have got away and fend for himself. He would have had an awakening in a most beneficial way. It is likely he will try it again, so if this is the case, *don't try to stop him*. He will eventually come to himself and profit much by the experience."

McKenzie encouraged Annie to let Don enlist in the New Year, but only in the artillery, feeling that the infantry would be too heavy for his youthful frame. McKenzie appears to have encouraged Don to enlist in the citizen militia, which was still maintained in Australia, not the separately-recruited AIF for overseas service. He would have been aware of one vital fact: Donald was merely 16 and would only turn 18 on April 10, 1918, the legal minimum age for recruits in the AIF, who even then required written permission from a parent before doing so. It is true that many younger men signed up, especially in the early years of the war when enlistment papers might note that the young man appeared to be 18 or more. Unlike today, most people did not hold a birth certificate as proof of age. But, by late 1916, recruiters were much more rigorous in preventing under-aged boys from signing up. For Don to enlist in the AIF earlier with parental permission would have required Annie to lie in writing about his age. However, it was possible for him to join the militia.

Hardly a surprising response from a mother, Annie was emotionally unprepared to do even this, which provoked a lengthy exasperated reply in January, 1917, in which McKenzie vented his frustrations in no uncertain terms, insisting that Don should enlist after his exams in February:

> Why hesitate longer. I *want* him to go and have already stated that he must go, so you are freed from all responsibility in the matter. Have no fears for him. The discipline will help him. He may "eat the pace." What matters nursing him at home won't save him so "hedge" no longer. If he is still at home you take him to the first recruiting officer that can be found and insist on him being put through and packed off to camp immediately. I do get more than annoyed at you *putting up* with his cheek and mourning laziness. I say here, now and for the *final time, he has to be cast out* and no more funking or nonsense about it. The only news I want to hear of him now is that he has gone to camp and left the home. So don't fool me in the matter any longer. Here I am suffering untold things every day I live here and have tried to help you all I know in the matter of Don. Every one of which suggestions you have turned down and so you shield him and thus encourage him in his laziness. To leave home will save him and he'll be saved no other way.[17]

He continued to insist that Don enlist in March, but in the meantime received the news that the young man was working on a farm alongside Colin, which pleased him, knowing he was out of the house and earning his own keep through hard harvest work. The situation gave both Don and his mother some relief.

But McKenzie continued to ask if Don was at the training camp yet. In August, he received "a lovely letter from Don. It was cleverly written, very frank and exceedingly encouraging to me. I have high hopes for Don and he will not disappoint me."[18]

Once Donald saw that he would be able to have more independence, things appeared to have settled down a little at home. Donald's school record was not all doom and gloom. He was in the First XVIII of the school's Australian Rules team in 1916–1917, and also represented the school in athletics, being named "Champion of the School 1917." He was also editor of the school magazine, a Cadet NCO and a sub-prefect in 1917.[19] Clearly he had talent and his leadership skills were recognisable, but they were not very discernible to his distressed mother.

Annie appeared to be out of her depth, not just with Don but with Colin and Gordon at times as well. The delayed letter in August announcing Don's conversion was counterbalanced by news of Gordon's "misdeeds" and that Colin had broken his arm in two places, but Annie forgot to tell him how.

"You are having some trouble with the boys in which you have my deepest sympathy and earnest prayer that God may give wisdom, grace and grit to help you thus," he wrote in reply. "Meanwhile, I trust that the young rascal may amend his ways."[20]

Then the letters that told of Don's relapse reassured him that Colin's arm was mended. He regularly monitored the younger boys' progress in school and encouraged them to continue their studies, particularly insisting that Colin apply his "ginger head" to staying at school throughout all of 1917. He did authorise Annie to terminate the boys' music lessons, but to begin Mavis with two a week, feeling that she would make "good headway."

Colin's progress at school and his leadership of soul-winning meetings at church was encouraging, as was Gordon's enthusiasm for Camberwell Grammar School, having joined Donald there at the start of 1917 from Camberwell State School.[21]

Mavis continued to delight, writing charming letters and starring in concerts. "I can imagine she throws her whole being into these 'goes' and I guess she does her part very well too," he wrote, clearly sharing the joy she brought to her audiences.[22]

McKenzie also wrote often to encourage and support Annie through her lingering discouragement. Her feelings can only be deduced from his letters, for while he asked her to preserve his, he was forced to destroy hers as he lacked a secure means to carry them around. When she repeatedly complained about a lack of mail from him, he defended himself, insisting that he wrote frequently and regularly, instead blaming the irregular mail service and German submarines, which had sent several mail-carrying ships to "the mermaids." He noted that he could go weeks without hearing from her as well.[23]

"I well know your deep anxiety for my welfare and thus I strive to keep you regularly posted," he replied to one complaint. He admonished her for feeling slighted by others, telling her that her cares were heavy "because you are so sensitive and self deprecatory. It is false that folks purposely neglect you. They may do so for want of thought but not otherwise." He lectured her to take proper holidays and "hang the expense," and repeatedly told her to find a new home that would reduce the need to walk so much when her feet were giving her trouble. At times, he challenged her victim mentality, urging her to take the initiative to relieve her worries rather than passively complaining. "Why be so helpless," he wondered. "Get over to Essendon, Box [H]ill or any suburb you fancy."[24]

He tried to affirm her work, praising her success in organising fundraising events, and he remembered her 41st birthday with special wishes. He sent her presents—a watch, spoons, Scottish mementoes, a bonnet and money for a holiday or for the children's school equipment—and also sent gifts to the children—coins, wallets, stamps, Christmas presents and war souvenirs, some were rings made from defused German shell nose caps "with which I had a nodding acquaintance."[25]

McKenzie encouraged Annie again to be cheerful and prayerful, despite her responsibilities and worries: "Yours is a heavy burden a trying task a lonely way but God is your helper and may He give you the needed daily strength." He also worked on improving the family finances, sending up to £100 at a time to be invested in War Loans—the interest of which would "more than pay for my insurance premium"—or Property Funds in Mavis's name to maximise tax efficiency. He also speculated about his post-war postings, hoping for Brisbane or Sydney, and occasionally wistfully noting some of his juniors in the Salvation Army who had been promoted to plum positions in his absence.[26]

McKenzie himself felt the separation deeply, "longing with intense yearning just to see you once again and get by the cosy 'jingle nook'," or "simply thirsting to see you all and have converse and fellowship with you." In 1916, he hoped to be home by Easter, 1917, but as the months passed without progress, he revised it to October, 1917, and then to April, 1918. He asked for a family photo "so that I can see how they have grown."[27]

During the most distressing times of the war, he developed the knack of imagining himself into the lives of his children as a means of retaining his sanity. "I get very heart hungry at times and home sick too," he wrote. "I long to see you all and clasp you to my breast. You are a great joy and comfort to me and I'm so glad you are mine. I lay for three hours last night having such kind thought of you and it did me good."[28]

For all of his insistence on Annie maintaining a proper Victorian vibrant positivity, McKenzie himself was suffering bouts of low emotions. In October, 1916, his war-weariness was such that he actually longed for death. With no victory in sight, only his family gave him the motivation to keep living:

> All goes well with me but I heartily wish the killing bis' was over. I've got almost to feel as if nothing now mattered, life is so cheap here. My thought is for your welfare with that of the children, otherwise I could gladly finish up here in a desperate and furious charge. To die for a worthy object such as one's country and in the vindication of righteousness and the liberty of the subject is sublimely grand and I'd *gladly do it*.[29]

Even as the news from home became more encouraging, McKenzie's own feelings continued at a low ebb, extending to twinges of spiritual doubt and exhibiting signs of the fatalism that was pervasive in the AIF.[30] By August, 1917, he was perplexed how Christian nations could behave in such a diabolical manner, speaking of the outcome of the war being in the lap of the gods and revealing that "I'm beginning to wonder if there really is a God after all who loves justice."[31]

His letters for public consumption were predictably less frank. His account to *The War Cry* of the overtaxing Sunday with 10 services admitted to the illness, but quickly concluded that he was "as right as a new Sunshine harvester again." While he acknowledged that the forward trenches would prevent services being held, he opined that "the great bulk of the men take a mighty different view of religion to what they did. They feel its need, and realise its power, and impressions have been made that cannot be effaced. A big revival must follow the war."[32] It made for excellent copy, and it reflected a belief that many clergymen and Christians in general shared,[33] but they were all to be disappointed when no such revival eventuated.

After running a successful day of meetings and concerts on Sunday, May 22, 1916—the day after coming out of the line—he left for England on two week's leave. There he met with leading Salvation Army figures, before travelling north to visit relatives in Scotland. The rest was badly needed, for recurring illness and family worries were not his only burden.

His campaign for people to write to lonely soldiers had been publicised in the popular press in Australia and its success was getting out of hand. With more than 3000 letters per post to deal with, as well as parcels and journals, he felt "swamped, overwhelmed, snowed under, snuffed out and given a task that is most taxing indeed." He feared this could reach 5000 letters per mail and was concerned about the "notoriety" that it generated for him. This notoriety ensured that his profile was publicised in civilian Australia as well as in the AIF, contributing to his growing status as a recognisable public figure. Apart from distributing the mass of mail, he had more than 450 letters to answer personally, writing up to 40 a day, and often writing until 2 am.[34] Little wonder his handwriting looked so rushed and untidy.

McKenzie was not the only one suffering from depression. Tom

Richards noted in his diary that he was in:

> a kind of hopeless groove. . . . We just live on and do so as best we can, that's all. To put up a bright side we occasionally sing Captain McKenzie's sunshine song,
>
> "Though the way be dark and the road be rough and dreary,
> "The sun is shining somewhere I know, I know
> "So to keep my heart from ever growing weary,
> "I carry my sunshine with me where'er I go."
>
> This song runs to a good swinging tune and has done a whole lot to tide us on our hard and grumbling way.[35]

This new composition embodied the classic McKenzie positivism and it became his trademark. For McKenzie made sure that his doubts and depression were confined to his letters to Annie. In front of the men, he presented the face of unalloyed cheerfulness that was such a tonic to their spirits. The new song's "good swinging tune" made it ideal for marching. It was a staple at his concerts during the war and regularly featured in his meetings with returned soldiers after the war. His concerts continued to be "rollicking affair[s]," with the men insisting that he preside, and he made sure Salvation Army songs featured prominently among the items.[36]

Later that year, battalion commander Iven Mackay made an effort to resurrect the battalion band, and asked his music-teacher sister to arrange some of McKenzie's songs for instrumentation. He claimed that one enterprising soldier in the battalion, Private William Cohen, had sold one of McKenzie's songs in Sydney, realising the princely sum of £40, and that it was being sung in Sydney's music halls.[37]

McKenzie finally gained some official recognition for his work at Gallipoli with the award of the Military Cross being gazetted in the King's Birthday Honours List on June 3, 1916. The citation read, "Continued courageous devotion to duty during the occupation of Anzac. Both in the trenches and out, his behaviour has set a good example to the men, in the fearless way in which he carried out his duties under fire."[38]

He received a personal letter of congratulations from General Birdwood, the AIF commander:

> My dear McKenzie, I cannot tell you how pleased I am to be able to write to congratulate you, as I do most heartily, on the award to you of the Military Cross, for I so well realise how thoroughly it has been deserved—none better, and, as I am sure you must realise, all our men are indeed most grateful to you for all the good work you have done for us during the whole time you have been with us.[39]

It is far more personalised than the routine Birdwood congratulatory letter that he wrote to every award winner.[40] While the General was famous for his common touch, it indicated that he held McKenzie in particular regard. At last he could feel that he had not been overlooked for honours compared to lesser chaplains in administrative roles, like New Zealand Salvationist Chaplain Greene, who had already won a medal.

If time in the "nursery" sector could produce discouragement, then the move to the Somme in early July bode ill, although a few like McKenzie remained optimistic. His antidote to the marching blues was "martial rollicking health-giving choruses to help things along on the march; the singing, whistling troops always march best and get less wearing and fatigued on the journey—the reason being the walk on 'the bright side' of the road." He believed that "an overwhelming victory [would] be recorded."[41] But General Haig's grand offensive began disastrously on July 1, resulting in the worst casualties ever suffered by the British army in a single day, as about 20,000 were killed and another 40,000 wounded, for only modest advances.

As part of the 1st Australian Division, the 4th Battalion arrived from Flanders to the Somme before the village of Pozieres, where several British attacks early in the month had made little progress against strong German defences. The ground was littered with the bodies and the fragments of the bodies of the dead, shattered by the concentrated artillery barrages from both sides. Immediately, "chaplain McKenzie took his jacket off (and soon afterwards, his shirt) as he toiled with pick and shovel to bury the impatient dead—more British than German. With a few words of comfort he would consign them to Glory." Another chaplain witnessed his repeated excursions into No-Man's-Land to carry out the wounded.[42] As on Gallipoli, the burial of the dead was the one task seen almost universally by the Anzacs as sacramental. The chaplain who would carry this out under fire—and there were quite a few like this in the AIF—earned the lasting respect of the men, and of their families in Australia.

Invited by the Anglican chaplain to address the Anglican church parade after the service on July 19, McKenzie told the men "in plain, straightforward words that many of us were attending our last church parade."[43] McKenzie's speech, very reminiscent of the sentiments he recorded before the Lone Pine battle, was no doubt his attempt to get them to make a spiritual commitment before their possible death, and soldiers appeared to have appreciated his frankness. Another man commented on this speech, describing it as "very solemn and impressive." It was certainly more effective than the whitewash that one chaplain unfortunately attempted on his congregation before Gallipoli—destroying his credibility in the process—"that it was not so very dangerous fighting. That there were almost as many dangers in times of peace with trains, cars and orange peels of all things."[44]

On July 23, the 1st Brigade attacked Pozieres. The 2nd Battalion captured a trench line to the south of the village and the 4th Battalion advanced through the 2nd into the village itself, meeting slight resistance as the Germans had withdrawn, but still struggling forward through a landscape so churned up by shells that movement was difficult and identification of location was almost impossible. The village itself had almost completely disappeared. Only smudges of red brick dust in the chalky soil indicated where buildings had been.

The battalion moved north-west across the main road through the village, past a captured German concrete blockhouse, later nicknamed "Gibraltar" and whose ruins remain to this day. Over the next two days, the Australian units consolidated their position, which pushed into the enemy lines, but they were subjected to a ferocious bombardment by the concentrated artillery of three German divisions on each side of the salient—the bulge of their advanced position.

By day, the heavy artillery played over the captured trenches, its unpredictability adding to the terror, destroying the trenches as fast as the Australians dug them. McKenzie wrote, "Many [men] were buried and dug out several times, others unable to get out and perished. Some went mad. Quite a few lost their nerve and some more blown to pieces."[45] All the while German counter-attacks had to be contained and repulsed by the shattered survivors. McKenzie worked with the Regimental Medical Officer, Captain Walter Stack, who set up his aid post so close to the front it was also under bombardment.

At night, the guns fell silent and McKenzie ventured into No-Man's-Land with the stretcher-bearers:

> The eerie silence was punctuated only by the groans of the wounded and the whoosh of an occasional flare lighting up the battlefield. Out in No-Man's-Land with the stretcher-bearers, sometimes silhouetted by flares against the tortured skyline, chaplain ("Fighting Mac") McKenzie of the 4th Battalion was despatching the dying and the dead to their final Reward. In the hot night air the stench of decomposing bodies was nauseating, stifling. He worked to the point of collapse with pick and shovel and Bible.

At one point, he stood on a mound of rubble in No-Man's-Land and sang his "Sunshine Song" in the darkness. Not a shot was fired at him.[46] He spent 10 days ministering to the wounded and collecting and burying the dead. "It was trying and at times risky work," he wrote in his diary, with some understatement.[47]

The 4th Battalion was pulled out of the line on July 27, having lost more than 100 dead and 300 wounded. The appalling bombardment endured by the Australians at Pozieres was one of the most intense of the war and 4th Battalion survivors emerged from the battle victorious but glassy-eyed.

However, at the northern end of the village, other Australian units fought on under an even worse bombardment. The desperate battle for The Windmill, which had once stood on the slight rise that offered excellent observation over the enemy lines, inflicted thousands of casualties. It was the scene of a heroic counter-assault by Gallipoli Victoria Cross winner Lieutenant Albert Jacka after the Germans overran his position in the early hours of August 7. Emerging from a dugout with only seven men, his furious attack from behind the advancing enemy inspired others, and the startled Germans were beaten off. But Australian losses in just six weeks of battle at Pozieres equalled those of the whole eight months of the Gallipoli campaign.

The respite from battle was too short for the 4th Battalion. The high command was desperate to pluck a significant victory from the terrible casualties they had suffered and the French were begging for relief from the massive German offensive around Verdun, so three Australian divisions were successively committed to advance to a farm atop a rise just 1.7 kilometres north-west of Pozieres. Its name was Mouquet Farm, but the Australians inevitably adapted it to "Moo Cow" or "Mucky" Farm. In the short period of rest, McKenzie ran services, concerts and sports to help relieve the men's stress. On August 6, the unit held a memorial service for the first anniversary of the Battle of Lone Pine.

A week later, McKenzie preached at a combined brigade church parade to about 5000 men in a large field, with General Birdwood present. Tom Richards recorded the event in his diary: "Rev McKenzie dealt with his favourite subject on St Paul and his troubles of a thousand kinds through all of which he stuck firmly to his hold on Christ. He then referred to the trifling troubles of all around him at this very moment. They have not the trials of St Paul to face, or trials out of common with the times, so it behoved them to stick more closely to their guns and with head erect stand up good and strong for the noble and righteous path."

Richards noted that this was followed by an "excellent, honest and morale-boosting" speech by Birdwood, who presented medal ribbons to some soldiers.[48] McKenzie was one of those called out, and Birdwood gave him the small purple and white ribbon of the Military Cross to stitch on his uniform. McKenzie told Annie that Birdwood said, "'I wish I had the Cross to give you but His Majesty the King will do that' and gave great congratulating words etc. After he had finished he called me to accompany him to review the troops in a march past. He said, 'come on Padre and let us . . .'."[49] Unfortunately, the rest of the letter is missing. However, Birdwood made a habit of asking McKenzie to accompany him while inspecting troops, feeling that the Chaplain gave him a better insight into the spirit of the men.[50]

The award of the Military Cross became the subject of another round of McKenzie mythologising, in part sparked by McKenzie himself. In a letter published in *The War Cry*, he claimed it was "much to my surprise" to be presented with the ribbon,[51] but this must be false modesty, since it had been gazetted two months earlier, and he had already received congratulatory letters from Birdwood himself, as well as from his old battalion commander, Macnaghten.

When asked by a journalist on one occasion what led to the award, McKenzie claimed he was given a leftover cross as he was passing a medal ceremony by chance at the time. The writer added, "You should have heard his laughter. It shook the tea things." McKenzie gave another light-hearted version of the event to another journalist: "I came in a bad last in a hundred yards sprint, but, owing to my weight, age and pluck for entering, was thought worthy of a consolation prize, and hence the M.C."[52] McKenzie could joke self-deprecatingly about it but actually he was very proud of his award.

In more recent times, several sources have tried to make much of this award, claiming that such an honour for a chaplain was "unheard of." But as Graham Wilson points out, 24 Australian chaplains were awarded the Military Cross, proportionally a very high rate given that they were not combat officers.[53] In fact, McKenzie felt he had been denied higher honours because of religious snobbery, writing to Annie in 1917 that "had I been a C of E Chaplain or even an R.C. I would have had the V.C."[54] He was not the only one to think he had earned more. Macnaghten wrote from Australia where he had been invalided, saying, "My most hearty and sincere congratulations, dear old Padre, on your Military Cross, but it ought to have been the D.S.O. [Distinguished Service Order]. However that will come, if not the Victoria Cross, and I know of no one more likely to gain it than yourself."[55]

Weeks after the award parade, a staff officer visiting the front at Mouquet Farm wrote:

> Great work was performed by Captain Chaplain McKenzie 4th Bn—he himself burying over 25 of our dead under shell fire and most trying conditions. Small service was held on grave of each. All their private documents were collected and a letter of sympathy sent to each one's relatives. I, personally, saw him on two occasions in the middle of this most noble and heroic work. He had been awarded a [M]ilitary [C]ross the week previous to this—but such man is none other than a "V.C." man.[56]

Archie Barwick wrote of McKenzie's Military Cross, "I'll bet his medal was one of the hardest earned there of any of them a V.C. would have been more like it." In 1937, a group of returned servicemen penned a tribute to him, claiming that his actions won "the V.C. again and again when no official eye was near to observe the deeds that are hallowed by heroism."[57]

In later years, the rumour grew that McKenzie had been recommended three times for the Victoria Cross, but various explanations are proffered as to why he didn't get it. One says that the officers who were recommending the award were killed before they could lodge their report, while others suggest that chaplains were not eligible for more than one medal. Again, there is no evidence to support that he was recommended, nor for the failure of McKenzie to receive it.[58] There were no restrictions at all regarding decorations for chaplains and in fact McKenzie's fellow chaplain and friend Walter Dexter received the DSO and the MC in France for his remarkable work.

The matter of decorations was always a vexed issue. The British handed out bravery awards in meagre quantities, especially when compared with the French, Germans, Russians and Americans, who dished out lesser awards like the Croix de Guerre or Iron Cross 2nd Class quite freely.[59] Winning medals depended on the good fortune of having one's bravery witnessed by a superior officer, who then survived to submit a recommendation—if he favoured you—then it being approved all the way up the chain of command.

Australians in particular felt aggrieved at a perception of not getting as many medals as the British, claiming it was anti-colonial prejudice at work. And Australian soldiers were in the habit of "awarding" the Victoria Cross rather liberally in their diaries and letters, frequently saying this man or that, or entire units should be so decorated. Even General Birdwood made such remarks, claiming to have told King George V that the Australians had earned 2000 VCs at Pozieres alone. As one soldier sagely remarked, many men had earned VCs and double VCs but got nothing.[60]

Jacka's heroics at Pozieres only earned him a recommendation for a Distinguished Service Order and resulted in the lesser award of the Military Cross, though opinions at the time and since have considered that it was a Victoria Cross-worthy exploit. Many in the 4th Battalion felt that they had been unfairly passed over for honours, especially as none of the VCs awarded for Lone Pine had been given to any of them, despite leading the attack. Eventually this became a matter of "fierce pride" and battalion commander Iven Mackay was deliberately frugal with recommendations in order to "maintain standards."[61]

Arguably McKenzie might have received a second or a higher award based on his constant activities for the wounded in No-Man's-Land, but there is no evidence to suggest that he was ever a serious contender for the Victoria Cross, despite the generous sentiments of various diggers. In any case on July 11, 1916, he was Mentioned in Despatches (MiD) for services on Gallipoli,[62] technically a decoration but one that came with a simple certificate rather than a medal, though it was effectively the British equivalent of the French Croix de Guerre or of the later American Bronze Star.

In any event, McKenzie did not receive more medals, but he was respected as a fighting man nonetheless. As at Gallipoli, McKenzie was fascinated by the art of war and rapidly absorbed even the finer aspects, becoming an authoritative voice in mess-room discussions. Soldiers told journalist F A McKenzie that his verdict on any technical point—for example, the trajectory of shells or the right height for a parados (defensive earthworks)—was taken as final. He was said to know more about fighting than anyone else in the battalion.[63]

This could be regarded as soldierly big-noting, more of the hyperbole dished up for public consumption by soldiers prone to talk things up—and McKenzie himself warned that the men told "some tall yarns of my doings"—but a battalion officer said more or less the same thing in a private remark to his father around the time McKenzie returned to Australia in early 1918: "Old padre Mackenzie [sic] should know more about the front than anyone if you should meet him." And this was after telling of a lieutenant his father could meet who was "some fighter, too."[64]

His labours also continued to attract high accolades from the men for their spiritual influence. A digger sergeant described his modus operandi in a letter to a friend, saying that:

> he is the greatest card, I think, I have ever met. Last night we were all sitting around our billets when we heard someone coming along shouting, "Come on, lads, we're going to have a concert. We've got two violins and all sorts of instruments down in the wood. Put away your cards (some were gambling) and let's have a good time!" Then away he goes, further along the street. Into the drinking houses, and everywhere he can get in he will go, and as all of the boys knew him, he gets a great reception. Before five minutes were up the men were all tramping off in the direction of the wood, and he soon

> put in an appearance and called for volunteers for a programme, which was soon filled, and a concert going in real good style.
>
> Captain McKenzie is not a "dugout chaplain" or "behind-the-line-worker." He is where the shells fall the thickest, and the cries for help are most numerous. That is where we always find him, and today I had the pleasure of seeing him receive his second decoration [MiD] for conspicuous bravery. These are the men who tell for Christianity in this great struggle. The men whom all the world might follow, and consider it an honour to be led by such a man.[65]

Archie Barwick of the 1st Battalion described another impromptu concert:

> Old Mac. had all the boys singing tonight, he came round to our billets where there is a small piece of vacant ground almost in the middle of the town, he started with just a handful, but you should have seen the crowd grow it was wonderful, in no time he had a sacred service in full swing nearly all singing you know, & with just a prayer in here & there, he is a grand fellow, the best of the boys will tell you in the A.I.F. he is almost idolised by the Australians you have no idea how that man is liked, I'll bet he can sway the whole of the Australians any way he chooses, & he would give you half of his last penny: such a man is Capt. Mackenzie [sic] a Salvationist.[66]

It was not unusual for him to sweep up whichever troops were within reach, regardless of unit or even nationality for these spontaneous concerts, ending up with mixed audiences of up to 1500 Australian, British, Canadian and even French soldiers, and on one occasion moving a French civilian woman to tears who was listening in the background. His Colonel noted that his particular hold on the men was based on:

> [his] remarkable versatility . . . surprising general

> knowledge and a vast understanding of human nature. Especially was he quick to judge the character of his fellow man. . . . He seemed to know everybody and as he moved freely among the troops, his invariable greeting was, "Hello! Hello! How are we?" The troops individually and collectively often tried to "take a rise" out of Mac, but he was far too clever for them and always got the best of the bouts of repartee.[67]

Just as striking was his capacity to move among the upper echelons of the army with ease. He was popular in the Officers' Mess, and he dined with Generals with equanimity.[68] His success can be measured in the unqualified praise he received almost without exception, whereas chaplains in general were subjected to mixed reviews. For example, Barwick hyperbolised McKenzie in his letters and diaries, but excoriated the efforts of his "wowseristic" co-religionists when they tried to lecture the men on moral issues.[69] His name crops up in a surprising number of soldier diaries and letters, affectionately noting his work in running services, funerals, entertainments and canteens, confirming that his own estimation of his impact was accurate. One diarist wrote that "his cheery, bluff personality endeared him to everyone."[70]

The battle for Mouquet Farm, which had begun promisingly, had now stalled and the 1st Division, hastily brought back up to strength during its two-week rest out of the line, was reintroduced in an attempt to hold out strong German counterattacks. The battalion spent several days capturing further sections of enemy trenches and repelling assaults before being withdrawn again on August 19, marching to billets in Amiens for a well-earned rest and reorganisation. Naturally the time in the trenches had been under heavy shell fire, and McKenzie was prominent again in bringing in the wounded from No-Man's-Land and conducting burials of British dead, sometimes in full view of the enemy.

McKenzie recorded in a letter to Salvation Army Commissioner Hay, published in *The War Cry*, experiences of a mystical nature while doing this:

> I had buried seven of these fallen heroes (all Sussex men) when my guardian angel said, "Get away from here quickly." I obeyed instantly, and had got away twenty-five yards in a slanting direction from the enemy's fire when a big shell landed right on the spot where I had been standing minutes before. I only got a shower of dirt. At all times of great danger I am quietly conscious of this guardian angel's presence while engaged on such work. I cannot see him, nor can I tell who or what he is like, but I hear his voice sometimes saying—"Do not go there," "Get in here," "Lie down in that shell hole," "Be careful," "You are quite safe," "Wait five minutes here," and such-like messages. I could give at least six instances within the past week where a prompt attention to his instructions has saved me from those big shells. I now know that if I pay heed and obey God, I will continue unharmed until my work is finished, so if I fall on the field you will know the reason. I'm ready to live or die! I have no fear or doubt; I only wish I loved God more, and was in possession of much more of the spirit and compassion of Jesus.[71]

To Annie, he wrote in similar terms, just out of the trenches:

> where we have had a very trying, dangerous time. Also many of my Australian boys now lie lifeless and many more wounded. Only for heeding the small voice of my guardian angel on several occasion [sic] I too would have been no more. It is most remarkable when I'm in great danger I am quite conscious of a guardian angel with me, who though I cannot see him tells me in times of peril just what to do and I have learned to promptly obey and so come off all right. Sometimes it is "go" others "do not go" and again "get away quickly," "lie down," "be careful," "go in there." It is very striking and has deeply impressed me. I am sure it is a guardian angel. Surely the Lord is good and His mercy endureth for ever.[72]

As in his youth and early ministry, McKenzie felt in direct communication with the Divine, making life-saving decisions based on these specific instructions.

He was also in awe of:

> the brave dauntless boys [who] have once more covered themselves with glory when taking trenches and booty from the enemy, laying low many of the arrogant usurpers of the lovely country. Their cheerfulness and fearlessness is something to wonder at [as] they dodge along battered trenches with their implements of war, water or rations without the slightest hesitation even when the five point nines [German 5.9 inch/150mm shells] are falling around us.[73]

A week later, he wrote again from the quiet trenches in Belgium, where the battalion rested until October, to his "dearest Muma," saying that he was well, though he had been suffering from persistent lice and the lack of being able to wash or even change clothes. He had worn the same undershirt for a month, but at last had got a chance to clean up. He had discarded his underpants two months earlier with no regrets, but the cool autumnal weather meant that he would need them again.[74]

The battalion was resting and rebuilding back in Flanders, having dwindled to 400 men. The 600 replacements needed to be trained for eight to 10 weeks before the battalion would be fit for more action. He deplored the war as a "ghastly business," a "destruction of robust manhood, the pick of Australia," but he was proud of their success, considering the Germans "poor fighters" and eager to surrender. He wrote of meetings he had taken with good success and of one scheduled with Canadian troops. Offered two weeks' leave in England, he turned it down:

> I did not want to leave the boys at this juncture. They need encouraging and cheering and they simply dote on me and are ready to do anything in reason that I ask them. The hold I have on the men is marvellous. They think that I am without fear in any place and I'm afraid

> tell some tall yarns of my doings. To the men of the 1st Brigade Engineers and Ambulance men I'll be a hero with a halo. There is no doubt they think a mighty lot of the Salvation Army.[75]

The next day he wrote to Annie again, having had 15 "seekers" at his meeting, including four British, one Canadian and a Jewish Australian. However, he was not satisfied with this, writing elsewhere, "but I asked myself, 'Why only fifteen?' There ought to have been twenty-five, or even fifty-five."

He was weighed down with the mails, again having a huge number to distribute and to write. He ran another concert, which included many Canadians for the first time, "so you guess we determined to have a ding-dong, slap-up, red-hot, unadulterated Australian 'go,' with lots of ginger in it, and you can rest easy on the result. It went like a succession of gun batteries. They heard us on the 'Sunshine' chorus half a mile away. The place was gorged, and the enthusiasm at boiling point."[76]

McKenzie was maintaining his punishing pace, now doing the work of four chaplains. He was the only Protestant chaplain left in the brigade as one was sick and the other on leave, and he complained that the Roman Catholic chaplain was ineffective and timid, never showing up near the front. However, in June, he was joined by Methodist chaplain James Dain, who worked collaboratively alongside him.[77]

He had also taken on a new project. He opened a brigade canteen, so the men would have ready access to refreshments at near cost price, cutting out the exploitative margins charged by opportunistic local merchants, and using the profits to buy practical gifts the men would appreciate, such as souvenir metal matchboxes that would keep matches dry in the trenches or special delicacies to lift the men's spirits. It was also aimed at keeping the men away from drink, for his canteen was naturally a "dry" one. Setting it up meant travelling to a supplier at Poperinghe, then hauling his stock back to the camp. Two soldiers helped him man the canteen and take care of stock and accounts, but the workload was huge.

McKenzie detailed a particularly hectic day's activities, which began with going to sleep at 4 am after writing letters, getting up at 7.40 am and cycling without breakfast over rough roads for 12 kilometres to conduct a burial, then returning for lunch and an interview. Then it was off to Poperinghe, returning at 7.30 pm with goods for the canteen. This was followed by a three-kilometre cart trip for tea, then at 9 pm a horse ride back over the 12 kilometres for more funerals. Finding insufficient graves dug, he had to rouse out 10 men at midnight. After the ride back, he then walked three kilometres to the new camp and retired at about 4.30 am, but was so exhausted that he only fell asleep at 6.[78]

The next day, he was back in Poperinghe for more supplies, where he met fellow Salvationist chaplain Benjamin Orames. Orames recorded the meeting as well, being surprised at meeting a debilitated McKenzie, for he always thought of him "as a wonderfully whole-hearted worker, and when he is the victim of some passing physical trouble—he never does anything half-heartedly." He rightly suspected that McKenzie was "war-weary" after two years' strenuous toil.[79]

Hardly surprisingly, such a schedule had its effect. "I had a very crook bilious attack this past week," he wrote to Annie. "Whenever I get real knocked out I invariably get a bad bilious attack, through nervous exhaustion. However, I recover in three days and feel OK once more."

But far from slowing down, McKenzie added to his workload, starting a second canteen, then running hot coffee and Bovril beef tea down to the men coming out of the trenches from fatigue-carrying duties in the chilly autumn nights between 6 pm and 6 am. No wonder he continued to have bouts of illness.[80]

His work was deeply appreciated, a 3rd Battalion officer writing:

> [McKenzie] rendered consistent and consecrated service of every kind, physical, social, mental and spiritual during this half year. He ran the Pipe Band of his Battalion (the 4th), he managed the 1st Brigade canteens: in everything he was a tower of strength to the officers

> and a comfort and keep to the men of his brigade. He never spared himself in any way.[81]

On September 25, 1916, he was made Acting Chaplain 3rd Class (Major) in recognition of his services, but some anonymous stingy army administrator made this without additional pay or allowances. Finally, on June 5, 1917, he was granted the full suite of allowances when he was officially promoted to Temporary 3rd Class Chaplain (Major).

In late October, the battalion returned to the Somme, enduring the winter in wet and mud-filled trenches. McKenzie maintained the positive outward frame, writing to *The War Cry* that "I rejoice in abundant health, a disposition for hard work, and a cheerful spirit to help keep my heart a-singing." He did his alliterative best to make light of the appalling conditions, both to keep up soldiers' spirits and reassure folks at home, writing:

> At present we are waging a woeful war in waders with slobbery, watering whirls wearily whisking round one's waist in some of the trenches, and withering wintry winds whistling round your withers. Ugh! It is calculated to cool the combustible characteristics of the fiercest fire-eater, and make him sigh for a little bit o' 'eaven 'ere, and 'ome, sweet 'ome, be it ever so 'umble.

The deep mud made movement laborious: he spent eight hours trying to reach Orames, but without success, and at one point he got stuck and had to be pulled out by others. He witnessed a soldier who was so bogged down that it required two horses to get him out of the mud. And all of this was under constant shell fire, some of it intense.[82]

If there were any doubts about his feelings on the justice of the war, he put them to rest with a chilling judgment in a letter to Annie. Outraged at the destruction of France, he hoped the Allies would break into Germany and destroy 200 of their cities and a thousand of their villages, even if a million German civilians died. He wanted to ensure that Germany was down for a long time.[83] This vengeful attitude also emerged in his sermons. In late October, before the men were committed to an attack on Delville Wood through almost impassable mud littered with hundreds of dead, a soldier recorded "that is what we are here for, to take our share in the great struggle of the world for right and freedom, which this war is, and which our own grand old padre (Captain Mackenzie) says is Armageddon." On a more humane note, the soldier added:

> Write, [McKenzie] said, to your mother and tell her she is the best mother in the world etc., well there is no need for me to tell you that, for you know I think and know you are, . . . However, he asked us to do so and I do it. He is a great man and looked up to and loved by all the men of this famous battalion and the men of the whole brigade in fact. We only sang two hymns, Onward Christian Soldiers and Lead Kindly Light and had the 23rd Psalm and his text was "Suit yourselves like men and fight" etc. and he speaks beautifully. We don't get much time for sentimentality or anything like that, but on an occasion like this of course we do.[84]

The trying circumstances lasted until mid-November when the battalion was bussed to billets north of Amiens. Heavy snow alternated with heavy rain, making the ground a quagmire. McKenzie claimed to be doing well despite a tenacious bout of the flu, a broken gold tooth plate and "a few other odds and ends to contend with—a trying cough, sleepless nights, bad heads, bleeding piles, sore bones and bleary eyes but these are really incidental to a soldier's life so we must give thanks, take heart to grace and press forward. It's pretty tough but it might be much worse." He thought the Germans were in a worse state. It was too cold, wet and dark for training or even for meetings, and finally he could take his much-deferred leave to Britain.[85]

Such were the conditions that the trip there took him four days. In London, he chased up instruments and music for the Battalion Band, visited Salvation Army friends, and spoke to an audience that included the Princess Louise, Duchess of Argyll, the daughter of Queen Victoria. He also met with two namesakes: the noted

Canadian journalist F A McKenzie and politician Sir Thomas McKenzie, as well as journalist Harold Begbie, who, he told Annie, will "be glorifying your hubby soon in the 'Chronicle'."[86]

He was also summoned to Buckingham Palace on December 13 to receive his Military Cross from King George V. McKenzie played this down in his published account of it but his pride could not be hidden. To Annie, he confided, "I called on the King who gave me a Cross to play with. He shook me twice by the hand. He said 'I have heard of, and know all about your great work for the men. I am proud of you. I congratulate you and hope your health will continue good until you see the war through.' This is 'well done' from the King." McKenzie felt ill at ease in the formal palace environment and took childish delight in dodging the ushers and their demands for tips, as well as the official photographers.[87] He did, however, keep the telegram inviting him to the investiture.

Offered a position in The Salvation Army headquarters in London, with the chance to have Annie by his side, he turned it down emphatically, labelling the British Salvation Army as detestable. In a later letter, he described a situation as having "much, too much, sleek, smug self-complacency, and highty-tighty hum-buggery, added to place-hunting, fandanglum bangers to suit a liberty-loving colonial." *The War Cry* diplomatically added, "This must refer to the conditions in Germany"—but it almost certainly referred to his feelings about England, and probably about The Salvation Army there.[88]

McKenzie was back in France before Christmas, having failed to get to Scotland, feeling "very well, though I have a trench cough, a trench foot, and a trench smell. Dirty, dowdy and dour though cheerful as a well fed louse and happy as Blithering Barney." Clearly, he found this environment more to his liking than palaces or administrative headquarters.[89]

He picked up where he had left off, but soon fell ill again. Two debilitating bouts of diarrhoea and vomiting showed that his Gallipoli condition was not out of his system, striking whenever he became exhausted. He admitted to Annie that he was war weary and in need of a spell.[90] He wrote much the same to Hay, who published it in *The War Cry*. "I am feeling OK," McKenzie claimed, "though the cold weather is a corker. I have a very sore throat and influenza, with strong retchings, violent pains, etc, for ten days, but Scottish hide and Australian grit made me sternly resist and hang on, so now I'm 'jolly good' once more." He reported that a shell had blown the end off one of his canteen huts, but fortunately no-one was in it at the time.[91]

In March, 1917, Begbie's article about McKenzie was reprinted in *The War Cry*. Begbie was conscious of writing appropriately for his audience, so it was not investigative or critical journalism, but his observations are revealing of the impact of McKenzie's personality, so it is worth quoting at length:

> Of all the ministers of religion on the battlefield, here, I think, is the strangest, and the most romantic. He is neither meek nor mild. He is neither tender nor gentle. And as for theology—well— . . .
>
> This Captain Mac is a big, solid person, with a brown Australian skin, black hair, black eyes, a black moustache, and a voice that would fill the Crystal Palace. His eyes shine and burn and twinkle with an animation so excessive that you cannot imagine how he doesn't explode, or how he manages to sit still for two minutes together. And his smile is of the kind that gives energy to the feeblest, and bestows good spirits on the saddest. A great, big, hearty man, overflowing with the joy of existence, bursting with energy, and longing, always longing, for a fight. . . .
>
> And Captain Mac, I am very certain, will die fighting, if not in France, then [fighting] the devil in Melbourne or Sydney.
>
> But let me tell you, the most interesting thing of all about this fighting Salvationist. He may not be a theologian; his language may be uncritical; and he may be the last man in the world to resolve a religious

> difficulty—except the biggest of all, namely how to get out of a bad life and into a good life; but, all the same, Captain Mac is a spiritual man in the most real sense of that word. Yes, this Australian is a mystic. . . . In spite of his hearty ways, his loud voice, his delight in his life, and his lust of fighting, here in sober truth is a man who lives with angels.

The front page of that issue featured a photo of McKenzie with "an extract characteristic of the man" from one of his letters.

> Things are going well with me. I have enough to eat, a place to lie nearly always—wet, hard, and cold at times—but it's a place to LIE, clothes enough to wear—need washing maybe, and the young recruits [lice] combed out—but they certainly bring one to the scratch, I have a fine, heavy pair of hob-nailed boots, a steel helmet, a gas respirator, a stout stick to kill the rats (here in millions), a brave heart, a chastened spirit, a cool head, a firm step, a strong fist, a dauntless soul, a gripping faith, a clear vision, a fighting fervour, a love of good things, a hatred of the devil, a hope of heaven, a vision of the glory. So I guess I ought to be happy.[92]

In some ways, the more McKenzie struggled to cope with his circumstances, the more his language became rhetorical and grand. These flourishes are rare in Egypt and Gallipoli, but are common in France by 1917, both in public and private correspondence. It is almost as if he was trying to persuade himself as much as his audience.

Through the early months of the year, the 4th Battalion moved in and out of the line, largely providing fatigue parties, doing the multitude of exhausting labouring jobs always needed behind the lines. The raw weather continued its miserable mix of snow, frost and rain. McKenzie had opportunity to preach to "monster" brigade parades, organise "monster" concerts and sports, rehearse his band to a high standard and distribute thousands of sheets of writing paper with a Salvation Army letterhead.[93]

He was again the only Protestant chaplain in the brigade: "One has gone mad and the other has gone to hospital with sore feet, they were both recent arrivals and have not stood it long," he wrote. "The other is a RC Chap and does very little, abominably frightened of shells. He thinks I'm the greatest hero of the war and says I'm an 'Oliver Cromwell' and a 'Teddy Roosevelt' in one." McKenzie was disgusted with the German behaviour during their strategic retreat in early 1917, systematically destroying French villages, and leaving booby traps behind. "They are human fiends incarnate and a positive disgrace to the human race, having no sense of decency whatever," he raged to Annie.[94]

Around the time that the 4th Battalion became involved in battles around Boursies and Demicourt in support of the First Battle of Bullecourt in mid-April, McKenzie was appointed chaplain at the AIF Depots in England. Despite his weariness, he could not keep himself away from the front, nor would he reduce the impossible load he had imposed on himself. A job description that had "fairly onerous" compulsory duties and "no limit" to the optional ones[95] was a recipe for trouble with McKenzie, who had poor boundaries when it came to how much work was enough. Even he was recognising that he was a spent force. But his philosophy of life advocated self-discipline, self-denial and self-sacrifice, while having nothing to say about self-care, for which he had little aptitude or experience.

The appointment to London was an attempt by his superiors to force him to rest. But McKenzie did not know how to slow down. The two months in Britain were consumed with rounds of hospital visitations, meetings with Salvation Army leaders, "red-hot" evangelistic meetings including one in Albert Hall, as well as a brief trip to Scotland to see family. He spent an enjoyable couple of hours with F A McKenzie, swapping stories, and was pleased with the write-up he had received in the *Philadelphia Ledger* the previous year.[96]

The Salvation Army in Britain continued to underwhelm him and he threw himself into trying to bring them up to his standards of fervour. "Things [Salvation] army are mighty slack around these parts and need a lot of shaking up. I am simply swamped with appeals for special meetings," he told Annie. In the end, observers described his time in London as a "busman's holiday," with one soldier speculating in a letter home that rather than resting, "I fancy he spent the greater part of the time visiting the boys in Hos[pital]. He arrived back here last Thursday evening, and received a cheer from the mob as soon as he put in an appearance."[97]

In mid-June, he made his way back to France to rejoin his battalion. The reunion was bitter-sweet. Hundreds of the men he knew and loved had been killed in the battles around Bullecourt in April and May. The battalion was out of the line for six weeks, rebuilding for the next assault. His letter to Annie anticipated a protracted struggle to end the war, with no real progress until at least mid-1918 once the Americans arrived in force. As a prediction, it was sadly accurate.

While McKenzie was in a more buoyant mood, his fatigue had reached the point that it affected his normally impressive memory. "I am absolutely war weary, my memory is fast failing and I'll have hard work to avoid a collapse later on," he admitted. "I'm quite perplexed over my lapses of memory and weariness of mind. However, a sea voyage should set me right even though I feel old." He was struggling to recall events on Gallipoli and details of his pre-war trip to the London Salvation Army Congress had disappeared. It could take him days to remember names of well-known people in Australia, yet his short-term memory seemed unaffected as he could remember several dozen messages for a trip into town. "I suppose it is the keen concentration of mind on the present and only the present," he mused.[98] He was at the point of no longer coping with the war, and the emotional burden of writing to bereaved families was almost more than he could bear.

The budding discipline of psychiatry was only just gaining recognition in its study of the emotional effects of war, and what is now called Combat Stress Fatigue, potentially leading to post-traumatic stress disorder, was labelled "shell shock" at the time, and was slowly gaining acceptance as a legitimate and recognisable condition brought about by prolonged exposure to combat. McKenzie could hardly be expected to be current with the latest theories of war trauma, so his lack of understanding of his urgent need for extended rest and therapy is not surprising. Given his self-expectation of maintaining impossibly high standards of devotion and service, an absence of grace toward his own deeply traumatised soul was predictable, but by expecting to bounce back after a short rest period, he unintentionally trivialised the seriousness of his condition.

He lasted only seven weeks back in France before it was clear to all that he would need to be replaced. During this time, he resumed his busy schedule of meetings, concerts, burials, canteens and sports. But he also suffered emotionally from the loss of mails in both directions as several mail boats were sunk in Germany's renewed U-boat offensive. One in particular hurt deeply—the loss of the *Mongolia*, sunk off Bombay by a mine laid by the commerce raider *SMS Wolf*, saw hundreds of letters to grieving families typed by a shorthand typist in London go to the bottom of the ocean.[99]

In the first three weeks of his return, he had two relapses of trench fever, ending up in hospital with a temperature of 103.8°F (nearly 40°C). After just a few days of sweating it out in hospital, he "bluffed the Doctor by telling him I was in the pink, feeling very fit and desired to be marked for duty, which he did and I left that same afternoon." He spent some time with Robert Henry, the Salvation Army chaplain designated to take over from him. McKenzie was impressed with Henry's work and again spoke disparagingly of the "double shufflers and quick change artists" who made up the leadership of the Salvation Army in England.[100]

He was soon back with the battalion and optimistically claiming that his health was the best since December, 1916, with no recurrences of his gastric troubles, and that he was actually regaining lost weight. His thoughts ran to speculation over the war and his post-war future. He continued to laud the fighting prowess of the Australians and damn the Germans, denouncing their latest weapon—the flame-thrower—as "diabolical."

"The Kaiser and his brood are the most unscrupulous scheming devils out of steel," he wrote. "I wish I could blow up a 100,000 of them."[101] He was also sick of war talk at all, rounding on those back home who exploited war stories to manipulate their audience's emotions. He wished to forget all about the conflict.

On the other hand, he had been transformed by it in positive ways:

> This war has given me much larger and wider views of human nature and made me much more tolerant, much less narrow and less bigoted than I was. For instance I can see lots of good in multitudes of Roman Catholics who are soldiers here and they fight pray and die as good and heroic as the best of them at the front. Indeed these things have made me take a different view of many things.

He added that his two Salvation Army chaplain colleagues felt the same way.[102] Ironically the great sectarian divide that was being bridged by the experiences of soldiers on the front was actually deepening in Australia under the strains of the bitter rhetoric of the two conscription referendum campaigns. Unfortunately, the soldiers' ecumenism failed to moderate attitudes at home after the war.

The paradox of secular soldiers exhibiting Christian virtues posed a dilemma for many chaplains, including McKenzie. Their Christian theology taught that the life without Christ was characterised by "the acts of the flesh": "sexual immorality, impurity, debauchery, idolatry . . . discord, jealousy . . . selfish ambition . . . and the like." On the other hand, Christians would exhibit St Paul's well-known list of "the fruit of the Spirit": "love, joy, peace, patience, kindness, goodness, faithfulness, gentleness and self-control" (see Galatians 5:19–23). These virtues, unnatural to the unregenerate man, were imparted to the Christian by the Holy Spirit's abiding presence, nurtured in the Catholic tradition principally by the administration of the Sacraments, and in the Evangelical Protestant tradition mainly by the devotional habits of Bible study and prayer.

Superficially, it was not difficult to recognise the "acts of the flesh" in many secular Anzacs: their capacity for blasphemy, drunkenness, gambling and immorality made the label an easy fit. But these same men often demonstrated stoic endurance under great trial, kindness, goodness and faithfulness to their mates and, above all, the ultimate Christlikeness. As Jesus famously said, "Greater love has no man than he lay down his life for his friends" (John 15:13)—and the Anzacs of all and no creed did so repeatedly.

The dilemma for the padres—and for other Christian soldiers—was that if men who did not acknowledge Christ or practice the Christian disciplines could still manifest these most godly of attributes, then Christian theology needed re-examination. Some padres found their faith weakened by the war; others adapted their beliefs to accommodate the observed phenomenon of unholy men performing holy deeds.

Padre James Gault summarised what he learnt about the Australian soldier and religion under six points: that the soldier believed in prayer; that he believed in life after death; that he saw sin differently from the church—but rather like Christ toward the Prodigal Son, not being concerned with drinking, gambling and swearing, but considering the absence of honesty, integrity and loyalty as true sin; that he admired above all things unselfishness, courage and sacrifice, all of which are best expressed in the life of Christ; that he had an utter disregard for denominational distinctions; and that he had taught the padre to see the greatness of "The Common Man." Gault concluded, "Digger! I salute you—No; I stand bareheaded as you pass."[103]

Like Gault and other chaplains, McKenzie quickly developed an enormous respect for the digger, and his beliefs became more accommodating and less judgmental, although McKenzie did not appear to have attempted any kind of systematic theological thought process. But his post-war ministry, while still as vigorous in seeking salvation for the lost, was less concerned with superficial sins such as drunkenness and swearing, and his instincts more surely recognised true virtues hidden beneath these surface faults. If he had been Catholic, McKenzie might well have used the terms "mortal sin" and "venial sin" to categorise the flaws that now did or did not exercise his principal moral indignation.

Finally, McKenzie's transfer to Australia was formalised, with Robert Henry due to succeed him on October 17, 1917. Sources vary on who initiated his return, some claiming the Salvation Army in Australia requested his return, others that battalion commander Mackay organised it.[104] Inevitably, McKenzie did not spend his final days on the Western Front quietly, for he was still running concerts and meetings and going up to the line during the 4th Battalion's attacks as part of the Battle of Broodseinde Ridge near Ypres in Belgian Flanders, the most successful operation of the extended Battle of Passchendaele. He was struck five times by dirt from shell explosions but was otherwise unhurt—though there are accounts of two incidents that suggest otherwise. One claimed that he nearly missed his battalion farewell, having been rendered unconscious by a shell, the other stating that as he said goodbye to the battalion commander, a shell killed a man nearby and a dismembered arm struck McKenzie a blow across the face. A fellow chaplain, the Methodist David Hunter attached to the 55th Battalion, was not so fortunate, being killed by a shell while returning from a visit to the men in the front lines.[105]

Chaplain Henry finally arrived on November 22 and McKenzie took his final church parade sermon on November 25, which was followed by special souvenir photo session of the battalion, and of various clusters of veterans who had served with McKenzie.[106] One final and rare honour awaited McKenzie three days later: Lieutenant-Colonel Mackay organised an official parade for his farewell, a ceremony more usual for a senior general than a lowly Chaplain-Major, and unique in the annals of the 4th Battalion. Mackay's biographer recorded the event:

> There was a farewell dinner, then a parade at which the bulky Scottish chaplain ("my acreage is great") listened, smiling, as Mackay traced his progression of names since 1914: The Bloody Parson, God Almighty, Salvation Joe, Holy Joe, Old Mac, Padre Mac, Fighting Mac. He

> recalled the padre's threat to punch Colonel Macnaghten on the nose for forbidding him to "hop over" with the troops in the charge at Lone Pine—unless he carried a rifle and bayonet.
>
> Mackay then brought the parade to attention and saluted the chaplain, "4th Battalion ready for your inspection, Sir." The regimental band struck up. A solitary bagpipe joined in. The entire 4th Aust. Inf. [Battalion] broke into the padre's own song, "Sunshine." As "Fighting Mac" strode through the ranks, a flood of tears poured down his cheeks.[107]

Mackay had made an effort to acquire a whole pipe band in time for the farewell but only one piper arrived in time. General Birdwood marked the occasion with an appreciative letter of farewell and McKenzie left the battalion for the last time, making his way to London a few days later.

He immediately made for Scotland to visit family, aware that such an opportunity might not arise again soon. However, army administration processes frustrated his hopes of a quick voyage to Australia before Christmas, so on his return to London, he made rounds of visits to Salvation Army leaders and to military hospitals, visiting thousands of wounded men.[108] He also took lively meetings for the Salvation Army in Sheffield and visited their institutions such as orphanages, running a schedule so busy that he was "fagged out" by Boxing Day. He was desperate to get home and hear news of the children, and found the delays "just purgatory." In the cold grip of an English winter, he was longing for the Australian sunshine.[109]

In December, *The War Cry* reprinted a *Sydney Sun* article by Keith Murdoch, titled "The Boys' Best Friend." Most of it was composed of material from an interview with McKenzie while he was still in France. McKenzie emphasised that the boys' best friend was in fact their mother, but careless readings of it in later years took it to mean that McKenzie was their best friend. It added to the myth surrounding him. McKenzie himself praised the supreme courage of stretcher-bearers, adding with Celtic pride that he had never seen a red-headed coward. Murdoch added stories of McKenzie, noting that he "has gone where shelling has made burial parties impossible to bury the dead. He has brought in wounded, and lasted out the most intense shell-fire with his men, so that he might cheer and comfort them. He has stayed afterwards to collect as much as two sandbags full of identity discs and paybooks off the dead." The article is notable as the first occasion on which McKenzie is nicknamed "Fighting Mac" in print, although soldiers' diaries record the moniker as early as 1916.[110]

Finally McKenzie was given a berth home on the *Corinthic* on January 10, 1918. Packed with his luggage was a trunk with the instruction writ large, "Never to be opened by anyone but myself. In the event of loss, or my death, it is to be destroyed—UNOPENED." In it were hundreds of IOUs recording loans McKenzie had made to indigent soldiers, whom he considered "brave and honourable and not capable of any wrongs that really mattered." His colonel noted that "McKenzie was particularly kind to all the 'lame ducks,' the drunks in the battalions of 1st Division, and gave them 'temporary loans.' Many of these, Mackay feared, were never repaid."[111] McKenzie kept the chits in order to give those who did repay the moral satisfaction of seeing their debt cancelled, but he had no intention of holding the unpaid debts against any man. In fact, for the rest of his life he continued to hand out cash to improvident ex-diggers who asked him for a loan to tide them over.

McKenzie arrived in Sydney in early March, 1918, and his AIF appointment was terminated on March 17. This brought to an end McKenzie's war service, but these three-and-a-half years remained the defining period of his long and active adult career. Except for a few years in China where his Anzac legacy was irrelevant, he would be remembered as the celebrated "Fighting Mac," Great War chaplain.

Consolidating the Legend

1. Ronald J Austin, *The Fighting Fourth: A history of Sydney's 4th Battalion 1914–19* (McRae, Vic: Slouch Hat Publications, 2007), page 99.
2. Capt Eric Wren, *Manuscript History of 3rd Battalion*, MSS0720, Australian War Memorial (AWM).
3. Lt Thomas James Richards, 1st Battalion, Diary, March 29, 1916, 2DRL/0786, AWM.
4. Letter to Annie, March 24, 1916, PR84/150, AWM.
5. Diary, undated, circa April 1–2, 1916, PR84/150, AWM.
6. Letter to Annie, April 16, 1916, PR84/150, AWM.
7. Leslie De Vine, Diary, April 25, 1916, 1DRL/0240, AWM.
8. Diary, undated, April–May, 1916, PR84/150, AWM.
9. For a valuable study of the nature of trench warfare, see Tony Ashworth, *Trench Warfare 1914–1918: The live and let live system* (London: Pan, 2000).
10. Adelaide Ah Kow, *William McKenzie M.C., O.B.E., O.F. Anzac Padre* (London: Salvationist Publishing and Supplies, 1949), page 46.
11. Edward Madigan, *Faith under Fire: Anglican Army Chaplains and the Great War* (London: Palgrave Macmillan, 2011), pages 120–125; Michael Gladwin, *Captains of the Soul: A history of Australian Army chaplains* (Newport, NSW: Big Sky, 2013), page 84.
12. Ah Kow, page 48.
13. Ah Kow, pages 48–49.
14. Letter to Annie, May 4, 1916, PR84/150, AWM.
15. Letter to Annie, May 4, 1916, PR84/150, AWM.
16. Letter to Annie, May 4, 1916, PR84/150, AWM.
17. Letter to Annie, January 30, 1917, PR84/150, AWM.
18. Letter to Annie, August 4, 1917, PR84/150, AWM.
19. Email from Trevor Hart, Archivist, Camberwell Grammar School, April 7, 2014.
20. Letter to Annie, August 6, 1916, PR84/150, AWM.
21. Email from Trevor Hart, Archivist, Camberwell Grammar School, April 7, 2014.
22. Letter to Annie, September 2, 1917, PR84/150, AWM.
23. Letter to Annie, July 16, 1917, PR84/150, AWM.
24. Letters to Annie, November 6, 1916; March 5, 1917; December 23, 1916, PR84/150, AWM.
25. Letter to Annie, July 16, 1917, PR84/150, AWM.
26. Letters to Annie, undated circa August, 1916; August 6, 1916; August 24, 1917; January 30, 1917, PR84/150, AWM.
27. Letters to Annie, February 4, 1917; September 2, 1917; August 29, 1916; August 6, 1916; October 10, 1916; July 16, 1917, PR84/150, AWM.
28. Ann Zubrick, Interview, October 28, 2013; Letter to Annie, undated, circa August, 1916, PR84/150, AWM.
29. Letter to Annie, October 20, 1916, PR84/150, AWM.
30. Gladwin, page 81.
31. Letter to Annie, September 2, 1917, PR84/150, AWM.
32. *War Cry*, July 8, 1916, page 3.
33. *Signs of the Times*, Vol 30 No 36, September 6, 1915, page 567.

34. Letter to Annie, May 24, 1916, PR84/150, AWM.
35. Thomas Richards, Diary, June 8, 1916, 2DRL/0786, AWM.
36. Letter to Annie, June 12, 1916, PR84/150, AWM.
37. Ivan D Chapman, *Iven G. Mackay Citizen and Soldier* (Melbourne: Melway, 1975), page 80.
38. <awm-public/cms_images/awm28/2/98/0010.pdf>.
39. Letter from Birdwood to Maj McKenzie, MC, 4th Bn, June 7, 1916, PR84/150, AWM.
40. See, for example, letter from Birdwood to James Caddy, MLDOC 3174, Mitchell Library, State Library of New South Wales.
41. Austin, pages 104–105.
42. Chapman, page 73; Harrie Joseph Cave, Letter 77, June 9, 1917, MLMSS 1224, Mitchell Library, State Library of New South Wales.
43. H G Hartnett, *Over the Top: A digger's story of the Western Front*, Chris Bryett (Editor) (Sydney: Allen & Unwin, 2009), page 53.
44. Arthur Edward Matthews, Diary narrative 2–3, 2DRL0219, AWM; Greg Kerr, Private wars: Personal records of the Anzacs in the Great War (Melbourne: Oxford University Press, 2000), page 147.
45. Diary, undated, July–August, 1916, PR84/150, AWM.
46. Chapman, page 76.
47. Not all chaplains were so calm under fire. An Australian sapper recorded having an unnamed chaplain rush into his dugout after being unexpectedly caught by machine gun fire. "It's the only time I've heard a padre swear and I'm sure he didn't realise he had done so. We looked at one another and didn't even laugh."—Henry Dadswell, Diary of a Sapper, 54, MSS0828, AWM.
48. Thomas Richards, Diary, August 13, 1916 2DRL/0786, AWM.
49. Letter to Annie, August 28, 1916, PR84/150, AWM.
50. *War Cry*, May 1, 1937, page 8.
51. *War Cry*, October 14, 1916.
52. Harold Begbie, "Captain Mac: A famous Australian Salvationist," *War Cry*, March 3, 1917, page 3; *War Cry*, December 21, 1918, page 16.
53. Graham Wilson, *Bully Beef and Balderdash: Some myths of the AIF examined and debunked* (Newport, NSW: Big Sky Publishing, 2012), pages 327–329.
54. Letter to Annie, March 28, 1917, PR84/150, AWM.
55. Letter from Macnaghten to McKenzie August 7, 1916, PR 85/049, AWM.
56. Noel Cuthbert, Diary, August 18, 1916, 2DRL/0560, AWM.
57. Archie Barwick, Diary, July 18, 1916, MLMSS 1493; *War Cry*, February 20, 1937, page 3.
58. Peter McGuigan, "A Man of Exceptional Courage," in (no editor) *In The Steps of the Founder: Celebrating the lives of 23 Australian recipients of the Order of the Founder* (Mont Albert, Vic: The Salvation Army, 1995), page 72; "William McKenzie," *Australian Encyclopaedia*, 6th edition (Sydney: Australian Geographical Society, 1996), Vol 5, page 1984; Wilson, pages 329–330.
59. A joke in the French army in the 1940s was that at the end of an action, the captain

would drop a handful of Croix de Guerre down the mortar barrel, fire it and whoever they landed on got it. About 2 million Croix de Guerre were awarded in World War I among a total of about 8 million French servicemen, and 5 million Iron Cross 2nd Class among 11 million Germans. French fighter ace Rene Fonck won the Croix de Guerre 29 times, once for each mentioned in despatches, each being represented by a palm leaf or star on the ridiculously long ribbon required to display them all.

60. Barwick, August 13, 1916, MLMSS 1493, Mitchell Library, State Library of New South Wales; George Makin, Letter, April 23, 1916, 1DRL473, AWM; Verner Cocks, Letter, June 13, 1917, MLMSS 1171, Mitchell Library, State Library of New South Wales; *The Presbyterian Banner*, March, 1917, page 7.
61. Chapman, page 77.
62. *London Gazette*, Supplement, July 13, 1916, page 6995.
63. F A McKenzie, *Serving the King's Men: How the Salvation Army is helping the nation* (London: Hodder & Stoughton, 1918), page 57.
64. Letter to Annie, August 28, 1916, PR84/150, AWM; Robert Horniman, Letter to his father, March 31, 1918, 1DRL/0358, AWM.
65. *Scottish Australasian*, August, 1918, page 6418.
66. Barwick, Diary, July 18, 1916.
67. Ah Kow, page 47.
68. Ah Kow, page 47.
69. Barwick, Diary, July 18, 1916; November 17, 1916; March 14, 1917; July 22, 1917; November 15, 1917.
70. Ben Champion, Diary, July 26, 1916, 2DRL/0512, AWM.
71. Letter dated August 20, 1916, in *War Cry*, October 14, 1916, page 3.
72. Letter to Annie, August 20, 1916, PR84/150, AWM.
73. Austin, page 119.
74. Letter to Annie, August 28, 1916, PR84/150, AWM.
75. Letter to Annie, August 28, 1916, PR84/150, AWM.
76. Letter to Annie, August 29, 1916, PR84/150, AWM; Letter dated August 30, 1916, in *War Cry*, October 28, 1916, page 3.
77. James William Dains, Diary, June 25, September 5, October 25, 1917, MLMSS 439, Mitchell Library, State Library of New South Wales.
78. Letter to Annie, September 18, 1916, PR84/150, AWM.
79. Ah Kow, page 46; Letter to Annie, September 18, 1916, PR84/150, AWM; *War Cry*, November 11, 1916, page 3.
80. Letter to Annie, October 10, 1916, PR84/150, AWM.
81. Eric Wren, September 25, 1916, Draft 3rd Battalion History, MSS0720, AWM.
82. Letters dated October 28, 1916, November 4, 1916, November 11, 1916, in *War Cry*, January 13, 1917, page 3.
83. Letter to Annie, October 10, 1916, PR84/150, AWM.
84. Robert Horniman, Letters to mother and sister, October 22, 1916, 1DRL/0358, AWM.
85. Letter to Annie, November 24, 1916, PR84/150, AWM.

86. Letter to Annie, December 23, 1916, PR84/150, AWM.
87. Letter to Annie, December 23, 1916, PR84/150, AWM.
88. *War Cry*, March 9, 1918, page 5.
89. *War Cry*, December 21, 1918, page 16.
90. Letter to Annie, February 4, 1917, PR84/150, AWM.
91. Letter to Hay, February 16, 1917, in *War Cry*, March 28, 1917.
92. *War Cry*, March 3, 1917, pages 1, 3.
93. Letter to Annie, March 28, 1917, PR84/150, AWM.
94. Letter to Annie, March 28, 1917, PR84/150, AWM.
95. *War Cry*, October 3, 1914, page 8.
96. Letter to Annie, May 11, 1917, PR84/150, AWM.
97. Letter to Annie, May 11, 1917, PR84/150, AWM; *Reveille*, March 1, 1933, 8; Charles Gifford Price, Letter, May 9, 1917, MLMSS 3444 ADD-ON 1255, Mitchell Library, State Library of New South Wales.
98. Letters to Annie, June 16, 1917, June 17, 1917, PR84/150, AWM.
99. Letter to Annie, July 16, 1917, PR84/150, AWM.
100. Letter to Annie, August 4, 1917, PR84/150, AWM.
101. Letter to Annie August 22, 1917, PR84/150, AWM.
102. Letter to Annie, August 24, 1917, PR84/150, AWM.
103. James Gault, *Padre Gault's Stunt Book* (London: Epworth Press, circa 1920), pages 173–175.
104. Ah Kow, page 51; Other Protestant Denominations Senior Chaplain Reports, August, 1914–October, 1917, AWM4 6/4/1; Chapman, page 96.
105. Chapman, page 96; Letter to Annie, October 10, 1917, PR84/150, AWM.
106. Battalion diary, November, 1917, AWM4 23/21/33; Leslie De Vine, Diary, November 25, 1917, 1DRL/0240, AWM.
107. Chapman, page 96.
108. Other Protestant Denominations Senior Chaplain Reports, August, 1914–October, 1917, AWM4 6/4/1, and January, 1918, AWM4 6/4/4.
109. Letter to Annie, December 29, 1917, PR84/150, AWM.
110. *War Cry*, December 22, 1917, page 9; Charles Monaghan, Diary, August 13, 1916, MLMSS 7478, Mitchell Library, State Library of New South Wales.
111. Chapman, page 96 and footnote.

CHAPTER 6

THE HERO RETURNS

AUSTRALIA, 1918–1927

William McKenzie anticipated that a sea voyage would set him right[1] and the two-month trip home must have been therapeutic. While there are no records of his activities, it is hard to imagine he was passive during this time. Running voluntary services and being involved in social life on board is almost a given. But it was a time free of external worry and stress. He was no longer dealing daily with traumatic wounds and death, and he would have had few formal obligations requiring him to be up early and late. By the time he arrived in Australia, he appeared ready to take up his busy schedule of ministry.

Of course, there were long-term effects from his war experiences. He suffered from nightmares for a long time afterward, often sleeping on the floor to avoid falling out of bed with his thrashing about. He would shout out in his sleep, reliving his war traumas, and occasionally would wander the room looking for a body blown apart or a trench system he wanted to visit. He admitted that the war had aged him 15 years, and his wife and close friends were alarmed at its impact on his mind and nerves. His memory was never the same again, although it lost little of its remarkable capacity to recall the names and faces of soldiers, and the events with which they were associated.[2]

Specialists in trauma treatment note a number of factors that aid in coping with past traumas, in particular a strong moral purpose and the ability to be active when under stress; a sense of safety; a feeling of belonging to a community; the capacity to articulate the trauma to an accepting audience; and a recognition of the trauma suffered.[3] By contrast, an absence of an accepting community can perpetuate a sense of shame in the trauma victim.[4]

A combination of these factors was helpful in McKenzie's recovery. His religious beliefs underpinned a strong sense of identity and calling, reinforced by his mystical connection with the Divine, which gave his spiritual worldview an experiential immediacy, as well as conferring on him a feeling of physical safety even in battle. He was returning to sure employment in a field he was passionate about, providing him with an ongoing sense of purposeful mission. He arrived home to widespread recognition and acclaim, and his speaking tour of the country provided the opportunity to process and articulate his trauma to audiences eager to hear and affirm his stories. Such audience acceptance minimised the aspect of shame that often attaches to trauma. And finally, but far from least, the warmth of his family relationships helped anchor his emotional wellbeing against the devastations he had experienced.

Yet there were elements of trauma recovery that McKenzie did poorly. Recognising and naming his own trauma was within his powers but he tended not to take seriously the owning required after the naming. Thus, giving himself permission to mourn did not rate on his to-do list. His inclination was to brush his own hurt aside as something he simply had to tough out, rather than allowing his soul to grieve and mourn. Interestingly, an expert in the field notes that compassionate men of high moral standard were likely to respond to trauma with symptoms of depression rather than rage[5]—a characteristic McKenzie had already demonstrated.

His arrival home was a much-anticipated event. Salvation Army Commissioner James Hay was advised by a Salvationist working on a hospital ship to expect huge crowds to welcome McKenzie, if conversations with sick and wounded men were anything to go by. When the *Corinthic* docked in Perth in late February, McKenzie was invited to speak at a patriotic fundraising meeting. The city's largest hall was fully booked at half a guinea per ticket, netting a handsome return for the war effort.[6] It was a foretaste of what was to happen in the eastern states, and an indicator of the reach of his popularity that he could draw such an audience in a state where he had never worked before the war and with whose soldiers he had had no official connection. Hay had written to the military authorities to ensure that McKenzie was to be disembarked in Melbourne, where his family was, rather than in Sydney, from where he had left Australia in 1914.[7]

The timing of his homecoming was ideal for maximising his reputation. The outcome of the war was delicately poised, with victory far from certain. The Russian war effort had collapsed during two revolutions in 1917, the latter bringing Lenin's Bolsheviks to power, and the Germans were able to move the bulk of their Eastern Front forces to the West, massing for an all-out offensive in the New Year. Worried Australians were keen to hear the latest news from a reputable source. If McKenzie had seen out the war overseas, he would have returned with the war won and out of the headlines. There would have been many prominent soldiers to share the spotlight and an Australian public far less interested in hearing "old" war stories. By 1919, war weariness at home meant that people wanted to forget the war and move on. But, in early 1918, McKenzie was primed to appeal to large audiences.

He had forged a national identity through his campaign for letters to lonely soldiers, resulting in thousands of people around Australia addressing letters to him during the war. The massive correspondence he had maintained with families of soldiers and word-of-mouth from thousands of returned servicemen added to the recognisability of his name. The Salvation Army had everything to gain by promoting him, as did civic authorities who needed something new to reinvigorate interest and support for the war effort from a jaded public, close to exhaustion after two divisive conscription referendum campaigns and the seemingly endless casualty lists published in the newspapers.

Achieved early in Egypt and sustained over the following years, McKenzie's fame and his remarkable charisma made him likely to capitalise on public interest. As a number of soldier commentators noted, he had an intuitive "understanding of the psychology of the masses," tuning in to his audience's mood and hitting exactly the right emotional notes to engage its heartfelt response. And by now, he was an accomplished public speaker, having had years of experience to polish his originally mediocre delivery. He communicated with warmth, humility, sincerity, a common touch and disarming humour.

His arrival in Melbourne on March 3 was publicised in *The War Cry*, which announced a "Welcome home" meeting in the Town Hall on Monday, March 11, with the expected overflow to be addressed in another meeting in the Athenaeum. The newspaper was delighted to report:

> This is what a returned soldier says of our comrade: "I say no man ever did more for the boys at the front. We have seen him coming in with a bunch of identification discs fastened to his belt after he had buried the bodies of the men; the discs represented the digging of the graves with his own hands. If any man deserves a welcome home it is the 'soldier's friend.'"
>
> "Chaplain McKenzie," another writer declares, "has attained a regard which has hardly been equalled by any other Chaplain who has gone to the front with the Australian Imperial Forces."[8]

In the meantime, McKenzie had a few days at home to reacquaint himself with his wife and children. They met him at the Victoria Barracks as the motorcade of disembarked soldiers was driven to the Base Hospital for a final check-up, but they had to compete for his attention with a crowd of returned soldiers and eager

Salvationists. He struggled to recognise the boys, Colin showing his disappointment at being forced to identify himself to his hero father. But he reported finding Annie unchanged and "in the pink." Through the babble of people trying to talk to him, he heard her say, "How well you look"—a compliment he was delighted to return.[9]

McKenzie had a couple of meetings with Salvationists, including one at the Training College, where he had begun his career as a Cadet. An account of the meeting said that Annie gave "some interesting glimpses of her inward soul-experiences during his absence." It would be fascinating to know what she said, but as there were no details given, it may be fair to assume that it was honest and therefore not totally positive. Of McKenzie's speech, it noted:

> It is by no means easy to describe the reception with which Chaplain "Mac" was greeted when he rose to speak, nor the emotions produced on his hearers by his thrilling words; but we believe they can be imagined to a great extent. The rapt and silent attention with which his words were followed were only broken here and there by spontaneous, irrepressible outbursts of enthusiastic appreciation. For close on an hour and a half his address lasted, and doubtless many present felt that they could have listened for twice as long. The Army's Chaplain is not only possessed of a humorous streak in his make-up, but he was able to move his audience to tears of sympathy as he described the "agonising experience through which he passed during his first few days and nights at Gallipoli.

On his first Sunday at home, he presented morning and evening talks at the Camberwell picture theatre, with 950 present. Three seekers came forward at his appeal.[10]

The venue of the planned public meeting was moved to the Exhibition Building in order to accommodate the crowd wishing to attend. People began queuing at 2 pm to be sure of a seat that night. More than 7000 people—of whom at least 1500 were returned servicemen—crammed into the building to hear several introductory speakers, including Colonel Le Maistre, former commander of the 5th Battalion, who welcomed McKenzie to the platform.

In his speech, McKenzie gave a pocket history of the AIF, praising the Australians' courage, patriotism and spirit, and throwing in several anecdotes about the actions of particular soldiers. He praised the various arms, but singled out the nurses, the stretcher-bearers (again noting that "the ginger chaps" were never cowards), the runners who were back and forth through shell fire with messages, and the chaplains.

He insisted that the Australians were not indifferent to religion: "They are not angels, I assure you—I do not want to make out that they are, but they have hearts to feel and manly natures that respond to the call of God Almighty, as multitudes have done." He noted many instances of religious sensitivity, including a mortally wounded Christian at Gallipoli who struggled to his knees in No-Man's-Land to recite the Shepherd's Psalm with the last of his strength. McKenzie estimated he had witnessed somewhere between 2000 and 3000 conversions during his war service, many of which would have been the fruits of his own ministry.

He also touched on a number of other topics, including the night bombing raids on London and the resilience of the British under great hardship, the accurate prediction that Germany's greatest threat would be over the coming three months (Germany launched the first of its five great spring offensives just 10 days later in a last throw of the dice to win the war), the superiority of Australia over other nations of the world, and he concluded by returning the Salvation Army flag that had been entrusted to him by Mrs Hay before he left. A transcript of the entire speech was published in *The War Cry* over the next two editions.[11]

A series of public engagements followed, under either the banner of The Salvation Army or of civic meetings organised for the general public. Each occasion was marked by huge turnouts of enthusiastic listeners as McKenzie shared some of his war experiences.

Returned soldiers organised to meet him at the Bourke Street Salvation Army headquarters, where speeches were made in his honour. In North Melbourne, the audience was too great for the Town Hall, while 2200 crowded the Brunswick Empire Picture Palace with hundreds more turned away. A civic reception in Ballarat attracted 3500.

There was a big reception at Bendigo, where McKenzie was met by a pipe band and honour guard of returned soldiers who carried him shoulder high into the hall, with "most enthusiastic" clapping. The mayor gave a speech, while the local paper reported on "the man who, although not a combatant soldier, has won fame by his devotion to duty and his conspicuous and consistent bravery. . . . [T]oday he holds the enviable record of being the most popular Chaplain who has laboured amongst the Anzacs." A song composed in his honour—"Captain Mac's Coming Home"—was sung. A sergeant eulogised him as "the most popular man who ever left Australia." Later, the city hosted a civic reception for him and 3500 people crammed into the Alfred Hall, "the accommodation of the hall being taxed to the uttermost."

Amid these events, McKenzie's appointment as Salvation Army Divisional Commander, Sydney Division, was announced. He had also been offered a government position, reputedly worth a lucrative £2000 per annum, but had turned it down.[12]

On his arrival in Sydney, McKenzie received the same celebrity welcome he had experienced in Melbourne—understandable especially as his battalion and brigade had been recruited from Sydney and its surrounds. "It was said that his feet never touched the ground from the time the returned men met him at the train till he landed on the town hall platform, where he was given—according to the Sydney *Daily Telegraph*, 'a welcome such as few are privileged to receive.'"[13] He was installed as Divisional Commander at The Salvation Army Easter Tent Meetings, where a separate tent was set up for his interviews with the throngs who wished to speak with him.

Hundreds of ex-servicemen came to meet him, as did family members of other servicemen, often travelling hundreds of kilometres and clutching a letter from McKenzie concerning the fate of a loved one. McKenzie never failed to recall time and place, giving grieving relatives a comforting final glimpse of their son, husband, brother or father. One woman exclaimed, "That dear hand! Oh may I kiss the hand that laid my boy to rest." So overwhelming was the demand for his time that he had to be smuggled out of the tent to eat or sleep.[14]

Despite the family's relocation to Sydney, Donald remained at Camberwell, and soon was able to achieve his ambition of enlisting in the AIF. On April 27, 17 days after his 18th birthday, he signed his papers, and was officially accepted on May 1. Among the paperwork was a statutory declaration from Annie that he was of age, and both his parents signed their approval on his papers. The army recognised leadership potential in the young man. He was promoted acting corporal then acting sergeant by October, having been sent to the training school for non-commissioned officers. This process was often a forerunner to a lieutenant's commission if the candidate continued to impress. The war ended in November, before Don could be shipped to France, and he was demobilised soon after, returning to Camberwell, where he served as prefect in 1918, and School Vice-Captain in 1919.[15]

A feature story on McKenzie in the *Scottish Australasian* gave an interesting account of Don's enlistment. It has him on his 18th birthday, meeting his father on the train at Melbourne and saying, "'Father, my conscience tells me that I should enlist.' 'Very well, my son,' said the father, 'I must not raise an objection,'" at which Don instantly took his papers and a pen from his pocket for his father to sign. "A chip off the old block!" concluded the journalist.[16] While not a strictly factual account, this embellished version of events must have come from McKenzie himself.

Cities and towns in New South Wales offered the same rapturous reception to McKenzie that he had experienced in Victoria. Everywhere he went, he was feted, with his appearances often hosted by the local mayor, and with leading figures—often generals—introducing him to the audience. He could speak for up to two hours and keep his audience entranced. At every meeting—whether civic or organised by The Salvation Army—there were numbers of people wishing to talk to him personally about someone who had served at Gallipoli or in France.

A brief return to Melbourne in May involved a string of meetings on one Sunday, including a "red-hot salvation meeting," before addressing a crowd estimated between 10,000 and 15,000 people in the Exhibition Hall for a Drumhead Commemoration Service, then another 1600 in Hawthorn Town Hall, with many unable to enter. His address at South Melbourne was described as "masterly." At Hawthorn, he spoke to a packed meeting mostly attended by non-church people. The mayor estimated that 1500 were turned away. "For one hour straight he poured himself forth, swaying the people at will, sometimes to laughter, sometimes to tears. His address was punctuated at many points by hearty applause. . . . It was a great address. Although this was the seventh meeting for the day, 'Chaplain Mac' could be heard in every corner of the hall."[17]

Back in Sydney, the *Daily Telegraph* reported:

> What is esprit de corps? If you wanted an illustration of it you should have been at the Anzac Buffet last night. Outside the rain beat down monotonously; inside was all the buffet building would hold—every one soldier, mother, father, sister, sweetheart connected with the Fourth Battalion who could get there. . . . The bluff padre talked with everyone, exercising his amazing memory as he pictured the feats of loved ones on the battlefield, or told some story of more restful fields. . . . So great was the crush that scores who would have liked to talk with "Mac."—the boys cut the "fighting" part out of his nickname—could not do so. But they heard from him a review of the doings of the Fourth that was simply all-embracing. Lieut-Col Storey welcomed him, and uttered a tribute to him that brought the protest, "Don't pile it on."
>
> "I can't pile it on enough, old fellow," was the retort.
>
> Then there was a good-humoured dispute amongst

> a couple of the men of the Fourth as to where they "picked 'Mac.' up."
>
> He settled that argument himself, and went on to tell delightful stories of the doings of the boys. Obviously between him and them there is a deep, sympathetic understanding, for many a sly joke they had between them that the uninitiated could only at best guess at.[18]

Storey's tribute included the statement that, "they say every cloud has its silver lining, and Padre Mac was ours, with his great-hearted personality and his famous Sunshine Song."[19]

The *Blue Mountains Echo* reported that a Katoomba audience had never been taken to such heights of hilarity or dregs of despair as those who listened to McKenzie's two-hour address. It continued:

> The address delivered by a strong man, with a strong personality, proved to a gem of the first water, and if the Captain of the Salvation Army could only coax "The Soldiers' Pal" back again for a second lecture two halls would not hold the audience. It was a genuine treat, smiles and tears alternating through the two hours. No mood was prolonged. From grave to gay the speaker kaleidoscoped, his anecdotes of the comparisons between the different Brigades being, perhaps, the masterpiece of a sterling lecture. He fitted admirably into every phase, and the audience cheered to the echo.[20]

The Newcastle press reported on his civic reception there at the Chamber of Commerce, with an honour guard to welcome him:

> After hearing Chaplain-Major McKenzie, one can readily understand the big influence he had with the troops, and the numerous appreciative references of which he has been the subject by soldiers. He has a bright, cheery style, combined with a vigorous and winning personality, that makes an irresistible appeal. Gifted with considerable power of expression, he moved his audience greatly as he recounted some of the epics of Gallipoli and France.

> Brigadier-General Meredith, who was a member of the original contingent, seconded the vote of thanks, and expressed his pleasure at being present to meet an old comrade in Chaplain-Major McKenzie, who got the name of "Fighting Mac" for being where he should not have been. (Laughter and applause). Men of his stamp have done more for the men than many generals.[21]

Despite still suffering from the effects of the war, McKenzie continued his non-stop schedule, and yet had to turn down numerous requests for speaking appointments as there were simply too many to accommodate. His presence was required at various high-level public engagements, hobnobbing with his characteristic ease with the Governor-General and invited to the State Government dinner for Edward, Prince of Wales (later Edward VIII of abdication notoriety) during his visit in 1920.[22]

As usual, the occasions he liked best were those where he could speak with ordinary people personally. He would travel long distances to visit an old comrade who was sick or dying, or with relatives of those who had been killed. Once he appealed for funds to relieve a widow in distressed circumstances whose son had died in the war, and soon £20 had been provided. Often he lent his own money.

On top of his administrative load and his heavy travel and public meeting commitments, McKenzie wrote a series of articles for *The War Cry*. The European battlefields became analogies for discussions of spiritual warfare as people were encouraged to show the same commitment to the spiritual battle as the soldiers had demonstrated in France.[23]

He found great encouragement from hearing of those who had become Christians through his war ministry. One wealthy squatter wrote to McKenzie to say that his only son found Christ at the Front, but that the father had been shattered when he had been killed. "I was tempted to despair, but somehow or other the spirit of my boy was calling in this dark and terrible hour in my experience to turn to God. And I have found Him—I have found Him!" the father wrote.

While a study of British chaplains found that on the whole they had little impact on allegiance to denominational religion, McKenzie's influence was great. Many men testified to their transformed attitude toward The Salvation Army during and after the war, from senior officers from the upper classes of society, such as Macnaghten and his father Sir Melville, to the working-class larrikins of the AIF.[24] One soldier said to McKenzie, "I'm not a religious man, but your damned religion'll do me every damned time!" Another man rang Commissioner Hay wanting to contact McKenzie. "'Any special reason?' he was asked. In an emotional voice came the reply—'Yes! he saved my son: he saved him in his body, and he saved him in his soul.'"[25] General Monash spoke "eulogistically" of the work of The Salvation Army, both during the war and after it, while General Birdwood specifically mentioned McKenzie during his tribute to The Salvation Army's contribution to the war effort.

In 1919, during a visit to Wagga Wagga, where he was met by "an extraordinary number of people at the railway station," who chaired him off the train to the car in a triumphal procession with bands to Town Hall and a guard of honour, the mayor made an "intimate, personal" speech, noting that his own son wrote his first letter home on Salvation Army notepaper. He asked his son if he had joined the church. He replied that The Salvation Army had joined the army.[26] The Salvation Army and the YMCA were perhaps the only two Christian organisations in Australia whose reputations were enhanced by the war, largely because they exerted so much effort in meeting the ordinary practical needs of soldiers.

It was not only others finding merit in The Salvation Army that enhanced McKenzie's reach; it was also his own recognition of the virtues to be found in other denominations—and in people of no professed faith. The war had taught McKenzie that goodness was not the exclusive possession of the saved in evangelical Christianity. This made him more collaborative with ministers of other religions, and his approach to the unsaved became less strident and more compassionate and empathetic. In particular, his reaction to the sins of the common man lost the condemnatory edge common among

Salvationists. He frequently overlooked what he now considered to be the superficial sins of drink, gambling and swearing because of the debt he felt to the truly noble, self-sacrificing character of the apparently irreligious Australians he had known at Gallipoli and in France. He now sought to connect at a deeper level than mere outward behaviour. His passion to save the lost was undiminished; what had changed in his ministry was a better tolerance for the foibles of humanity, and greater gentleness in dealing with other's failures.

Back in France in mid-1918, an officer in the 4th Battalion heard of McKenzie's reception, writing to his mother, "Am very pleased that old Padre Mac. got such a splendid reception in Australia. But he more than deserves anything he gets like that, for he has helped wonderfully in making the A.I.F. what it is and I might say that at present our force in France, through these recent happenings, are considered by everyone to be nothing short of marvellous."[27]

McKenzie's fame reached the ears of Salvation Army Commissioner Henry Howard, Chief of Staff at the UK headquarters, who decided during a visit in 1919 to test how closely it matched its reputation. Against strong advice, he insisted that McKenzie accompany him from the Army's Goulburn Street office to the Sydney Town Hall to check on arrangements for a meeting. The distance was just more than two city blocks, a mere 500 metres or so. An hour later, the visitor was back. When asked about the Town Hall, "he exclaimed in mock disgust, 'Town Hall! I have not seen it. I haven't been out of this street.'" The pair had hardly made any progress because of the press of people on the street who recognised the giant figure of McKenzie and stopped to talk to him.[28]

Among the demands for McKenzie's time were continuing requests from the public arena. Of these, only one was accepted. In November, 1919, New South Wales Premier William Holman asked for and was finally granted McKenzie's services for three months by The Salvation Army to help resolve a problem with repatriated men. Several hundred soldiers who had been settled on farms had grievances that they wanted addressed by an independent arbitrator.

McKenzie was the ideal choice and he was equipped with a special railway carriage and secretarial assistants. He was authorised to settle claims of up to £100 on his own authority.

He was characteristically thorough, visiting practically every convalescent home in the state and every soldier settlement. The Premier was delighted with the report, for it allowed him to claim that most of the problems were of the soldiers' making rather than of government departments. "I am glad to know that many men have derived substantial relief as the result of chaplain McKenzie's inquiries, and much misunderstanding has been removed," he said. Grateful soldiers later said of this incident that his "capacity for organisation proved almost Napoleonic."[29]

McKenzie led his Sydney Division with his usual energy, overseeing the expansion of its numbers and in particular initiating a program for girls, which he titled "Life Saving Guards." In the 17 centres established, girls were taught domestic work such as sewing, darning and knitting, cooking, swimming and life-saving, and physical culture. Achievements were celebrated with badges and demonstrations, and McKenzie felt that the movement helped girls develop positive life attitudes and skills.

He was given the Salvation Army's Long Service Order on October 17, 1919, in recognition of his 25 years of service. In 1920, he was one of the 16 chosen to receive the inaugural award of The Order of the Founder, The Salvation Army's highest honour recognising service that would have commended the recipient to Salvation Army founder William Booth, for his work among the troops during the war.

In January, 1921, McKenzie was appointed Divisional Commander, Brisbane, moving there with Annie, Gordon and Mavis. Donald and Colin stayed behind in Sydney, the restless Donald failing to fulfil his intellectual potential, while the gentle Colin commenced a degree in architecture. McKenzie was the subject of an extended interview in the *Brisbane Courier*, where he impressed with his energy, spirit of hopefulness and commitment to action. He outlined his vision as "the advancement of the cause of righteousness in its broadest and highest sense" and hoped to establish Life Saving Guards in Brisbane.[30]

McKenzie remained in Brisbane until April, 1923, when he was made Field Secretary of the relatively new Australia Southern Territory, responsible for Salvation Army activity in Victoria, South Australia, Tasmania and Western Australia. His new post involved even more travel than his Divisional commands, including a trip to New Zealand in 1923. However, with the boys leaving home to forge their own lives during these years, Annie and Mavis were increasingly able to accompany him.

His work continued to be a mix of Salvation Army meetings and public memorial services, a sample of which demonstrate his continued status as a high-profile member of the community. He was honoured by the Royal Caledonian Society of Melbourne at a dinner in March, 1923, where in deference to his teetotal principles "the Rosebery Cup went round during Mac's visit, but, by way of gentle variation, it was filled with lemonade." He unveiled a war memorial at Finley, New South Wales, on Empire Day, 1923, and a huge reception of Scottish flavour was staged for him in Freemantle in 1924.

In Melbourne, he gave the main 1925 Anzac Day address at the United Memorial Service in the Exhibition Building before the Governor General in the morning and in the afternoon spoke to the widows and bereaved mothers of members of the AIF and Australian Navy. The same year, he took an "impressive" dedication ceremony of Memorial Gates in Oakleigh in the presence of 3000 in memory of 164 pupils of Oakleigh State School who had served overseas in the Great War.

In 1925, he delivered the Christmas address to the influential members of the Melbourne Legacy Club, composed of business and commercial men who served as officers of the AIF. "The greatness of our nation, I need not remind you, does not rest upon the possession of arms and goods and gold," he told these leading businessmen. "These are secondary to the ideals and high ethical standards that make a great nation."[31]

McKenzie became a regular at Anzac Day services, where he was mobbed by people who would bring photos of loved ones. He would identify them and tell the family the details of their career and of how they died. Of all the dignitaries at these occasions, McKenzie was most in demand, and would spend all day there, returning home late at night absolutely worn out emotionally and physically. He also maintained a voluminous correspondence with families of soldiers regarding their fate. Historian Michael McKernan notes that on occasions his hand was seen to be bleeding by the end of Anzac Day, the result of it being shaken by so many people. While there is no other evidence for this, his eldest granddaughter considers it possible.[32]

On Salvation Army business, he wrote a long recruiting article to young people to volunteer for service as Officers in The Army in 1924, delivered an "intensely interesting" address to an enthusiastic Yarrawonga Corps audience in the Atheneum Hall in October, 1925, then presided over the 41st anniversary of the Corps at South Richmond in November. In March, 1926, he conducted holiness meetings, giving a personal testimony of his own experience of conversion and sanctification. He was also appointed by The Salvation Army General Bramwell Booth—whom he had met in London during the war—to represent the International Headquarters at the March annual Territorial Congress in New Zealand. While there, he toured both islands, taking meetings everywhere he went.[33]

McKenzie continued to be a target for those in financial need, especially returned servicemen. A good number of these were hopeless alcoholics, but McKenzie could not help giving them a loan in the light of their wartime courage. He had always been generous with his own funds, but his giving reached the stage that imperilled the family finances. He would keep a pocket full of silver florins on purpose for the panhandlers exploiting a hard-luck story.[34]

On one occasion, Commissioner Hay laboured with his soul over the matter, but McKenzie was unconvinced. Later that day, Hay found McKenzie staring with delight at an anonymous cheque for £1000 that he had just been sent. "That seems to solve the problem," he said, handing over the money. Others sent him money as well, which was placed in a trust fund to help needy ex-soldiers. One donor gave his reason for his gift: "McKenzie saved me once—body and soul."

Other returned soldiers also targeted McKenzie, just wanting to catch up or to say thank you. Some soldiers arrived beaming, girl on their arm, hoping that he could conduct an on-the-spot marriage service. His secretary in Melbourne in the mid-1920s recalled acting as impromptu bridesmaid several times a week.[35]

In October, 1926, McKenzie's promotion to Lieutenant-Commissioner was announced, as well as the end of his tenure as Field Secretary. His next appointment as Territorial Commander would be overseas, due to a new policy that Commanders could not take office in their home country. He prepared for a trip to Headquarters in England without knowing where he would go next. Asked if he had any anxiety about his future, McKenzie replied, "None at all! My ways are in the hands of the Lord."[36]

A round of farewell visits began, at which McKenzie was eulogised "for what kind of man he is." Congratulations on his promotion poured in from various quarters, including from Dr Maloney, Member of the House of Representatives, Mr E Turnbull, State President of the Returned Soldiers and Sailors Imperial League of Australia (forerunner of the RSL), "and not least a prisoner at Pentridge," who had heard McKenzie speak at a recent meeting there.[37]

He was officially farewelled at a huge event in the Independent Church on Collins Street on October 25, 1926. The next day, McKenzie and his wife Annie set sail to London on board the *SS Naldera*, taking with them 18-year-old Mavis. She had just finished high school, winning a scholarship to a prestigious school, but as the baby of the family—and McKenzie's favourite—she could not be left behind.

The family spent several months in England meeting with Salvation Army leaders and grabbing the opportunity to visit Scotland over a free weekend. Early on the following Monday morning, McKenzie got a literal dusting-down from a colleague, showing up in the

London editorial office in a frock coat covered in dust, having come directly from the train station. He had slept on the carriage floor all the way from Glasgow, with Annie and Mavis sleeping on the two seat benches.[38] In the English winter, the McKenzies visited the High Wycombe Corps in a snow-storm, wading through drifts to get there. For the ladies it was a novel experience: they hadn't seen falling snow before.[39]

In the meantime, McKenzie was awaiting the news of his next appointment.

1. Letter to Annie, June 16, 1917, PR84/150, Australian War Memorial (AWM).
2. Adelaide Ah Kow, *William McKenzie M.C., O.B.E., O.F. Anzac Padre* (London: Salvationist Publishing and Supplies, 1949), page 57.
3. See, for example, Judith Lewis Herman, *Trauma and Recovery* (New York: Basic Books, 2007), for more on the process of trauma recovery.
4. Jeffrey Kauffman (editor), *The Shame of Death, Grief, and Trauma* (New York: Routledge, 2010), page 7.
5. Herman, page 58.
6. Ah Kow, page 53.
7. National Australian Archives: B2455, MCKENZIE, W.
8. *War Cry*, March 9, 1918, page 5.
9. *War Cry*, March 2, 1918, page 3; March 9, 1918, page 5; March 18, 1918, page 1.
10. *War Cry*, March 16, 1918, page 5.
11. *War Cry*, March 23, 1918, pages 5, 7; March 30, 1918, page 2.
12. *War Cry*, March, 30, 1918, pages 4, 5; August 6, 1947, page 5.
13. Ah Kow, pages 53–54.
14. Ah Kow, page 54.
15. Email from Trevor Hart, Archivist, Camberwell Grammar School, April 7, 2014.
16. *Scottish Australasian*, August, 1918, page 6419.
17. *War Cry*, May 3, 1918, page 5.
18. Quoted in *War Cry*, May 11, 1918.
19. Ah Kow, page 54.
20. Quoted in *War Cry*, September 14, 1918, page 6.

21. Quoted in *War Cry*, September 28, 1918, page 2.
22. *War Cry*, June 5, 1920; Ah Kow, page 56.
23. *War Cry*, February 15, 1919; February 22, 1919; March 1, 1919; March 22, 1919.
24. Letter to Annie, January 31, 1916, PR84/150, AWM.
25. *War Cry*, August 16, 1947.
26. Edward Madigan, *Faith Under Fire: Anglican Army Chaplains and the Great War* (London: Palgrave Macmillan, 2011), pages 151–152; Norman Campbell, "Fighting Mac," undated news clipping circa 1926, McKenzie file, Salvation Army Heritage Room, Bexley North, Sydney; also quoted in Dale, "Fighting Mac," and quoted in *War Cry*, August 9, 1947, page 6; January 24, 1920, page 3; January 3, 1920, page 8; November 15, 1919, page 5.
27. Robert Horniman, Letter to mother, June 9, 1919, 1DRL/0358, AWM.
28. Ah Kow, page 57.
29. *War Cry*, August 9, 1919, page 4; Ah Kow, page 56; "Grievances. Returned Soldiers. 'Fighting Mac's inquiries," *Sydney Morning Herald*, November 5, 1919, page 10; *War Cry*, February 27, 1937.
30. "Fighting Mac: Noted Salvation Army Leader Lieut.-Colonel MacKenzie Interviewed," *Brisbane Courier*, January 7, 1921, page 7.
31. *War Cry*, May 5, 1923, page 6; June 9, 1923, page 16; March 15, 1924, page 16; April 18, 1925, page 10; May 2, 1925, page 8; January 2, 1926, page 10; January 9, 1926, page 9; <www.electricscotland.com/history/australia/melbourne12.htm>, accessed September 9, 2013.
32. Ann Zubrick, Interview, October 28, 2013; Jean Newall, interview, October 30, 2013; Michael McKernan, "William McKenzie," *Australian Dictionary of Biography*, <http://adb.anu.edu.au/biography/mckenzie-william-7391>, accessed December 16, 2013.
33. *War Cry*, July 26, 1924, page 3; October 31, 1925, page 10; November 14, 1925, page 7; March 6, 1926, page 9; March 13, 1926, page 10; May 22, 1926, page 8.
34. *War Cry*, June 3, 1961, page 2.
35. Ah Kow, pages 58–59.
36. *War Cry*, May 14, 1927, page 8.
37. *War Cry*, October 9, 1926, page 9; October 16, 1926, pages 1, 8; October 23, 1926; March 12, 1927, page 9.
38. *War Cry*, August 13, 1948.
39. *War Cry*, April 2, 1927, page 8.

Chapter 7

Front Line Again

China, 1927–1930

McKenzie's new appointment was announced in February, 1927. He was to be Territorial Commander of North China, based in what was then called Peking (today's Beijing). Many of the missionary Officers in China were Australian.[1] When asked to go to China by The Salvation Army Chief of Staff Edward Higgins in London, he replied,

> "I am more than ready to go to China. There are no reserves in my consecration, 'Anywhere with Jesus' is my unchanging attitude."
>
> "Thank God, thank God," exclaimed the Chief, with a manifest relief.

Four Officers had already declined the appointment to a country wracked by a civil war that specifically threatened the wellbeing of Westerners.[2]

Strangely, McKenzie's diary dates the interview with the Chief of Staff as July 24, 1927—clearly a mistake as he was already in China by that time. The interview must have been in late February, 1927, for he wrote that he immediately boarded a ship for his voyage.

When interviewed about the appointment, McKenzie said, "I go gladly to that disturbed country, believing God will work for us and through us," adding, "When we get on the spot I only hope my health keeps good. It is a difficult path, but I delight in a conflict with devils and darkness, for surely God is our Refuge and Strength. . . . I only wish I could speak the Chinaman's language, and so get under his skin, the better to reach him and help him to see the beauty of Jesus." As usual, he saw the opportunities, not the problems.[3]

In what was characteristic for missionaries of the period, McKenzie received no training in Chinese culture or language, being expected to manage in the completely foreign culture from his own very Scottish–Australian resources.

The McKenzies were farewelled from London by a large crowd, notwithstanding other major Salvation Army events happening at the same time.[4] They travelled by train to Liverpool and took a ship first to Belfast, then across the Atlantic to Canada. Naturally, McKenzie held Salvationist meetings on board every afternoon in steerage, "attended by great crowds singing splendid."

His diary lists their port of arrival as St John's, which is a small fishing port in Newfoundland, but as he states they then caught the train to Montreal—difficult to accomplish as Newfoundland is an island bereft of railways—he probably miswrote the name, meaning Saint John, New Brunswick, a major Canadian port for trans-Atlantic shipping, and a straightforward train ride to Montreal. From there, it was across Ontario to Winnipeg in Manitoba, where McKenzie led out in a big meeting for 1400 people, "a mighty enthusiastic affair."

Next was the long and tedious trip across the prairies, where McKenzie found the prairie towns to be "bleak and bare," with unpainted wooden houses. However, this changed on April 11, as they spent all day rolling through the Canadian Rockies. "Scenery surpassing all my expectations," enthused McKenzie. "It was a delectable feast to the eyes and senses; Visibility extraordinarily good. Could see for 50 miles with perfect pleasure. Landscape is a delight—the hills sing to my heart and Highland blood, 'I to the hills will lift mine eyes.' Nothing mean or petty about them—truly magnificent grandeur."

They arrived in Vancouver the next day, and McKenzie found its spectacular harbour-side setting impressive. From there, they sailed on the *Empress of Asia* at noon for Tokyo.[5] One wonders if McKenzie knew of his connection to the ship: when the *Emden* was sunk in December, 1914, by *HMAS Sydney*, the *Empress* had carried the captured wounded German sailors to Colombo.

McKenzie organised Sunday services on board, arriving in Yokohama on April 17, 1927. The McKenzies travelled the short distance to Tokyo, meeting 140 Salvation Army Officers and Cadets there and running successful meetings, but the train ride left McKenzie feeling ill as the narrow 3'6" (1.05 metre) gauge rocked badly. It must have been something, for McKenzie never recorded being seasick on his many ocean voyages! The next leg was across the straits to Korea, before travelling to Beijing by train from Seoul.

In 1927, China was disintegrating into chaotic civil war. Its government, initially led by Sun Yat-sen of the Kuomintang Party, had held a tenuous grip on power since the revolution that had deposed Puyi, the last Emperor of the Qing Dynasty in 1911. The Kuomintang held a mix of socialist and nationalist policies, wanting to modernise China while expelling foreign influences, and it wished to establish traditional Confucian ideals as the centrepiece of national law and education. But it had to negotiate the implementation of its policies with powerful local warlords who only paid lip-service to the central government, which had direct control only over a relatively small central coastal region. As a result, China was marked by unrest, lawlessness and political intrigue.

When Western powers failed to help Sun defeat the warlords, he turned to the Soviets, who—with political cunning—backed both him and the small but growing Chinese Communist Party led by Mao Zedong. Under Sun, the Communists more or less cooperated with the Nationalist Kuomintang, with sporadic campaigns against particular warlords. But when he died from cancer in 1925, the Communists increasingly contested power with his successor, Chiang Kai-shek, who sought to eliminate the rising threat of Mao's grass-roots movement. Having defeated a coalition of warlords in 1926, Chiang purged his forces of Communists, leading to a civil war between the rival parties from April, 1927.

To complicate matters, many warlords were still active and the conflict degenerated into a complex series of engagements between Chiang's forces, various warlords and the Communists. Invariably, the peasants suffered most, being exploited and pillaged by ever-shifting coalitions of forces and, in the power vacuums that occurred, by bandits—often unpaid conscripts who deserted—who took advantage of the endemic lawlessness.

Adding to the chaos for Westerners were the deliberate attacks on non-Chinese institutions. Assaults on Western citizens followed in Nanking—present-day Nanjing[6]—soon after its capture by Chiang's forces from the local warlord in March, 1927.

For centuries, China had regarded itself as the superior civilisation surrounded by barbarians and resented the way Western imperialist powers had trampled on its sovereignty during the previous 100 years. It had lost a string of wars against foreign states, including Japan, and had been forced to accept many humiliating "unequal treaties," as the Kuomintang accurately described them. These treaties mandated paying huge indemnities, conceding unfair trading rights and being forced to continue such injustices as the opium trade, to the financial benefit of the British in particular, while making opium addicts of tens of thousands of Chinese. Among the terms of these treaties was the granting of extra-territorial rights to many European states, joined by the United States and Japan, in key places, mostly trading ports. These Concessions were operated under the law of the controlling power, and were garrisoned with their police and military. In scenes reminiscent of the anti-foreign Boxer Rebellion of 1899–1901, it was easy for the Kuomintang to arouse its followers to assaults on Western "foreign devils" and their Chinese supporters who they saw as corrupting China's purer heritage and values. Naturally, missionaries with their alien religions were prime targets.

This was the perilous situation that McKenzie was going to. With Westerners under attack in parts of the country, Annie and Mavis remained behind in Korea until McKenzie had time to establish whether it was safe for them to join him. He left Seoul on April 27, 1927, by train, Annie recording that, "He went off in that same brave spirit that he manifested when he left us at Bendigo to go to the war. He stood in the doorway of the train and waved till we were out of sight." In the meantime, the two ladies ran successful meetings in Seoul.

McKenzie found Beijing in turmoil as Southern Chinese (Cantonese) forces were threatening the city. Women missionaries were evacuated to Tientsin (Tianjin), Beijing's port town and considered marginally safer as foreign warships could evacuate their citizens.[7] The local authorities had ordered all foreigners into the Western Concessions where they could be better protected by their own military.

A group of 60 Salvation Army Officers met McKenzie at the station. A welcome meeting was organised on Thursday night, April 28, with a great crowd in attendance at the Territorial HQ at 71 Morrison Street (now Wangfujing Street, Beijing).

For the first time, McKenzie preached through an interpreter, finding that this fettered his natural style. But by the time of his next talk with an interpreter on the following Sunday night, he had adapted to the process and "did better." However, he never learnt to master a style that was readily translatable, and his energetic and colourful language remained a challenge for his interpreters for the rest of his stay. At one stage, he used the term "as mad as a hatter," forcing the creative translation of "The man was so angry that his head got very hot and then threw his hat off.'" McKenzie only mastered a few words of the local dialect of Chinese, principally the words "Hui Kai," meaning "repent."

At a meeting in Tientsin on Saturday, May 7, he received "a fine generous welcome." The next day he dedicated three Chinese babies and held meetings at several Corps in the city, including the

Slum Corps. He noted the great unrest and fear manifest among the Chinese, who were afraid to mix with foreigners owing to anti-foreign feeling. He found the Chinese very shy of coming to the penitent form "but we must fight and win out by the Holy Spirit."[8]

In reality, the concept of coming to the penitent bench was alien to Chinese culture. McKenzie and most of his colleagues were so thoroughly Western, especially Anglo-Western, in their outlook that they struggled to adapt their faith to the culture they found themselves in but did not fully understand. All the same, real efforts were made by a good number of missionaries, including Salvationists, to overcome their cultural biases, learn fluent Chinese and present a gospel that resonated with Chinese culture. McKenzie's success in China was probably more due to his charismatic empathy that transcended linguistic barriers, for he was not reflective enough to work out how Salvationist principles of British origin might be contextualised in China.

Having Annie by his side as he travelled made a huge difference. Annie showed some sensitivity to issues of language and culture, and doubtless she helped her husband bridge some gaps that his more energetic disposition overlooked.[9] She demonstrated a poise and leadership that might have astonished those who only had McKenzie's wartime letters to go by. Gone was any evidence of the "extreme self-consciousness and numbing nervousness"[10] that McKenzie had worried over earlier.

The change may have been due to any combination of factors. She no longer had the worry of the boys who, as young adults now, were away from home. She was clearly more comfortable in her role as mother to her daughter Mavis, and this in itself might have made her more relaxed. While the situation in China was difficult, at least she had the constant support of McKenzie by her side. And furthermore, he had returned from the war in a weakened state from which he had never fully recovered. No longer the omni-competent man—though still a perpetual-motion machine—his memory lapses and need of emotional care may have reduced his formidableness down to manageable size, and his vulnerability gave her a definable role in supporting him that affirmed her own worth. In China, she carved out for herself a career that paralleled and supported his, but was still distinctly her own achievement. It was marked by incredible hard work, endurance of hardship and commitment to improving the lot of women in China through practical means.

McKenzie relished the challenge posed by China. Its population of 359 million represented "a vast ant heap," while the country as a whole was subjected to war, violence, corruption and soon a massive famine. The Salvation Army's resources in China were about 250 Chinese Officers, fortunately none of whom had been killed in the troubles, but many of the Army's properties had been looted or confiscated.

The violence and the famine of 1928–1929 provoked levels of atrocity and horror greater than the things he witnessed during the Great War. Yet his first biographer Adelaide Ah Kow considered that the years in China provided welcome relief from the constant "poignant reminders of the great, stressful days of 1914–1918." She felt that the change in scenes, conditions and ways of living was good for him, proving "most beneficial."[11] This can be hard to believe. China may have provided some valuable relief, but the nature of his work was taxing in the extreme, both emotionally and physically.

"I saw some sickening, soul-searing things during the Great War, but I met stark, grisly horror face to face in China," he wrote. "I know of happenings in that strange land too dreadful to whisper," adding that he knew of human flesh for sale in remote parts of China. Elsewhere he spoke of "unprintable happenings, dwarfing in sickening horror the worst things of the Great War."[12] The emotional difference in China was that the human horrors he witnessed were inflicted largely on people he did not know personally and with whom he had no bond of shared blood and culture, so it lacked the intensity of Gallipoli and France. In China, he had his wife with him—and, for a while, his daughter—to offer emotional support and he did not return from China in the same exhausted, traumatised state that he had from the Great War. But it still must have been hard on his soul to witness again such traumatic events.

For the first few months, McKenzie's work was confined to the coastal regions but, as things settled down, he was able to expand his journeys to other parts of northern China. Annie and Mavis were able to join him in due course. He felt positive about the work in China, being delighted at how easy it was to attract a crowd, often holding an audience numbering up to 2000 for an hour or more, sometimes in very cold winter conditions. He was his energetic self, travelling by any means possible—train, boat, bus, cart and often on foot—and not sparing himself in commitment.

Once he arrived at a centre after a tiring journey, had a cup of tea and discovering that no meeting was scheduled until 7 pm—three hours distant—refused a rest, instead immediately launching into an impromptu open-air meeting. This story was repeated many times during his time in China. Where possible, Annie accompanied him on his travels, taking Women's Meetings. His other companions were usually an expatriate local Officer and his translator, Ensign Kuo, who had spent a year in London and was responsible for translating many Salvation Army publications. Mavis occupied herself teaching English and music, while studying Chinese.

On November 30, 1927, McKenzie left for his first country tour, returning to his headquarters on December 12. Following this tour in detail from McKenzie's diary gives an idea of his work. He left with Kuo and Staff Captain Cederval at 7 am from Beijing. The train trip to Paotingfu was supposedly four hours but took eight and a half, a delay that in no way surprised any of the train's occupants. At Paotingfu, they had to talk the military guards at the city gates into permitting the night meeting, despite the curfew. One new Salvation Army soldier—a railway Station Master—was enrolled but no-one came to the penitent bench. Only three of the 17 soldiers in the local Corps could be found. Most of the others had been conscripted as soldiers or coolies in warlord forces, McKenzie euphemistically noting that many of these overworked and abused coolies were probably "now enriching China soil." He found the atmosphere of the city "electric with very sinister feeling about military affairs."

The next morning, the party left by bus at 7 am for Kao Yang, running meetings for large crowds on market day, but without any soul-saving result. An early morning walk of 14.5 kilometres took them to Chiu Ch'eng through 15 centimetres of snow. Arriving at noon, a cup of tea was all the refreshment they took before attracting a crowd of 400 by marching with two drums beating. Five meetings between noon and 9 pm resulted in five recruits and one seeker.

Then it was a cart ride to Jen Co'u Hsien, though McKenzie walked as it was too cold to sit still. They were met by an impressive reception committee, the military governor and the mayor sending buglers, drummers and heavily armed police, who escorted them to the Salvation Army Hall. They had a crowded audience for two meetings, despite this being a strongly Muslim area, and McKenzie wanted to make it a Sectional centre on the strength of its local Corps. The next two days involved visits to surrounding villages, with excellent results from a number of meetings, then back to Jen Co'u Hsien for packed stirring meetings in the evenings, but without results at the penitent bench.

They were unable to take a boat to their next destination—an island village—as the lake had frozen over and the ice would not yet bear an ice-sled "with the added weight of 17 stone of animated corruption imposed upon it"—a creative way for McKenzie to describe himself—so they aimed for Tientsin, 200 kilometres away. Unfortunately, the regular bus that day was destroyed by a smoking bus driver who got too close to the open petrol tank, but they managed to catch another that fortuitously arrived on a trial run from Tientsin. They were gratefully received as passengers: as members of The Salvation Army, they proved influential in negotiating the transit through eight successive military roadblocks.

Eighty kilometres short of Tientsin, they approached an ancient ramshackle bridge full of gaps and holes over a fast-flowing river. Reconnoitring ahead of the bus, McKenzie was met on the other side by seven men in black, who insisted on inspecting the bus. This was not unusual, but these "inspectors" turned out to be bandits. Holding pistols to their heads, the bandits searched the bus, then through their baggage, tossing their belongings carelessly in the dirt.

They seemed angry at the slenderness of the pickings, including the pitifully small total of petty cash, but McKenzie challenged their decision to keep his overcoat.

At this point, Ensign Kuo intervened, warning the bandits that his party was part of the Chiu Shih Chün—The Salvation Army—under the protection of the local dictator who would hunt down anyone who harmed them. The bluff worked immediately and the bandits returned the goods with alacrity, ensuring all was in order and politely farewelling them. McKenzie reported feeling "not the slightest tremor" during the incident. Despite having a pistol within centimetres of his nose, he regarded it all as "a great joke!" As it had during the Great War, physical danger acted as a stimulant rather than a discouragement to his personality.

Arriving in Tientsin at 2.30 am, they moved straight on to Sheng Feng, where the Army's reputation had been damaged by an Officer who had murdered his child and attempted to murder his wife. A good crowd attended all five meetings but without result. Next they walked 12 kilometres to a village and attracted an audience of 1000 on market day. McKenzie's talk on the gospel was done "in simple effective language illuminated by Chinese incidents"—and won five seekers. Two of them were young and a delighted McKenzie reported the words of one of them: "I have been seeking truth for a long time, but I have found it at last and it makes me happy."

The next village involved a blistering 25-kilometre walk, the trio arriving "limp and limping" but running bright meetings with six seekers, followed by more walking to arrive at dusk at the next village. The group then retraced their steps to Sheng Feng, running meetings at every stop, but again with poor results at the penitent bench. This concluded the mission trip.

McKenzie evaluated the results of the tour, regarding most Chinese Officers as lacking in initiative for "stirring in the way of extra meetings," requiring "specialists"—meaning expatriates—to keep them up to the mark. He felt there were "illimitable possibilities" for work among China's large population of children and youth, but he realistically recognised that 50 per cent of his converts would be lost due to the circumstances of the war.[13] To be fair to the Chinese Officers, they were working under the most difficult circumstances and, until McKenzie's arrival, they had received little real support from Territorial Headquarters.

A gruelling 17-day tour comprised McKenzie's second trip, beginning on January 2, 1928, with Ensigns Sowton and Kuo as his companions. The hard winter weather added to the difficulty, which began when McKenzie had to be shoved and dragged head first through a train window to get into an overcrowded third-class carriage. It seated a theoretical 120 but had nearly 500 crammed into it. Despite the unavoidably snug accommodation, the broken train windows made for a freezing journey. At their inn that night, they were three times interrogated by soldiers, finally grabbing a little sleep between 2 and 4 am.

The trip involved more transport adventures, many very early mornings and late nights, and frequent days with infrequent meals snatched at odd hours. They arrived two days late at one Corps, who had feared that they had been executed by the Red Spears, a rural vigilante self-defence group who dispatched any interlopers they suspected could upset local conditions. When not travelling, each day was packed with meetings and McKenzie also took time in each place to instruct his Chinese Officers, many of whom were very inexperienced and in some cases rather ignorant of basic Christian doctrine. As much as anything, his work was to lift the morale of the local Officers, whose situation was miserable in the extreme during these unsettled times. For many Officers, it was their first Headquarters visit in three years. They often had little outside support, their buildings were vandalised and they felt threatened by the many anti-Western groups.

The trip home was an epic of endurance, the usual five-hour train trip taking more than 20 hours through intensely cold conditions. McKenzie described the voyage in his usual vivid way: "'The Chinese National Anthem pertained throughout the journey. This National Anthem consists of continual hacking, coughing and spitting. Their yells and smells are pungent enough to poison a polecat. Believe me it's some fun riding in a third-class carriage in China." He noted that the ticket prices had doubled, courtesy of the generals who owned the railways and milked them for personal gain. He arrived home at 9 pm, days late, where Annie patiently awaited him, always with a hot meal ready, never knowing when he might suddenly appear. Asked once if the rumour of him coming home on top of a goods train in the middle of winter with just a blanket was true, she dissented on only one point: it was a coal truck. One can imagine the state he was in coming through the door.

As a postscript to the tour, he noted that he had wrenched his leg while jumping from the train on the first evening. Despite this, he walked an estimated 400 kilometres over the next 17 days, yet seemed surprised that all the walking had not cured the problem. Instead, his leg swelled up until he was nearly lame. Typically, he shrugged it off with "we'll get over it sooner or later just as we have got over many other things."[14] While the sheer physicality of these trips was enough to challenge a robust young man, the portly McKenzie was nearing 60 but still no more likely to concede anything to age or personal need.

On another trip in April–May, 1928, his experiences included a train carriage that caught fire from a carelessly dropped cigarette, and a hearty and encouraging 173 penitents over the course of the tour that also included unproductive visits to bandit towns—where converts were threatened with violence—and villages recently held by the Communists. A number of his converts were well-educated businessmen or civil servants. At one stage, the firebox of the engine towing their train fell off while going up a steep incline. Stranded while another engine was sent for, McKenzie started a Salvationist meeting on the train, discovering several Chinese Salvationists who happened to be on board.

The record of a trip in May, 1929—accompanied by Annie, Adjutant Bruce and interpreter Ensign Kuo—included a preaching duel with a band of Communists, before the Communists abandoned the field after an hour, leaving the victorious McKenzie with an uncontested audience of 800 and a very sore throat. There were also long tiring walks over ploughed ground and soft sand, sometimes through terrible dust storms. This tour was during the height of the dreadful famine that accompanied the drought in northern China, and he recorded one Salvation Army Porridge Kitchen that fed 9800 per day in Saratai. The Swedish Mission there was astonished at his 52 seekers, having suffered the heart-rending loss of 23 foreign missionaries to typhus and bandits in the previous five years.[15]

The drought-induced famine of 1928–1929, exacerbated by civil war, corruption and banditry, which hampered the government's ability to harness resources, brought the most appalling conditions. It is estimated it cost about 3 million lives. At its worst, people were literally falling dead in the streets of towns and villages across northern China. Violence was rife, with bandits stealing food and instances of cannibalism recorded.

McKenzie oversaw the establishment of food kitchens, but appealed to Australian Salvationists for financial support in a circular letter published for the annual Self-Denial Week in February, 1929. He detailed the enormous work that the Porridge Kitchens had achieved over the winter months, serving 740,361 large bowls of porridge to the starving and distributing 2000 padded winter garments to the poor. Hot tea was supplied to rickshaw coolies, and food and shelter given to many homeless White Russian girls—refugees of the Russian Revolution who eked out a precarious existence in northern China—while Chinese war refugees were housed, clothed and fed. The Girls' Homes in Beijing and Chengtingfu looked after 100 girls, including ensuring that they got an education. Several thousand patients were treated at medical centres, while a hospital was being built. But even then, demand was greater than supply for all services.[16]

By late 1929, he reported that political unrest and anti-Christian sentiment added to the difficulties created by poverty and famine: "We are opening our porridge kitchens on December 1 and will be feeding 10,000 in Peking and some more thousands in Tientsin, besides many thousands in the famine district."[17]

To Benjamin Orames, his one-time colleague in France and eventual successor in the Northern China Command, he wrote of

100,000 mostly unemployed civil servants left begging in Beijing, while respectable businessmen committed suicide out of shame and despair. The southern supporters of Sun Yat-sen brought their aggressively anti-business, anti-Western and anti-Christian attitudes to the north (which was ironic as Sun had drawn strong inspiration from Christianity for his movement). Chinese Christians were scattered, many were killed, many fled and many others abandoned their faith.

"This, you will see is a serious state of affairs," wrote McKenzie. "Our back is to the wall, our faith is in God, our colours are flying top mast, we refuse to be dismayed or discouraged and with the unsheathed sword to Black Devils, blue devils, brown devils, yellow devils or dirty white devils, come one come all and we will overthrow you in the mighty power of our God."

In these circumstances, he was still about to open the first Territorial Conference in four years. He pleaded for prayer and material help, as his porridge kitchens supplied the only food for many in the face of a government that didn't seem to care.[18]

One unusual and distressing role that McKenzie assumed in Beijing demonstrated his continuing capacity to earn the trust of the hierarchy, in this case that of the Chinese authorities and of the foreign consulates. At the height of the troubles, when executions were common, McKenzie would each morning identify the corpses of non-Chinese people beheaded in Tiananmen Square overnight. He undertook this grisly task in order to help the families of those executed achieve some certainty over the fate of their loved ones. It was eerily reminiscent of his work during the Great War.[19]

McKenzie's excellent relationships with well-placed officials saw him tipped off that Mao and Chiang were mobilising for another round of fighting, and that this would take up all the rail traffic. Plans had been made for Mavis to go to London to study medicine, but the news meant she had to leave immediately if she wanted to get out. McKenzie accompanied her to Harbin in the north of China and stayed overnight with the British consul, who had married a White Russian. The next day they travelled to Vladivostok. Mavis then travelled 4th class on the Trans-Siberian railway, then across Europe to London, where she took an arts degree at London University and played the organ in the Holloway Corps. She later completed a medical degree at Sydney University and married a fellow Salvationist Officer, Kingsley Mortimer, serving for many years as missionaries in Africa.

There was an odd sequel to this story. In 1955, Mavis returned to Australia to pack up the family home after her mother's death. While there, she heard a knock on door. An immigration official had arrived asking if anyone could identify a distressed refugee woman who claimed residency status in Australia as a British citizen because she had been married to a British consul, naming the McKenzies as supporting witnesses. Demonstrating a memory for faces that would have made her father proud, Mavis recognised her as the wife of the consul in Harbin from an overnight stay some 25 years earlier and the woman was able to get papers to stay in Australia.[20]

Along with the major issues were some petty ones. McKenzie wrote to Australian Salvationists to alert them that often they were not putting enough postage stamps on letters to missionaries in China and the unfortunate recipients were being fined for it. He himself received no fewer than 14 and had to pay out a handsome sum to have them released by the post office. This created financial difficulties, unwelcome on top of the very heavy local taxation and the inadequate mission budgets. He reminded his readers that a 3-penny stamp was the minimum needed for a letter to China.[21]

In the meantime, trouble was brewing at Salvation Army Headquarters in London. The 73-year-old Bramwell Booth's generalship was coming under increasing criticism over perceptions of its erratic decisions, dictatorial manner and nepotistic character, but Booth refused to resign even after losing the support of his sister Evangeline—later elected as fourth General in 1934—and his brother-in-law Frederick Booth-Tucker. McKenzie discussed the denominational politics obliquely in a letter to Orames, suggesting that Booth had suffered a mental breakdown. He seemed to support a change in the administrative processes that would create more transparency in the selection of the Army's General, taking it out of the hands of the General himself to appoint his successor. McKenzie's choice to replace Booth—should he "suddenly pass out"—was Commissioner Henry Mapp.

Things came to a head in 1928 as Booth's health deteriorated. It provided the excuse to convene the first ever meeting of the High Council of The Salvation Army, to which McKenzie, as a senior church administrator, was invited, travelling to London for the occasion. The sessions were held in January and February, 1929, voting Booth out of office by a huge majority after he again refused to resign. While Booth unsuccessfully contested the outcome in court, Army leadership elected the Chief of Staff, Edward Higgins, as the new General.

Given McKenzie's disgust at the slack state of affairs in the London Headquarters of The Army, it is unsurprising that he fully supported the actions of the High Council and considered the result a good one, noting that the disintegration of The Army that some feared did not eventuate, with not a single Officer resigning over the crisis and Salvationist numbers growing in key Territories.[22] Ironically, McKenzie's preferred candidate Mapp, was dismissed by Evangeline Booth for personal misconduct in 1937.

In early 1930, McKenzie's term as Commander of Northern China came to an end. Higgins had dropped the policy of not appointing Commanders to their home Territories and McKenzie was given the Australian Southern Territory, with headquarters in Melbourne. On May 7, he and Annie left China for Australia. They left behind them a reinvigorated Salvation Army in northern China. The organisation was much more sound in its finances, recovering from the great damage inflicted by years of civil war and famine. The first class of Cadets had completed their training and the new Officers were commissioned by McKenzie before his departure, ensuring vigorous new Chinese leadership of Corps in the years to come. Above all, he had instilled in his Officers and Corps the same "all-absorbing, over-powering passion for souls."

Of his term of office, it was said, "His powers of endurance, his fearless leadership and his rare gift of attachment entrenched him firmly in the hearts of Chinese Salvationists during a period of exceptional distress and hardship. To the Australian missionary Officers he was a veritable father." With characteristic humility, McKenzie reflected that "China has done more for us than we have been able to do for China."[23]

1. *War Cry*, March 12, 1927, page 9.
2. McKenzie minute book, 95, Archive Box R15, Salvation Army Heritage Archives, Melbourne.
3. *War Cry*, May 14, 1927, page 8; May 21, 1927, page 10.
4. *War Cry*, May 21, 1927, page 10.
5. McKenzie minute book, 95–96, Archive Box R15, Salvation Army Heritage Archives, Melbourne.
6. Nanjing was used as the new capital of China from 1927 until its brutal capture by the Japanese in 1937.
7. *War Cry*, June 18, 1927, page 8; June 25, 1927, page 8.
8. McKenzie minute book, 98, Archive Box R15, Salvation Army Heritage Archives, Melbourne; Adelaide Ah Kow, *William McKenzie M.C., O.B.E., O.F. Anzac Padre* (London: Salvationist Publishing and Supplies, 1949), page 64.
9. *War Cry*, June 28, 1930, page 13.
10. Letter to Hay, January 9, 1915, PR85/815, Australian War Memorial.
11. *Melbourne Herald*, June 14, 1930, page 271; Ah Kow, page 59.
12. *Melbourne Herald*, June 14, 1930, page 271; "Fighting Mac: Notable Salvationist, Distinguished Padre," *Adelaide Chronicle*, July 24, 1930, page 52.
13. McKenzie minute book, 101–105, Archive Box R15, Salvation Army Heritage Archives, Melbourne.
14. McKenzie minute book, 105–109, Archive Box R15, Salvation Army Heritage Archives, Melbourne; Ah Kow, page 65.
15. McKenzie minute book, 110–114, Archive Box R15, Salvation Army Heritage Archives, Melbourne.
16. Letter, circa January–February, 1929, Archive Box R15, Salvation Army Heritage Archives, Melbourne.
17. *War Cry*, January 25, 1930, page 8.

18. Letter to Colonel B Orames, October 28, 1928, Archive Box R15, Salvation Army Heritage Archives, Melbourne.
19. Ann Zubrick, Interview, October 28, 2013.
20. Zubrick, Interview.
21. *War Cry*, July 7, 1928, page 10.
22. Letter to Colonel B Orames, October 28, 1928; "Fighting Mac: Notable Salvationist, Distinguished Padre," *Adelaide Chronicle*, July 24, 1930, page 52; *Melbourne Herald*, June 14, 1930, page 271.
23. Ah Kow, page 66; *War Cry*, February 6, 1937, page 7.

CHAPTER 8

CULMINATION

AUSTRALIA AND RETIREMENT, 1930–1947

A stern test for any celebrity's popularity is the reception received after having been out of the public eye for a time. After three years in relative obscurity in China, followed almost only by Salvation Army press, McKenzie was coming home. Events showed that he was still forefront in the minds of many Australians, not only those of his co-religionists. A program for a "Great Public Welcome to Lt-Commissioner and Mrs McKenzie" was published. The venue was the Melbourne Town Hall, set down for Monday, June 16, 1930. It was presided over by no less a figure than the Lieutenant-Governor, Sir William Irvine, KCMG, KC, and included an additional address by Lieutenant-Colonel A F Burrett, DSO, on behalf of the Returned Soldiers. The back cover gave a pocket history of McKenzie, calling him about the best-known Salvation Army Officer in the country due to his war work and his post-war lecture tour.[1]

The *Melbourne Age* reported his arrival on June 11, 1930, noting the large crowd at Spencer Street Station, despite his return being generally unknown. Among the crowd were several hundred Salvationists but also many returned soldiers. McKenzie was given "an enthusiastic welcome. Cheer after cheer was given, and there were greetings of 'Good old Fighting Mac,' 'Welcome back to Melbourne,' from all sides." It took time for McKenzie to free himself of the crowd, delivering a short speech, then driving directly to the Bourke Street Headquarters, "where the new leader settled down to work without delay." The article described him as "one of the best-known officers and probably the most popular in the army in Australia. He is a man of splendid physique, radiating strength, energy and geniality."[2]

The *Melbourne Herald* featured him in its magazine section, captioning a photo of him with, "There is no more picturesque personality or better-loved man in Australian than Commissioner W. M. McKenzie, M.C., of the Salvation Army."[3]

In fact, the welcome everywhere was as if he had never left. His travels around his new command, encompassing Victoria, Tasmania, South Australia and Western Australia, were greeted with laudatory write-ups in the local press and civic receptions presided over by the highest local authorities, retired military officers, respected clergymen from the major denominations and representatives from various community organisations. The speeches honoured both McKenzie's outstanding war work as well as The Salvation Army, with praise for The Army's "highly effective" social work, behind which "was the great spiritual aim to lift men and women out of the gutter and to make them worthy citizens of God's kingdom."[4]

At last, Annie was able to be constantly by his side. Without children to be responsible for, she had the freedom to travel with him and she made important contributions at their engagements. To both civic and church groups, she spoke movingly and effectively especially about the needs in China, often dressed in traditional Chinese garb for added effect, and received considerable plaudits for the warmth of her public speaking. She became a popular speaker in her own right with a fund of stirring stories. By early July, the couple had 25 speaking engagements for July and August, with more yet to be confirmed, in locations as widely separated as Ballarat, Adelaide and Perth.[5] These distances represented much wearying travel in an era before regular air services.

The McKenzies returned to a nation in the grip of the Great Depression, the world's worst economic crisis. Australia was particularly vulnerable, dependent on exports mainly to Britain and, with huge overseas loans to repay, the government was unable to respond effectively. Unemployment was rampant and governments at every level were baffled as to the right strategy to restore the situation. The new federal Labor government of James Scullin was divided over whether to pursue risky inflationary or conservative deflationary policies, while radical New South Wales Labor Premier Jack Lang threatened to repudiate his state's massive debts.

The dire economic situation greatly impacted the work of The Salvation Army. Donations and tithe income were down, while the demand for social welfare skyrocketed. McKenzie led the Army's response by cutting the salaries of Officers, with the bigger cuts coming to those at the top of the command chain. Some Officers were working for little more than food and clothing themselves. The Army was forced to run its budget at a significant deficit, amounting to £10,000 in a total of £92,000 by 1932. It sheltered thousands of men, women and children. A serious problem was the theft of equipment from its homes by the desperate people it served. One of the men's homes in Melbourne lost 2000 pieces of cutlery in three years, while 100 sheets disappeared, wound around the bodies under the shirts of men who were leaving. Replacing the items represented an unwanted additional cost.[6]

The McKenzies had strong views about the economic situation. Annie considered the crisis to be a call to righteousness, "declaring that she was certain that all would be well if God was given His right place in the heart of the individual, in the home and in the nation."[7] McKenzie urged a spiritual solution leading to self-sacrifice and an active engagement with the needs of others. His essential social and political conservatism emerged again when he castigated the Labor governments and the striking trade unions in a private letter to his Salvation Army colleague Benjamin Orames. He badged the Left as "the Devil's orchestra," accusing them of "seeking to create red ruin." He feared for Australia's international reputation. In particular, Lang came in for some vitriol for his "extravagance" and government debts.

"To speak the truth," he wrote, "I would like to see the whole bag and baggage of the whole Australian Labor parties, from one end to the other go into the wilderness for a period of twenty-five years and give the country a chance. The bulk of them are incapable, dishonest, dastardly, demoralizing dabblers in politics." He accused them of self-serving cronyism, though he did admit that there were a few on the other side of politics who were similar.[8]

In November, 1930, McKenzie travelled to London for a meeting of all 42 Territorial Commanders and the General of The Salvation Army. Doubtless the meeting discussed their collective response to the social crisis that followed the worldwide economic collapse that had multiplied The Army's work, while significantly reducing its available funds. He returned home in December.

Both McKenzie and Annie maintained their busy schedule of travelling, preaching, encouraging and evangelising throughout their term of office, as well as writing articles for *The War Cry*. His standing in the public eye was demonstrated when he was asked to be one of three speakers at the public Memorial Service held after the funeral of the distinguished Australian General Sir John Monash on October 11, 1931, who had died three days earlier. Held at the Melbourne Shrine of Remembrance, the principal speaker was General Sir Harry Chauvel, followed by brief addresses to the 30,000 listeners by RSSILA Victorian President George W Holland and then McKenzie.[9]

In May, 1932, McKenzie was promoted to Commissioner by the General, Edward Higgins, announced in a public meeting at the Exhibition Centre in Melbourne, to acclamation from Salvationists and the general public. In November, his transfer to the command of the Eastern Territory, encompassing New South Wales and Queensland, was announced. The couple undertook a farewell tour of their Territory through December, 1932, to February, 1933, often giving their own personal testimony and receiving moving tributes everywhere they went.

In one Armistice Day address, attended by the mayor of Coburg and other dignitaries, McKenzie's speech drew tears. "It is not gold, or goods, or weapons, that make a nation strong and great," he said. "It is love, unselfishness, brotherly kindness, and, above all, righteousness." A local councillor gave the vote of thanks at the end, remarking, "I am not ashamed to confess that I am a much better man through coming here this afternoon."[10]

In response to heartfelt tributes from Army and civic officials at a meeting in Tasmania, a visibly affected McKenzie replied, "I am bewildered and touched by the enthusiastic and generous sentiments expressed here this evening as well as the wishes for our future welfare. I am a Salvationist by conviction and by the will of God."[11]

McKenzie's reception on their arrival in Sydney was predictably large. A massive reception was held in the Town Hall, and AIF soldiers could be heard calling out "Good old Padre" and "Good old Mac!" McKenzie was saluted by a grey-haired "Australian of Australians"—an Aboriginal digger who had impulsively leapt onto the stage and was quickly swallowed up in McKenzie's powerful embrace. *The War Cry* described the meeting as featuring "a galaxy of Sydney's leading men," including his old colonel, now Brigadier-General Iven Mackay, speaking on behalf of the AIF's officers. Speeches praising McKenzie's wartime heroics "were continually interrupted by vociferous applause," which increased when the representative of the ordinary soldiers spoke.

"No man in Australia is better known, or more firmly entrenched in the affections of thousands of her citizens than William McKenzie," the *War Cry* journalist wrote.[12] The Returned Soldiers official journal *Reveille* reported the "magnificent reception" attended by hundreds of Diggers, along with the Salvation Army and public "to make his welcome worthy of the great MAN [sic] he is."[13]

Despite the passage of time—or perhaps more truthfully—because of the passage of time, McKenzie remained hugely popular with returned soldiers. "The idols of the war years remain public idols still; the Diggers are always quick to recognise and acclaim them," wrote a journalist for the *Melbourne Herald*. "One of the best-known and best-liked is Commissioner McKenzie, M.C., of The Salvation Army."[14]

The *Sydney Morning Herald* reported his reception at an Anzac Day reunion in superlative terms: "From the moment he appeared at the returned soldiers' reunion in the Sydney Town Hall yesterday, he was the central figure." It described the "deafening burst of cheering, and a rush on all sides to shake his hand . . . the gathering rose as one man and lustily sang 'For he's a jolly good fellow'." McKenzie led the singing of many choruses, but when he tried to speak the men demanded more songs. The report continued:

> Never, perhaps, has a public speaker's voice been drowned so good humouredly. "Fighting Mac" proved himself too good a soldier to be beaten. Before they were aware of the sway of the Commissioner's personality over them, hundreds of Diggers were singing in perfect rhythm "When the Roll is Called Up Yonder I'll Be There". So "Fighting Mac" had given them a sermon of song. Even then they were not satisfied. Men filed before the Commissioner in a seemingly endless stream, grasping his hand as they passed and recalling some incident of a soldier's life. Never was there such a spontaneous levee.[15]

Such reunions remained a feature of his time. As before, wherever he went he was received at public receptions by high dignitaries who sang his praises. Standing with him on public platforms were federal and state leaders and politicians, local mayors and councillors, governors, retired senior military officers, heads of servicemen's associations, senior clergy from mainstream denominations, heads of community organisations and, from time to time, prominent rabbis. In many ways, they came not just to honour him but to share in the honour accorded him. He was a celebrity figure and it was in many people's interest to be identified with him.

The raw enthusiasm of returned soldiers at various meetings seemed to have grown with time, as their traumatic memories faded but their nostalgic affection for McKenzie remained. Records of some meetings speak of "tumultuous" scenes as veterans competed with Salvation Army groups to express their enthusiasm. Processions were characterised as being like Royal Progresses, such was the public response to McKenzie's appearances. As in Melbourne, he was a prominent figure at Anzac Day services, leading out in various capacities and constantly beset by long queues of people wanting to talk to him.[16] In 1933, the Returned Soldiers' journal *Reveille* published a feature article about him as part of its "Celebrities of the AIF" series, which had other features on notable generals, officers and ordinary soldiers who had in some way distinguished themselves.[17]

Naturally, he continued his busy schedule of travel and meetings, accompanied again by Annie. He was the first Eastern Australia Territorial Commander to have had experience in the Territory, and within a month of taking up command, the couple had visited all six Divisions in New South Wales, as well as the Central Queensland Division. In his second month he conducted the first Easter Campaign in Prince Alfred Park, with congregations peaking over 1200, resulting in 150 seekers for salvation or for holiness.

By this time, Mavis had returned to Australia as a Salvation Army Lieutenant and eventually took up medical studies at Sydney University. She sometimes travelled with her parents and was a popular vocal soloist at Army events—her childhood voice lessons had paid off as McKenzie had hoped.

McKenzie also maintained his voluminous correspondence. One who wrote to him in 1935 was Joe Cocking, a Salvationist at the Tighes Hill Corps in Newcastle that McKenzie had founded during his first posting as an Officer in 1890. Cocking's radical socialist-pacifist beliefs made him increasingly disenchanted with The Army and his confrontations with his Corps commanders made him feel virtually pushed out of the organisation. He took exception to a claim that McKenzie was in favour of compulsory military training, writing to the Commissioner for clarification, but McKenzie replied that he favoured it because it would give young men physical exercise and prepare them for an unstable world. In particular, McKenzie feared the revived Germany.

Cocking had this "lovely 'Christian' letter published in the daily rag, which evidently made the Scotch fire-eater afraid that some of his dupes would censure him for his heathenism," for McKenzie promptly published an article denouncing war, particularly Italy's designs on Abyssinia. Cocking found this hypocritical, and in 1939, he wrote that he hoped that "Billy" (McKenzie) would not "contaminate" The Army's new General, McKenzie's old friend George Carpenter.

As a new war loomed, Cocking denounced the military as anti-Christian, writing that "there is little doubt that many of the heads of the churches will favour compulsory military training; and most of the leaders of The Salvation Army will aid and abet [Prime Minister] Menzies in this crime. 'Fighting Mac' will probably be delighted to find that 'Thou shalt not kill' is to be flouted and ignored again." He added a poem he had written "of the whole diabolical business" that was published in the *Common Cause*, the Coal Miners Union journal, in November, 1939. Its fifth stanza ran:

Though fighting Macks and jingo Jacks
Compulsion have applauded,
Yet, when coerced and loudly cursed,
The lads will be defrauded.[18]

But there was nothing hypocritical about McKenzie's stance. His was a militant Christianity—as indeed was that of The Salvation Army—seeing itself pitched in a war between the kingdom of Christ and that of the devil. The whole idea of a Salvation *Army* was militant, predicated on a literal spiritual war on the devil's strongholds. This war required vigilance and vigour to bring down the devil's kingdom, and not just in the spiritual realm, for the conflict manifested itself in the material world as well, through such evils as drink, gambling, Sabbath-breaking, poverty and sloth.

For McKenzie, physical warfare was an extension of the spiritual conflict he was engaged in. He did not like war but he hated evil even more and was prepared to condone the war conducted by political states if he saw it as protecting righteousness, because for him "righteous[ness] comes first." He had seen the Great War in that light, and was seeing the same in the looming conflict that would pit the British Empire and its allies against Fascism and Japanese imperialism.

If his vision was limited, it was in failing to see any great difference between the values of a Protestant British world and those of Christianity. But given a choice, he favoured peace. The editor of *The War Cry* in 1933 wrote about Anzac Day, decrying any association of glorifying war with the Anzac Day marches, saying that McKenzie, who was still prominent in Anzac Day services, "is the passionate pleader that the peace of God may reign in all hearts, and fill the whole world with its fruits. . . . True Anzacs are anti-war." And McKenzie's 1936 Christmas message expounded on the beatitude of Christ—"Blessed are the peacemakers"—stating that "war is wicked and wasteful, and is the outcome of sin and selfishness," and that "every Christian's influence should be eternally opposed to devastating war."[19]

In the first year of his term, he instituted Divisional Congresses for each state centre, which was considered "a striking success," resulting in many people joining The Army and its influence being more widely felt. A tour by General Evangeline Booth in 1935 featured a public meeting with Lieutenant Governor Sir Philip Street, Premier Bertram Stevens and former Prime Minister William Hughes. The State Governor's wife Lady Hore-Ruthven attended the women's meeting.

Despite the lingering effects of the terrible depression, McKenzie was able to allocate nearly £100,000 for capital works, building new or restoring old Corps buildings and other facilities across the Territory. New Corps and Outposts were established, and the various organisations within The Army, such as Home League, seniors' and young people's activities, were multiplied. A Training Farm at Riverview, Queensland, provided probationary prisoners in the last six months of their sentence an opportunity to learn farming skills, and the People's Palaces in New South Wales and Queensland were remodelled and modernised. The St Peter's Men's Industrial Home, housed in a large "paper shed"—probably a warehouse for paper products—provided relief employment, while the Home for Homeless Men opened in Goulburn to relieve emergency distress, providing 3000 free beds. In 1936, the new Gill Memorial Home for 80 boys was opened on the Winderadeen estate near Goulburn, a property named after a wealthy squatter donor. It replaced the Dee Why boys' home, was proclaimed "the most up-to-date and nearest-to-perfection Boys' Home in the whole Army world," and was opened by Prime Minister Joseph Lyons.[20]

While he did not enjoy administration, McKenzie's success in that role rested on several things. He always saw this role as the servant of the workers in the field; administration as an end in itself or as a power base was anathema to him. Thus he cut through red tape and ensured that all processes were as efficient and effective as possible. His innovative mind devised new methods of ministry and his energetic personality ensured quick implementation.

Working in the strongly hierarchical Salvation Army reduced the expectation among those he led of collective or consultative decision-making, which happened to suit his direct and decisive operational style. He was disposed to rapid decision-making, and his capacity to inspire his colleagues and subordinates meant people were usually swept up in the energy of the initiatives. Allied to this were his formidable work ethic and his rock-like integrity. Above all, his administration never lost sight of the people it was designed to serve; the employees and members of the church, and the general public always felt that they were the centre of his attention.

But in keeping with his established practice, he often escaped the office and ran as many Field Campaigns as possible, in order to have direct contact with people. He was still driven by the imperative to save all the souls he could, believing as he did that time was running out for the world. While he continually pursued the large agenda of his Territory, he was still most at home talking with people one-on-one and was legendary for his solicitous concern. He inquired after the comfort of his Officers, ensuring their homes and offices were adequate, and he felt bad when he discovered that excesses of his enthusiasm had created a huge workload for his secretarial staff. Wherever he went, he took time out for the ordinary people in public life who served him. He was known to disappear on long train trips because he was counselling with a member of the train staff. Most of all, he was tender with those who had let him or The Army down. He was tough on wrongdoing, but gentle with those who were repentant, rather than dealing out harsh discipline.[21]

His post-war ministry embodied the maturation of his outlook during the war years. While his passion for souls remained undiminished, his approach demonstrated a broader sympathy and considerably less fire-and-brimstone. The harshness of his Presbyterian heritage was softened by a greater empathy for those he sought to save, and a tolerant understanding of the foibles and weaknesses of humanity.

In the King's Birthday Honours List of June, 1935, McKenzie was appointed an Officer of the Order of the British Empire in recognition of his services to the Australian people, particularly his welfare work, but also for his war service and service to returned soldiers.[22] A six-week tour of evangelistic meetings in Queensland in 1936 also offered the opportunity for a radio broadcast in his old hometown of Bundaberg, and the dedication of his grand-nephew Darrell McKenzie Deighton.[23]

Unfortunately, McKenzie's health was suffering under his workload. The symptoms that had led to his return from France during the war again asserted themselves, and his memory lapses reached the point of creating major embarrassments for McKenzie and The Army. In September, at the instruction of the General Evangeline Booth, McKenzie took leave and sailed to England for a furlough designed to restore his health. Annie and Mavis farewelled him and, during his absence Annie carried a larger responsibility with many engagements in the Eastern Territory in children's, women's and men's homes, and in hospitals and retirement homes.[24] In England, McKenzie attended the Salvation Army Congress at the Royal Albert Hall, returning to Sydney in late February. The rest had done him visible good, *The War Cry* proclaiming that "he was re-invigorated in body and mind."[25]

But the problems quickly reappeared. In February, 1937, the

General replaced him at his administrative post and asked him to return to China as a travelling evangelist, where his memory problems would not cause difficulties. Some Officers in Australia questioned the reasonableness of sending the McKenzies overseas again at a moment's notice, "but the Officer himself, nodding sympathetically at his wife's wry smile, salutes and starts to pack up their personal belongings—they're off again!" When it came to commitment, Annie's was of much the same stamp as her husband's, saying that "a fundamental principle of Army teaching which had to be demonstrated in practice, was the denying of self and the devoting of one's life, in whatever circumstances or environment it might be placed, to the highest welfare of the people."[26]

They began another farewell tour, again marked by an outpouring of heartfelt tributes from Army officials and from leading Australian citizens and former soldiers. In Bundaberg, McKenzie was able to reunite with his extended family. A group of returned soldiers sent a letter of tribute to be published in *The War Cry*, asking McKenzie to put his Scottish reserve aside and allow the letter to be published. It was. In it they wrote, "The memory of your courageous vitality, your overflowing humour, your fund of good stories, your stainless integrity and Christian character will remain with us while life shall last."

The last farewell event was in Sydney where a huge audience listened to many speeches in his honour. His son Donald asked to speak and gave an "affectionate tribute" to his parents, citing "a number of instances of their wonderful influence and example, and especially referred to Mrs McKenzie's spirit of bravery and sacrifice in the war days, when the father was with the troops on Gallipoli, and in Flanders." He considered his own volunteer Christian work on several nights each week to be "a real tribute to the godliness of his parents." Deeply moved, McKenzie replied, concluding with a challenge to the young people present to advance the cause of righteousness against the forces of evil, in particular drink, gambling and "Sabbath-breaking." The McKenzies left on April 21 on *SS Taiping*.[27]

Landing in Hong Kong on May 11, the McKenzies swung immediately into action, running meetings and meeting with 140 seekers in just three days. Then it was on to Shanghai and Tientsin (Tianjin), where he met many Officers and soldiers whom he had known during his earlier service there, "surely the sweetest possible reward for faithful teaching and example."

McKenzie's timing could not have been worse—or better, depending on whether one adopts his point of view, which was always drawn to a crisis—for the Japanese launched their invasion of China on July 7, with Beijing and Tientsin as their immediate objectives. McKenzie's heroics in refusing to look for shelter during bombing raids and artillery bombardments were reported in the Sydney press, which noted that "Commissioner McKenzie and his wife spent most of their time on the railway station, cheering up people who were seeking to get away to safer regions. They had no thought for themselves."

They spent their final week there conducting a campaign, attracting 800 people and gaining 36 seekers. In the meantime, eight porridge kitchens fed 15,000 people per day, many of whom had been displaced by the recent fighting that would capture the city at the end of July.[28]

The war forced the premature departure of the McKenzies, who returned to Australia. He was in no condition to resume the heavy administrative tasks he had held before, so he continued to run campaigns for souls with as much vigour as he had, making no concession to his advancing years or poor health. He conducted the annual young people's meeting at Petersham in November, 1937, presenting prizes and telling stories of China, and had nine campaigns during December.

For the first six months of 1938, the McKenzies ran a series of meetings across Victoria and Tasmania, finally taking up residence in the Sydney suburb of Earlwood in late June. They received a welcome from the local Salvation Army Corps, the mayor, and the local branch of the RSSILA, with an honour guard of former AIF soldiers.[29]

McKenzie formally retired on March 1, 1939. At his insistence, this took place in a small room at Salvation Army HQ in Sydney. Others wanted a large public gathering of The Salvation Army, civic leaders and returned soldiers, but McKenzie had had enough of hearing his own praises sung. "Thus it was among 'his ain fowk' he and Mrs McKenzie, in the Board Room, sat and enjoyed a farewell cup of tea, listened to words of appreciation of a magnificent service, and themselves in valedictory words expressed gratitude, and passed on words of blessing and strength." General Evangeline Booth sent a tribute message, and Annie was given a basket of red roses by a young Salvation Army girl.

Annie spoke of her service in The Army:

> From the time she went to the Goldfields in Western Australia, forty-three years ago—and she was still in her 'teens—there had not failed one of all God's promises concerning her. Those were pioneering days, fraught with poverty, difficulty, sorrow and bereavement, but there had been an overwhelming joy in it all. She had found the comradeship of The Army a most precious heritage, and she was still on the altar for sacrifice and service.

McKenzie made a similar speech of ongoing commitment.[30] *Reveille* wrote, "The Commissioner retires with the goodwill and affection of tens of thousands of Salvationists, and hundreds of thousands of those who know little of The Army, but know without mistake the practical meaning of The Army's religion, as it has been presented to them by this man of practical godliness."[31]

In June, McKenzie made his way north to see his three brothers in the Bundaberg district. Later that year, he celebrated 50 years as a Salvation Army Officer. Mavis, now a Captain, was living with them at Earlwood, completing her six-year medical training at Sydney University, and working at Prince Alfred Hospital, with the intention of going overseas on medical missionary work once she graduated.[32]

In retirement, McKenzie walked the streets of his suburb, running meetings wherever he could gather an audience, and he became a familiar figure in his local community. But his health deteriorated again in 1939. Perhaps the declaration of war against Germany in September triggered awful associations that caused his memory to decline even further. He found it difficult to be sidelined during that conflict and attempted to volunteer again for service at the age of 69,[33] but he was in no condition to make a meaningful contribution. He was photographed shaking hands with the first Salvation Army chaplain of the Second AIF, George Sandells. The caption read in part, "Memories, sad, poignant and unforgettable are with Commissioner McKenzie." His physical decline is visible, for he looked old and distant in the photo.[34]

As time progressed, his memory loss degenerated into dementia, although it didn't seem to affect his capacity to recall old soldiers he had known. He would wander the streets of Earlwood searching for men by name, but he was easily disoriented and couldn't find his way back. Local residents would take him in, give him cups of tea and despatch a child to his house to tell Annie where he was or to escort him home.[35]

In 1943, Mavis left home for good. Adjutant Dr McKenzie went to London to marry Adjutant Dr Kingsley Mortimer, then on to Northern Rhodesia (today's Zambia) to work as a medical missionary. It was left to Annie to make the farewell speech, remembering the "red-letter days" in Mavis' life: her dedication as an infant, her conversion, time at training college, her commissioning by her father, and her first appointment, as well as her travels and university studies.[36]

The home in Earlwood now held just McKenzie, with his wandering mind, and the devoted Annie who nursed him through his long and distressing decline, although visitors were regular. Donald lived in Sydney so was able to visit his parents and grandchildren stayed from time to time. Donald's eldest daughter, Jean, spent many happy days at her grandparents' home. However, Colin, an architect in Melbourne, was seriously unwell and couldn't travel. He was to outlive his father by just eight months, leaving behind a widow and two young daughters. Gordon had emigrated to Canada.

In 1945, General George Carpenter visited. Choked with emotion at seeing his old friend reduced to such a state, he broke down in the middle of his prayer. McKenzie calmly picked it up and finished it for him.[37] Despite his condition, he never lost his spiritual zeal. Annie would often find him kneeling on their front lawn, hands clasped in prayer, pleading for those who were lost. Hospitalised once, he overheard the Matron tell a visiting doctor about changing double rooms to singles, saying, "And here is another one that has been converted." She was startled to hear McKenzie's weak exclamation, "Another convert—Hallelujah!" A weekly visitor sang with him mixes of old Scottish songs and hymns. McKenzie's favourite—"Jesus! He flooded me with melody"—prompted a flash of energy. "That's the stuff to give them—'Jesus! He flooded me with melody'." For a moment, a younger McKenzie was visible.[38]

At the annual reunion of the Gallipoli Legion in 1947, Salvation Army Brigadier Arthur McIlveen, who had been a popular chaplain at Tobruk in World War II and also nicknamed "Padre Mac," told the men:

> I have been to see your old padre, "Fighting Mac." If he were here, I know he would have you singing, "I Carry My Sunshine Wherever I Go."
>
> With one accord the 150 or more men, all over the building, spontaneously burst out singing the words of the familiar chorus. Afterwards, crowding around the Brigadier, they begged him to take their greetings to "Fighting Mac." One officer wrote his name on the souvenir programme, saying, "Because of what 'Fighting Mac' did for us, I would like to write my wishes in three words: 'God bless you.'"[39]

On June 21, 1947, the couple celebrated their 48th wedding anniversary. It must have been bitter-sweet for Annie. In early July, George Carpenter rang Annie to inquire after McKenzie, and could hear him singing in the background, "When fade my earthly joys, Jesus is mine."[40]

William McKenzie died in the early hours of Saturday, July 26, at home in Earlwood, Sydney, aged 77. His funeral, held in the Salvation Army Congress Hall, Sydney, was predictably large and the building was "entirely inadequate" to hold the mourners. Retired Commissioner James Hay led the service. A large contingent of returned soldiers was present, many of whom wept unashamedly. Representatives of the Gallipoli Legion of Anzacs, the RSSILA, the Australian Legion of Servicemen, the Rats of Tobruk Association and the 4th Battalion Association were there, as well as a representative for the Deputy Commissioner for Repatriation, and Colonel Mann representing Lieutenant General F H Berryman, GOC, Eastern Command. Many tributes were read, with some referring to him as a "Greatheart."

Mastering her grief, Annie spoke of the privilege of the "companionship of such a noble soul." Donald, the only child who was able to be present, called him "a hero, a knight in shining armour, who had taught his children the highest ideals, particularly chivalry. . . . He walked and talked with Jesus, and Jesus was his Master; he combined humility, purity, goodness, and the gentleness of a saint, with the strength of a giant." He concluded, "It is a great honour to be his son, and, incidentally, a very great responsibility. He set a standard which is extremely hard to maintain."

After the service, a procession made its way to Rookwood Cemetery. The city footpaths were lined with mourners as the hearse, a procession of dignitaries, the Salvation Army Headquarters Band, Returned Soldiers, Salvation Army members and others marched past. A Guard of Honour formed at Wentworth Avenue. A mounted police troop escorted the cortege to Rookwood Cemetery, where a large crowd had gathered. He was buried at sunset, as The Last Post was played by two trumpeters, one of whom was a former soldier who had served with him. The gravediggers covered his grave with wattle bloom and stood reverently throughout the service, which touched Annie.[41]

A memorial service was held in Melbourne and tributes were read out there, including a message from the RSSILA President saying, "To tens of thousands, Major McKenzie was never anything but 'Fighting Mac'—the 'Salvo' who was one of themselves, who shared their burdens, their joys, and their sorrows," noting that he was "no back-lines chaplain."

The fearless warrior was at last at rest from his battles and infirmities. In the grand phrase used in The Salvation Army, he had been "Promoted to Glory."

1. Reception Programme, Archive Box R15, Salvation Army Heritage Archives, Melbourne.
2. *The Age*, June 12, 1930, page 7.
3. *Melbourne Herald*, June 14, 1930, page 271.
4. "Commissioner McKenzie's Visit; Civic Welcome," *Hobart Mercury*, February 10, 1931, page 2.
5. *War Cry*, July 5, 1930, page 15; July 23, 1932, page 8; December 5, 1932, page 9; December 10, 1932, page 9.
6. Adelaide Ah Kow, *William McKenzie M.C., O.B.E., O.F. Anzac Padre* (London: Salvationist Publishing and Supplies, 1949), page 67; "Fighting Mac Salvation Army Chief Visit to Brisbane," *Brisbane Courier*, February 20, 1933, page 13.
7. *War Cry*, February 21, 1931, page 8.
8. Letter to Orames, 1928, Archive Box R15, Salvation Army Heritage Archives, Melbourne.
9. "Service at Shrine," *Melbourne Argus*, October 12, 1931, page 7.
10. *War Cry*, November 26, 1932, page 8.
11. *War Cry*, January 14, 1933, pages 8–9.
12. *War Cry*, February 18, 1933, page 8.
13. *Reveille*, March 1, 1933, page 8.
14. Quoted in *War Cry*, May 13, 1933, page 10.
15. "A Soldiers' Hero," *Sydney Morning Herald*, April 25, 1933.
16. *War Cry*, March 4, 1933, page 9; March 11, 1933, page 9; May 15, 1933, page 10; July 25, 1936, page 9; February 27, 1937, page 7; *The Musician*, September, 1947, page 8.
17. *Reveille*, March 1, 1933, pages 8–9.
18. Joe Cocking, Diary, <www.newcastle.edu.au/Resources/Divisions/Academic/Library/Cultural%20Collections/pdf/Cocking-U-1939-1940.pdf>, accessed September 9, 2013.

19. *War Cry*, May 20, 1933, page 8; December 26, 1936, page 10.
20. Tragically, some of the most notorious cases of child abuse in the 1940s–1970s were perpetrated in two of these institutions, the Gill Memorial Home and the Boys Home associated with the Riverview farm. Both were closed by the 1980s. The Salvation Army recently offered an apology and compensation to those affected.
21. *War Cry*, April 24, 1937; Ah Kow, pages 68–69.
22. *War Cry*, June 15, 1935, page 8.
23. *War Cry*, August 29, 1936, page 10.
24. *War Cry*, September 14, 1935, pages 8 14; December 14, 1935, page 15.
25. *War Cry*, March 14, 1936, page 8.
26. *War Cry*, April 1, 1933, page 9.
27. *War Cry*, February 6, 1937, page 7; February 20, 1937, pages 3, 7; February 27, 1937, page 7; March 6, 1937, page 7; March 27, 1937, page 7; May 1, 1937, page 8; Letter to William (Fighting Mac) McKenzie from his Bundaberg cousin William McKenzie, circa February, 1937.
28. *War Cry*, June 26, 1937, page 9; July 24, 1937, page 3; October 9, 1937, page 8; October 27, 1937, page 8; March 18, 1939, page 9.
29. *War Cry*, December 4, 1937; January 1, 1938, page 8; June 25, 1938, page 10.
30. *War Cry*, March 18, 1939, page 9.
31. Quoted in *War Cry*, July 15, 1939, page 8.
32. *War Cry*, July 15, 1939, page 8.
33. Ivan D Chapman, *Iven G. Mackay Citizen and Soldier* (Melbourne: Melway, 1975), page 153 footnote.
34. *War Cry*, January 20, 1940, page 8.
35. Ann Zubrick, Interview, October 28, 2013.
36. *War Cry*, July 31, 1943, page 5.
37. *War Cry*, August 16, 1947, page 5.
38. Ah Kow, pages 71–72.
39. *War Cry*, June 7, 1947, page 7.
40. *War Cry*, August 16, 1947, page 5.
41. *War Cry*, August 16, 1947, page 5; August 23, 1947, page 7; August 30, 1947, page 6.

Chapter 9

The Best-known Man in the AIF?

The Legacy of "Fighting Mac"

In countering many myths about Anzac, a recent historian has debunked the idea that McKenzie was the most famous and best-loved figure in the AIF—or even the best-known and best-loved chaplain in the AIF. Graham Wilson shows a huge respect for McKenzie and his achievements, but urges—as does this author—that the best way to honour him is to respect his actual life, not the mythical one. Wilson considers that his influence was limited to the 4th Battalion and the 1st Brigade, or at the very best the 1st Australian Division, and that he had little direct contact with other brigades or divisions. He considers that McKenzie may not even have been the most famous chaplain at the time, noting the reputation of men such as Walter Dexter and Michael Bergin.[1]

Wilson states that such claims are "simply ridiculous" and "the sheerest nonsense," arguing that the huge crowds that greeted the returning McKenzie in Australia in early 1918 were mostly Salvationists. He argues that McKenzie's popularity was subject to significant post-war inflation, especially under the stimulus of well-executed Salvationist publicity, "in much the same way as the myth of Simpson expanded after the war."[2] The comparison with John Simpson, the legendary Man with the Donkey immortalised in bronze outside the War Memorial in Canberra, is interesting.

It is true that Salvationists turned out for McKenzie's return, encouraged by *The War Cry* to make a good showing, although Salvation Army archivist Lindsay Cox considers most of the 6000-strong audience at the Melbourne Exhibition Building to have been returned servicemen and their families.[3] It is also true that McKenzie's reputation spread further after the war. But the sheer number of people who flocked to his meetings over the following months and years was simply too numerous to be made up primarily of Salvationists.

However, his claims to earlier fame deserve examination. One of the earliest evidences of his reputation is from the diaries of a Gallipoli soldier, Archie Barwick, who considered McKenzie to be one of the two outstanding personalities on Gallipoli, alongside no less a figure than General William Birdwood. Barwick went on to note McKenzie regularly in his letters home. His diary records in 1916, "He is a grand fellow, the best of the boys will tell you in the A.I.F he is almost idolised by the Australians you have no idea how that man is liked, I'll bet he can sway the whole of the Australians any way he chooses, [and] he would give you half of his last penny."[4]

A judgment like this carries weight, because it was delivered early in the war by a soldier on Gallipoli. Admittedly, the AIF was still small at that point but, having established his fame early and as other divisions were formed in part by taking men from those early battalions to form new ones, it is not hard to see the reputation of a high-profile, larger-than-life performer like McKenzie being spread by word-of-mouth across the AIF.

A year later, another soldier wrote home describing McKenzie as "the Daddy of the lot in the A.I.F.," a man who had won "undying popularity" because of his actions.[5] War correspondent and official historian C E W Bean, who was as well-placed as anyone to make such a judgment, stated in his radio eulogy that "Fighting Mac was the most famous chaplain of the First AIF. Though we had many fine chaplains (a number gave their lives for their men) his fame came foremost and earliest." Bean considered his work in Egypt, particularly his vigour in keeping men out of the brothels, to be the foundation of his reputation.[6] While this comes from a funeral tribute and hence is not likely to be a critical observation, Bean's assessment of McKenzie's influence is still significant and deserves weight, especially as Bean was the son of a clergyman himself.

McKenzie's colleague and supervisor Chaplain Frederick Miles made it clear several times in his reports that McKenzie was a cut above the other chaplains he knew. He stated that, "It is doubtful if any other padre equalled, certainly none surpassed, this magnificent all-round service. He was a big man in every respect; he rendered full and faithful service in matters physical, mental, social, moral and spiritual. He leaves this force with the high esteem and appreciation of all ranks."[7] McKenzie's replacement as 4th Battalion chaplain, Padre Robert Henry, wrote, "He has been loved and venerated and men will continue to cherish his memory all through life."[8] While not evidence of the extent of his popularity, it is one of its depth and endurance, and one that the passage of time proved true.

By early 1918, the *Melbourne Herald* trumpeted that "No man is better known among Australian soldiers at the front than Chaplain-Major W. McKenzie, of the Salvation Army,"[9] although there is probably journalistic licence in the statement, given that an Australian-based journalist could hardly be an authority on the opinions of 100,000 men in France. The newly returned McKenzie allowed for positive propaganda, when the nation was war-weary and the outcome of the struggle was still far from clear, at a time when to exaggerate McKenzie's achievements made good journalistic and political sense. Still, for the claim to be made suggests there was some evidence in its favour and that it was not wholly without foundation.

In 1926, noted journalist Norman Campbell stated that "there is no more striking personality or better-loved man in Australia than Lieut-Commissioner W. McKenzie, of the Salvation Army."[10] As previously noted, Michael McKernan claims that after Anzac Day marches—probably referring to those of the early 1930s—his hand was observed to be bleeding from the sheer number of men who shook it, and his popularity at Anzac Day marches at this point rivalled that of "The Little Digger," wartime Prime Minister Billy Hughes.[11] Both of these observations are of McKenzie's post-war reputation and neither offers any supporting evidence, but—again—they may be discounted but not dismissed, for McKernan is a most meticulous historian.

There is considerable evidence that McKenzie reached a wide circle of soldiers during the war itself, more than just his own battalion, brigade or even division. He also became known to civilians at home with his phenomenally successful campaign for people to write to anonymous soldiers, which generated tens of thousands of letters over the course of the war, addressed to him by name for him to distribute. Even before this, his name was being spread as rural newspapers reprinted his letters from *The War Cry*. By September, 1915, he noted that he was receiving "many" letters of inquiry from people in Australia, including 40 just that week, as a result of these country reprints.[12]

On the ship to Egypt, he ministered to more than 2000 men. His church parades in Egypt grew to include more than half of the 1st Brigade, outnumbering the parade attendances for the other three chaplains combined. His concerts in Egypt and France were legendary, with audiences often numbering more than 1000, drawn from any and every nearby unit, including other nationalities at times.[13] His Egypt diary notes services taken for a variety of troops across both his brigade and other brigades, making him a familiar figure at the very least to most of the 1st Division, and he worked for and with Salvationists from many other units, including the New Zealanders. On Gallipoli and on Lemnos, he was for some time the only chaplain serving the 1st Brigade, and he is named in the diaries of men in divisional units, the 2nd Brigade, the artillery and the Light Horse when he took church services for those units as well.[14] Between 1914 and 1917—in camps, on ships, at the front, in hospitals, in transit and in England—he met literally many thousands of soldiers, running formally organised and impromptu meetings and concerts at every conceivable opportunity, and impressing the majority with his energy, cheerfulness and sincere care.

No other individual is as frequently singled out in the history of the 4th Battalion. Where most battalion histories never mention their own chaplain, let alone one from another battalion, his activities are also noted in the histories of the 2nd, 3rd and 10th Battalions, and commanders in other brigades commented on his influence on their men. Significantly, he was the only member of the 4th Battalion of the Great War to feature in the official history of the 2/4th Battalion of World War II. Its pages record, "He was a legend and a by-word: not just in the battalion or brigade, but indeed throughout the whole A.I.F.", quoting an original member of the 4th Battalion speaking of him more than 40 years later: "The late Padre McKenzie was one of the great men of the A.I.F."[15] The unit war diary for Chaplains, Other Protestant Denominations, records his widespread activities across many units, noting that in just one month before he left England for Australia in January, 1918, he visited about 1000 men in British hospitals, most of whom would have had no connection to his brigade.[16] In reading many hundreds of surviving diaries and letters of members of the First AIF, no chaplain is as frequently named, and few officers either, and they would usually be the senior generals such as Birdwood.

McKenzie was the last person to consider which unit a man belonged to: he behaved as if all humanity was his parish and he expended himself for the needs of whichever soldiers he happened to come across. He counted many senior and influential officers among his personal friends, not least of whom was Birdwood. Despite having had no formal connection with Sir John Monash during the war—McKenzie returned to Australia months before Monash took command of the Australian Corps in France—as previously noted, he was one of only three speakers at Monash's post-funeral public memorial service, alongside indisputably national Anzac figures Sir Harry Chauvel and the RSSILA president. Such an honour can only have been accorded if he was seen by a majority of people to represent the voice of the AIF.

Doubtless, the vast majority of Australian soldiers, spread across the five infantry divisions in France and the Light Horse units in Palestine, never met him personally, but they probably didn't personally meet any of the other legendary figures of the AIF, such as Birdwood, Monash and Hughes. There probably is hyperbole in the claims of his almost universal fame, but there is no doubt that his reputation extended far beyond the sphere of his personal influence, as wide as that already was.[17]

Wilson is right to note that other chaplains worked as hard as McKenzie, with the same degree of personal and spiritual integrity, and greatly influenced the men they served. Men like Dexter and Bergin, as well as others such as T P Bennett, James Gault and Andrew Gillison were admired, respected and deeply loved by the Anzacs. What set McKenzie apart was his larger-than-life personality, his energetic charisma and his overflowing vitality, which had a powerful effect on his audiences. McKenzie's service was not superior to those of other great chaplains in commitment and integrity, but as a function of his personality, it reached a wider audience in a more memorable way. He exceeded them in fame, not in moral stature.

It is also true that his fame grew after the war: his prominent leadership role in the Salvation Army made it easy for that organisation to capitalise on his reputation. Although there is little evidence that The Army did much deliberate publicising, McKenzie's own big personality and leadership roles rendered the need obsolete. Already, in Egypt, he recognised how his military service might give him a public profile that would be a launching-pad for his post-war ministry, saying to Annie that his work "will lend me considerable prestige in coming days and you my dear must seize with me this opportunity."[18] Ambitious as he was though, he never sought publicity for himself, always seeking to lift up the work of The Army and put forward the claims of Christ. If he talked about the war, he focused almost exclusively on the heroism of the men he served. Of his own actions, he was invariably self-deprecating, being characterised several times by critical observers as the soul of humility.[19]

In any case, debate over the title of "the most popular man in the AIF" is useless, as it is one that can never be accorded with any kind of certainty. No means exists of testing its validity. What can be said for sure is that his was a well-known name in the AIF and Australia during the war, and that post-war he attained and maintained the status of a celebrity. It is difficult to find in any literature the kind of adulation that he received for 20 years after the war being accorded to any other figure of the AIF. Large turnouts would characterise the funerals of many notable former AIF figures, especially its generals, but few other living men were such a consistently powerful and emotional drawcard for thousands of people around the country, based on their reputation from the Great War.

At a meeting in Lidcombe in 1933, the local president of the RSSILA said, "We are proud of him, and there was no man in the A.I.F. held in higher esteem."[20] His former commander Brigadier-General Mackay spoke in 1937 of his influence being "enlarged, until not only the men of the 4th Battalion, but the 1st Brigade and, in time, the whole of the Australian and New Zealand forces got to know him as well as Salvationists in Australia did. The Generals, no less than the men, appreciated him."[21] In World War II, several Salvation Army chaplains and welfare workers were nicknamed "Mac" by the diggers in his honour, regardless of their surnames.[22]

Reveille's tribute to him said, "His understanding of the psychology of the masses, particularly that of the Digger, is the secret of his success as a man among men."[23] His fame endured for the lifetime of the men he served. In 1953, an incident was published in *The War Cry*:

> "I see that you belong to The Salvation Army," said a man to Senior Major Mildred Hoepper, while they were

> travelling through a Sydney suburb on Anzac Day. Then he told her that on the day before, he and some of his mates had been out to the cemetery to visit the grave of "Fighting Mac."
>
> "We cannot do anything for him now," the man said, "But we have done all that we can do out of respect for his memory." He did not know that he was speaking to a niece of the late "Fighting Mac."[24]

But as these soldiers and their families passed away, so too did the popular memory of McKenzie. Naturally, The Salvation Army strove to keep it alive, as an inspiration for following generations. Adelaide Ah Kow's biography of McKenzie was published in 1949, with a foreword contributed by Field Marshal Lord Birdwood. It was serialised twice in *The War Cry*, in 1954–1955 and in 1965. Other Salvationists wrote about him as well in pamphlets and articles.

His story has been featured in other Christian media, the majority of which have repeated and sometimes exaggerated the various myths that have accrued around his story. The most recent is evangelist Col Stringer's book on McKenzie, which has imaginatively expanded on many of these myths as part of his attempt to claim Australia's Anzac heritage for Christianity. Among its various examples of historical carelessness, he associates McKenzie with the Light Horse at Gallipoli instead of the infantry. Stringer does not set himself up as a historian, so it may be unfair to be excessively critical, but the book only exacerbates various untruths and overstatements about McKenzie.[25]

With the boom in publishing on Anzac themes of late, McKenzie has also been featured in secular works, including a chapter in John Laws and Christopher Stewart's *There's Always More to the Story*,[26] but again this chapter is happy simply to repeat earlier versions of the story without verifying their accuracy.

Graham Wilson's critique of the mythologising of McKenzie draws parallels to the mythologising of John Simpson, the stretcher-bearer who is now famous as the man who rescued the wounded with a donkey. Both stories have been subjected to mythological inflation, but there are significant differences between the two. As two useful studies have shown, Simpson was not particularly well-known on Gallipoli, rather achieving his legendary status after his death through the efficient functioning of domestic political propaganda machines desperate for a suitable story to boost sagging enlistment rates. One of the studies even shows how some soldiers on Gallipoli backdated their diary entries in order to include an account of a man they discovered was famous from reading the newspapers sent from Australia.[27]

The glorification continues to this day, with his statue outside the Australian War Memorial in Canberra reminding every visitor of his story, and ongoing calls by organisations and politicians to have this mythologised hero awarded a belated Victoria Cross. Essentially, Simpson's fame was political and posthumous, resting on the needs of government and society at large for a hero whose life could be moulded into a eulogy capturing the significance of Gallipoli for all generations. It had little to do with the actual John Simpson Kirkpatrick and his actions.

On the other hand, McKenzie's fame was personal and spontaneous. It rested on the relationship he had forged with the men of the First AIF under fire, and the care he invested in them out of the line and in their families at home. There is no doubt that his reputation was also cultivated: McKenzie himself saw his personal reputation as a springboard for the spreading of the mission of The Salvation Army, and soldiers invented stories about him and embroidered others, a process that continued between the wars and continues to this day. However, McKenzie was genuinely famous with the men of the AIF and the exaggerated stories were largely attempts to honour a man who was widely loved to the point of veneration.

Ironically, a key reason his story has not remained in the public imagination is precisely because it was personal rather than institutional fame. As a living legend, he did not have statues and other permanent memorials built—although some returned soldiers wished for it, both to commemorate his wartime service and his work for veterans after the war. One wrote:

There were numbers of us who felt, and still feel, that you
should have been immortalised, but alas!
We had not skill enough your worth to sing,
For we which now behold these present days
Had eyes to wonder, but lacked tongues to praise.[28]

But his story is also less susceptible to moulding into the ideal Anzac. The meaning of Anzac has been shaped into a powerful unifying national myth and has attained the status in the eyes of many observers as Australia's national secular religion, complete with national temple (the cathedral-like War Memorial with its reverentially-lit exhibits), local places of worship (RSL clubs and the multitude of local war memorials in cities, towns and hamlets across Australia) and a national day of worship (Anzac Day) with its own ceremonies and cults. The Anzac myth even provides it with a populist dogma remarkably resistant to informed historiography. The iconic Anzac has been represented in film by actors such as Chips Rafferty and Paul Hogan, whose public personas bear little resemblance to McKenzie. Like Simpson, they can embody the myth of the larrikin, irreverent, practical, secular digger in ways that the earnestly evangelistic, teetotaller, non-swearing, anti-gambling, Sunday-keeping clergyman McKenzie cannot. Even Simpson's Englishness has been successfully expunged from popular memory as he has been reshaped into the ideal Australian bushman.

The Anzac story has been fashioned from its raw historical material to meet national needs. While the vast majority of the detail of the myth and legend of Anzac has a sure historical foundation, its meaning has been reshaped largely by what has been left out. The forgotten men of Anzac tend to be those who don't fit the national stereotype: those of British birth and outlook who made up about one in five of the Anzacs; those Anzacs of urban origin who made up four out of five of what has since become a bushman-Anzac legend; the "Bad Characters" whose criminal or cowardly behaviour was a serious stain on the Anzac character; the devoutly Christian, who were far from invisible at the time but have since been submerged in the secular legend, and so on.[29]

McKenzie does not easily fit the current popular conceptions of the Anzac, yet he was a favourite among the Anzacs themselves. He made a characteristically Australian transition from rank outsider to the ultimate insider, beginning the war as one of the least likely to be popular and ending it as an Anzac icon. Maybe it is time to restore McKenzie and his legacy to the bigger picture of what Anzac means. After all, he meant so much to the actual Anzacs who are behind the Anzac legend. We who wish to honour the Anzacs could do a lot worse than to remember the man those Anzacs honoured.

1. As previously noted, Dexter served for the entire war, a feat that McKenzie could not manage, and won the DSO and the MC. Bergin may just be the most curious Anzac of them all. An Irish Jesuit priest, he was a missionary in Damascus at the start of the war and was interned by the Turks. Released in 1915, he attached himself to the Australians in Egypt and served on Gallipoli and in France. He was killed by shell fire at Passchendaele in October, 1917, and awarded a posthumous MC. The closest this Anzac ever got to Australia was Egypt!
2. Graham Wilson, *Bully Beef and Balderdash: Some myths of the AIF examined and debunked* (Newport, NSW: Big Sky, 2012), pages 322, 327–344; Wilson, Emails to the author, August 12, 2008; March 9, 2009.
3. Lindsay Cox, "Lone Pine 1915," *War Cry*, April 24, 1999, page 1.
4. Archie Barwick, Diary, September 12, 1915–March 28, 1916, 41–42, MLMSS 1493 Box 1/Item 2, Mitchell Library, State Library of New South Wales, published as *In Great Spirits: The World War One diary of Archie Barwick* (Sydney South: HarperCollins, 2013), page 65.
5. Harrie Joseph Cave, Letter 77, June 9, 1917, MLMSS 1224, Mitchell Library, State Library of New South Wales.
6. Transcript of radio broadcast for "News Digest," July 28, 1947, by C E W Bean, PR 84/150, Australian War Memorial (AWM).
7. Other Protestant Denominations Senior chaplain report, August, 1914–October, 1917, AWM4 6/4/1; AWM4 6/4/4, January, 1918.
8. *War Cry*, February 9, 1918, page 5.
9. Quoted in *War Cry*, February 16, 1918, page 5.

10. Norman Campbell, "Fighting Mac," undated news clipping circa 1926, McKenzie file, Salvation Army Heritage Room, Bexley North, Sydney; also quoted in Dale, "Fighting Mac," and quoted in *War Cry*, August 9, 1947, page 6.
11. Michael McKernan, *Padre: Australian chaplains in Gallipoli and France* (Sydney: Allen & Unwin, 1986), page 3; Michael McKernan, "William McKenzie," *Australian Dictionary of Biography*, <http://adb.anu.edu.au/biography/mckenzie-william-7391>, accessed December 19, 2013.
12. William McKenzie, Letter to Hay, September 23, 1915.
13. William McKenzie, Letters to Annie, March 5, 1915; March 16, 1915.
14. Roy Rowe, July 4, 1915, PR04297, AWM; Henry Tucker, Diary, May 30, 1915, MLMSS 1013, Mitchell Library, State Library of New South Wales; Victor Rupert Laidlaw, Diary, September 5, 1915, MS 11827, State Library of Victoria; Albert Arthur Orchard, Diary, January 31, 1916, February 1, 1916; *Diary of an ANZAC: the front line diaries and stories of Albert Arthur 'Bert' Orchard M.C.: Gallipoli & the Western Front 1914 to 1918*, compiled by Arthur Orchard (Otago, Tas: A F Orchard, 2010); Ernest Murray, Diary, October 3 & 10, 1915, MLMSS 2892, Mitchell Library, State Library of New South Wales.
15. William McKenzie, Letters to Hay; William McKenzie, Letters to Annie; Eric Wren, *Randwick to Hargicourt: History of the 3rd Battalion, A.I.F.* (Sydney: Ronald G McDonald, 1935), pages 34, 134; F W Taylor and T A Cusack (compilators), *Nullis Secundus: A History of the Second Battalion, A.I.F. 1914–1919* (Swanbourne WA: John Burridge Military Antiques, 1992 [original printing 1942]), page 52; Unit History Editorial Committee (editors), *White over Green: The 2/4th Battalion and reference to the 4th Battalion* (Sydney: Angus and Robertson for 2/4th Australian Infantry Battalion Association, 1963), page 22; Robert Kearney, *Silent Voices: The story of the 10th Battalion AIF in Australia, Egypt, Gallipoli, France and Belgium during the Great War 1914–1918* (Sydney: New Holland, 2005), page 61.
16. Australian Imperial Force unit war diaries 1914–18, Senior Chaplain, Other Protestant Denominations, Headquarters AIF, London, August, 1914–October, 1917, AWM4 6/4/1-4.
17. Campbell, "Fighting Mac."
18. Letter to Annie, January 8, 1915, PR84/150, AWM.
19. *War Cry*, February 20, 1937, page 3; August 16, 1947, page 5.
20. *War Cry*, March 22, 1933, page 9.
21. *War Cry*, May 1, 1937, page 8.
22. *War Cry*, March 7, 1970.
23. *Reveille*, March 1, 1933, page 9.
24. *War Cry*, May 9, 1953, page 4.
25. See, for example, Barry Gittins and Faye Michelson, "Wars and Rumours of Wars," *On Fire*, Vol 9 No 8, April 26, 2008, page 9; *The Boys' Best Friend* (Written and Directed by Michael Bennett), Anglican Media, 44 minutes, 1999; *Fighting Mac: The story of William McKenzie* (Written by Daniel Reynaud, Directed by Mal Hamilton), It Is Written Oceania/Adventist Media Network, 23 minutes, 2012; John Banton. "I Dare You," <www.johnbanton.org/John_Banton_web_sermons/

ANZAC_DAY_2004_I_Dare_You.htm>; "The Fighting Padres," <www.acctv.com.au/featuredetail.asp?id=987>, accessed August 31, 2007; Col Stringer, *'Fighting McKenzie', Anzac Chaplain* (Robina, Qld: Col Stringer Ministries, 2003).

26. John Laws and Christopher Stewart, *There's Always More to the Story* (Sydney: Macmillan, 2004).
27. Peter Cochrane, *Simpson and the Donkey: The making of a legend* (Melbourne: Melbourne University Press, 1992); Graham Wilson, *Dust, Donkeys and Delusions: The myth of Simpson and his donkey exposed* (Newport, NSW: Big Sky, 2012).
28. Letter by James MacPherson, representing other soldiers in *War Cry*, February 20, 1937, page 3.
29. L L Robson, *The First A.I.F.: A Study of its Recruitment, 1914–1918* (Melbourne: Melbourne University Press, 1970); Peter Stanley, *Bad Characters: Sex, Crime, Mutiny and Murder and the Australian Imperial Force* (Sydney: Murdoch/Pier 9, 2010); Robert D Linder, *The Long Tragedy: Australian Evangelical Christians and the Great War, 1914–1918* (Adelaide: Open Book, 2000).

ACKNOWLEDGMENTS

The goodwill and cooperation of many people has contributed to this book.

Lindsay Cox, archivist at The Salvation Army, Melbourne, was my starting point and his assistance in finding materials has been outstanding, while his wide-ranging knowledge of Salvationist history and culture and witty advice has been helpful in critiquing the manuscript. It was his idea that I produce a biography of McKenzie. His assistant, Yasmin Van Gaarlen-Pentice, went the extra mile in chasing up photos despite her own busy schedule.

George Hazell, archivist at The Salvation Army, Bexley North, Sydney, provided some telling memories and anecdotes of McKenzie, while Garry Mellsop, Territorial Archivist for The Salvation Army in New Zealand identified the slender materials relating to McKenzie's stay in that country.

In researching the McKenzie family, I was helped by Val Messer, Research Officer of the Bundaberg Genealogical Society, Rhonda Symonds, great-niece of William McKenzie, and Patricia Davies, Head Teacher at Biggar High School in Lanarkshire, Scotland.

Jean Newall, McKenzie's eldest granddaughter, provided personal memories of her grandfather, while her daughter Miriam was an important link in the chain of communication. Their kind assistance is greatly appreciated. Special thanks to Ann Zubrick, McKenzie's youngest granddaughter, for offering not just family memories of McKenzie but also a big-picture critique of the manuscript as it evolved. Her searching questions made for a more rigorous text.

I am indebted to the staff at the Research Centre of the Australian War Memorial and the State Libraries of New South Wales and Victoria, whose unfailing helpfulness has smoothed the process of identifying key documents.

Dr Michael McKernan has kindly provided the foreword to this book and I acknowledge that I have been working in his shadow, after he pioneered the study of the Anzac chaplains. Professor Peter Stanley has also been generous in supporting this project.

I had the privilege of spending a total of 10 days at Gallipoli during the course of two trips, courtesy of It Is Written Oceania, filming documentary episodes in relation to the stories of the Anzac chaplains.

I am grateful to the staff at Signs Publishing, particularly the editor Nathan Brown who has facilitated the publishing of this book, and more importantly has ensured that it reads much better than my original text did. But, as always, any lapses in the text remain mine to own.

My employer, Avondale College of Higher Education, has provided me with not only an enjoyable place to work but also research leave during which I was able to walk over McKenzie's battlefields in Belgium and France, and accomplish the bulk of the writing. I greatly appreciate the collegiality of my fellow lecturers in the Faculty of Arts and Theology.

And, as so often is the case with writing projects, my family has put up with my enthusiasm on the subject of McKenzie for many years, enduring with equanimity each fresh discovery or new anecdote that I could not resist telling them, and listening patiently as I repeated these to many friends and acquaintances. For love and support, I thank you, Emi, Etienne and Bianca.

Bibliography

Archival material

Australian War Memorial

1DRL/0162 Eric Burgess

1DRL/0192, Herbert G Carter

1DRL/0240 Apcar Leslie De Vine

1DRL/0296 Robert Pearce Flockart

1DRL/0358 Robert Horniman

1DRL/473 George Makin

1DRL/619 Chaplain Donald B Blackwood

2DRL/0219 Arthur Edward Matthews

2DRL/0512 Ben Champion

2DRL/0560 Noel Cuthbert

2DRL/0786 Thomas Richards

3DRL/3906 Howard John McKern

3DRL/4104 Charles F Bosward

PR 01463 Percy Smythe

PR 01507 Francis Godlee

PR 04297 Roy Rowe

PR 84/150 Chaplain William McKenzie

PR 85/412 Sidney Charles Dewey

PR 85/815 Letters of Major W McKenzie

PR 91/192 Richard Asaph Edwards

PRMF 0015 Chaplain T P Bennett

National Australian Archives

B2455 MacGregor, J

B2455 McKenzie, W

Salvation Army Archives

Archive Box R15, Salvation Army Heritage Archives, Melbourne.

File J139653, Salvation Army Heritage Archives, Melbourne.

McKenzie file, Salvation Army Heritage Room, Bexley North, Sydney.

Mitchell Library, State Library of New South Wales

MLDOC 3174 James Caddy

MLMSS 1013 Henry Frederick Wallace Tucker

MLMSS 1171 Verner Cocks

MLMSS 1224 Harrie Joseph Cave

MLMSS 1493 Archie Barwick

MLMSS 2765 George Thomasson Gill

MLMSS 288 Ralph Ingram Moore

MLMSS 2886 Alfred Prichard Kington Morris
MLMSS 2892 Ernest Murray
MLMSS 3432 Terence Ward Garling
MLMSS 3444 ADD-ON 1255 Charles Gifford Pryce
MLMSS 439 James William Dains
MLMSS 5480 Lennox Douglas
MLMSS 7478 Charles Monaghan

State Library of Victoria

MS 11827 Victor Rupert Laidlaw

Newspapers and magazines

Adelaide Chronicle, 1930
Age, 1930
Brisbane Courier, 1921
Daily Mirror, 1959, 1981
Hobart Mercury, 1931
London Gazette, 1916
Melbourne Argus, 1931
Melbourne Herald, 1930
Methodist, 1915
Musician, 1947
On Fire, 2008
Pipeline, 2012
Presbyterian Banner, 1917
Reveille, 1933, 1934
Scottish Australasian, 1918
Signs of the Times, 1915
Spectator, 1915
Standard, 1948,
Sun, 1915, 1972
Sydney Morning Herald, 1919, 1933
War Cry, 1898–1948, 1959, 1980, 1999
Young Soldier, 1949

Journal articles

Cook, Tim, “Fighting Words: Canadian soldiers’ slang and swearing in the Great War,” *War in History*, Vol 20 No 3, July, 2013.

Websites

Banton, John, “I ‚Dare You,’ <www.johnbanton.org/John_Banton_web_sermons/ANZAC_DAY_2004_I_Dare_You.htm>; “The Fighting Padres,” <www.acctv.com.au/featuredetail.asp?id=987>, accessed August 31, 2007.

Cocking, Joe, Diary, <www.newcastle.edu.au/Resources/Divisions/Academic/Library/

Cultural%20Collections/pdf/Cocking-U-1939-1940.pdf>, accessed September 9, 2013.

Hazell, Envoy George, Podcast, <www.chr.org.au/audio/fighting-macKenzie-podcasts/MacKenzie-Track-01.mp3>, accessed July 25, 2013.

McKernan, Michael, "William McKenzie," *Australian Dictionary of Biography*, <http://adb.anu.edu.au/biography/mckenzie-william-7391>, accessed December 19, 2013.

<www.electricscotland.com/history/australia/melbourne12.htm>, accessed September 9, 2013.

<www.salvationarmy.org.au/en/Who-We-Are/History-and-heritage/Opposition-and-acceptance-of-The-Salvation-Army/>, accessed August 26, 2013.

DVDs

Fighting Mac: The story of William McKenzie (Written by Daniel Reynaud, Directed by Mal Hamilton), It Is Written Oceania/Adventist Media Network, 23 minutes, 2012.

The Boys' Best Friend (Written and Directed by Michael Bennett), Anglican Media, 44 minutes, 1999.

Unpublished sources, interviews and emails held by author

Cox, Lindsay—Archivist, Salvation Army, Melbourne, Interview, July 26, 2007.

Hart, Trevor—Archivist, Camberwell Grammar School, Email correspondence, April 7, 2014.

Hazell, George—Archivist, Salvation Army, Sydney, Interview, December 17, 2007.

Newall, Jean—Granddaughter, Interview, October 30, 2013.

Symonds, Rhonda—Descendant of Donald McKenzie Snr, Bundaberg, Family papers.

Wilson, Graham—Historian, Email correspondence, August 12, 2008, October 8, 2008.

Zubrick, Ann—Granddaughter, Interview, October 28, 2013.

Monographs and book chapters

Adam-Smith, Patsy, *The Anzacs*, Melbourne: Penguin, 1991.

Ah Kow, Adelaide, *William McKenzie M.C., O.B.E., O.F. Anzac Padre*, London: Salvationist Publishing and Supplies, 1949.

Ashworth, Tony, *Trench Warfare 1914–1918: The live and let live system*, London: Pan, 2000.

Austin, Ronald J, *The Fighting Fourth: A history of Sydney's 4th Battalion, 1914–1919*, McCrae, Vic: Slouch Hat, 2007.

Australian Encyclopaedia, 6th edition, Vol 5, Sydney: Australian Geographical Society, 1996.

Barwick, Archie, *In Great Spirits: The World War One diary of Archie Barwick*, Sydney South: HarperCollins, 2013.

Bond, Lieut-Colonel, *The Army that went with the Boys: A record of Salvation Army work with the Australian Imperial Force*, Melbourne: Salvation Army, 1919.

Brugger, Suzanne, *Australians and Egypt 1914–1919*, Melbourne: Melbourne University Press, 1990.

Cameron, David W, *The Battle for Lone Pine: Four days of hell at the heart of Gallipoli*, Melbourne: Penguin Viking, 2012.

Chapman, Ivan G, *Iven G Mackay Citizen and Soldier*, Melbourne: Melway, 1975.

Cochrane, Peter, *Simpson and the Donkey: The making of a legend*, Melbourne: Melbourne University Press, 1992.

Collier, Richard, *The General Next to God: The story of William Booth and the Salvation Army*, London: Fontana, 1969.

Crotty, Martin, *Making the Australian Male: Middle-class masculinity 1870–1920*, Melbourne: Melbourne University Press, 2001.

Dale, Percival, *Fighting Mac (William McKenzie M.C., O.B.E., O.F.)*, Salvation Army Liberty Booklet, not dated.

Doran, Christine R, "Separation movements in North Queensland in the Nineteenth Century," in B J Dalton (editor), *Lectures on North Queensland History*, Third Series, Townsville, Qld: James Cook University of North Queensland, 1979.

Eley, Beverly, *Ion Idriess*, Sydney: ETT, 1995.

Gammage, Bill, *The Broken Years: Australian soldiers in the Great War*, Canberra: Australian National University, 1974.

Gault, James, *Padre Gault's Stunt Book*, London: Epworth Press, circa 1920.

Gerster, Robin, *Big Noting: The heroic theme in Australian war writing*, Melbourne: Melbourne University Press, 1997.

Gladwin, Michael, *Captains of the Soul: A history of Australian Army chaplains*, Newport, NSW: Big Sky, 2013.

Hartnett, H G, *Over the Top: A digger's story of the Western Front* (Chris Bryett, editor), Sydney: Allen & Unwin, 2009.

Herman, Judith Lewis, *Trauma and Recovery*, New York: Basic books, 2007.

Kauffman, Jeffrey (editor), *The Shame of Death, Grief, and Trauma*, New York: Routledge, 2010.

Kearney, Robert, *Silent Voices: The story of the 10th Battalion AIF in Australia, Egypt, Gallipoli, France and Belgium during the Great War 1914–1918*, Sydney: New Holland, 2005.

Kerr, Greg, *Private Wars: Personal records of the Anzacs in the Great War*, Melbourne: Oxford University Press, 2000.

Linder, Robert D, *The Long Tragedy: Australian Evangelical Christians and the Great War, 1914–1918*, Adelaide: Open Book, 2000.

Madigan, Edward, *Faith Under Fire: Anglican Army Chaplains and the Great War*, London: Palgrave Macmillan, 2011.

McGuigan, Peter, "A Man of Exceptional Courage," in (no editor) *In The Steps of the Founder: Celebrating the lives of 23 Australian recipients of the Order of the Founder*, Mont Albert, Vic: The Salvation Army, 1995.

McKenzie, F A, *Serving the King's Men: How the Salvation Army is helping the nation*, London: Hodder & Stoughton, 1918.

McKernan, Michael, *Australian Churches at War: Attitudes and activities of the major churches 1914–1918*, Sydney & Canberra: Catholic Theology Faculty and Australian War Memorial, 1980.

__________, *Padre: Australian Chaplains in Gallipoli and France*, Sydney: Allen & Unwin, 1986.

Orchard, Albert Arthur, *Diary of an ANZAC: The front line diaries and stories of Albert Arthur 'Bert' Orchard M.C.: Gallipoli & the Western Front 1914 to 1918* (Compiled by Arthur Orchard), Otago, Tas: A F Orchard, 2010.

Reynaud, Daniel, *Celluloid Anzacs: The Great War through Australian cinema*, Melbourne: Australian Scholarly Publishing, 2007.

Robson, L L, *The First A.I.F.: A study of its recruitment, 1914–1918*, Melbourne: Melbourne University Press, 1970.

Rohr, Richard, *Adam's Return: The five promises of male initiation*, New York: Crossroads, 2004.

Schweitzer, Richard, *The Cross and the Trenches: Religious faith and doubt among British and American Great War soldiers*, Westport, CT, & London: Praeger, 2003.

Seal, Graham, *Inventing Anzac: The digger and national mythology*, St Lucia, Qld: University of Queensland Press, 2004.

Snelling, Stephen, *VCs of the First World War: Gallipoli 1915*, Gloucestershire: Sutton Publishing Limited, 1995.

Stanley, Peter, *Bad Characters: Sex, crime, mutiny and murder and the Australian Imperial Force*, Sydney: Murdoch/Pier 9, 2010.

Stevenson, Robert C, *The 1st Australian Division in the Great War, 1914–18*, Melbourne & Cambridge: Cambridge University Press, 2013.

Stringer, Col, *'Fighting McKenzie' Anzac Chaplain: Tribute to a hero*, Robina, Qld: Col Stringer Ministries, 2003.

Taylor, F W, and T A Cusack (compilators), *Nullis Secundus: A history of the Second Battalion, A.I.F. 1914-1919*, Swanbourne, WA: John Burridge Military Antiques, 1992 [original printing 1942].

White over Green: The 2/4th Battalion and reference to the 4th Battalion, Unit History Editorial Committee (editors), Sydney: Angus and Robertson for 2/4th Australian Infantry Battalion Association, 1963.

Wilson, Graham, *Bully Beef and Balderdash: Some myths of the AIF examined and debunked*, Newport, NSW: Big Sky Publishing, 2012.

__________, *Dust, Donkeys and Delusions: The myth of Simpson and his donkey exposed*, Newport, NSW: Big Sky, 2012.

Wren, Eric, *Randwick to Hargicourt: History of the 3rd Battalion. A.I.F.*, Sydney: Ronald G McDonald, 1935.

INDEX

Ah Kow, Adelaide: 2, 11, 15, 44, 67, 84, 111, 240
AIF: 1, 54, 55, 56, 57, 59, 64, 65, 66, 77, 80, 81, 111, 131, 139, 143, 144, 146, 147, 165, 172, 182, 184, 188, 191, 218, 220, 226, 228, 233, 234, 235, 237, 238, 239, 241
Units:
Divisions
1st Division: 54, 72, 124, 146, 172, 233, 236
2nd Division: 118
5th Division: 124
Australian Light Horse: 55, 131, 236, 238, 240
Brigades
1st Brigade: 55, 65, 67, 82, 86, 95, 106, 113, 118. 120, 147, 158, 159, 233, 236, 239
2nd Brigade: 73, 86, 95, 103, 118, 236
3nd Brigade: 86, 95
Battalions
1st Battalion: 105, 107, 112, 113, 124, 125, 154, 233
2nd Battalion: 77, 107, 113, 114, 124, 147, 237
3rd Battalion: 67, 81, 107, 115, 119, 159, 237
4th Battalion: 55, 65, 67, 72, 95-96, 97, 99, 107-108, 111, 113, 115, 118, 121, 124, 125, 131, 132, 146, 147, 148, 149, 152, 157, 159, 161, 164, 165, 167, 170-171, 186-187, 189, 235, 237, 239
5th Battalion: 73
6th Battalion: 73
7th Battalion: 118
8th Battalion: 96
10th Battalion: 237
11th Battalion: 96
14th Battalion: 74
55th Battalion: 170
56th Battalion: 124
Field Ambulances
1st Field Ambulance: 67, 79
2nd AIF: 2/4th Battalion: 237
Anglican/Anglicanism/Church of England: 13, 19, 56, 58, 60, 63, 73, 81, 89, 124, 147, 151
Anzac myth & legend: 3, 242
Arnott, Arthur: 49, 53n
Baptist: 56, 73
Barwick, Archie: 125, 126, 151, 155, 234
Bean, C E W: v, 84, 99, 235

Begbie, Harold: 109-110, 162, 163
Bennett, Alfred: 93n, 97
Bennett, T P: 126, 238
Bergin, Michael: 126, 233, 238, 243n
Birdwood, William: 1, 124, 126, 146, 150, 152, 188, 234, 237, 238, 240
Blaskett, William: 49, 53n
Booth, Bramwell: 117, 192, 211
Booth, Evangeline: 52n, 211, 222, 224, 227
Booth, William: 19, 28, 43, 52n, 190
Booth-Tucker, Frederick: 210
Brethren: 56
Bridges, William: 95
Cameron, David: 114
Campbell, Norman: 236
Carpenter, George: 48, 52n, 221, 228, 229
Chaplain/s: v, 1, 56-60, 72, 73, 79, 80, 83, 87, 168-169
Chauvel, Harry: 217, 238
Chiang Kai-shek: 199, 209
Churches of Christ: 56
Cocking, Joe: 221
Congregationalist/Congregationalism: 56
Corinthic: 172, 179
Cox, Lindsay: 234
Crotty, Martin: 70
Dain, James: 158
Dale, Percival: 3, 111
Deighton, Darrell McKenzie: 224
Dexter, Walter: 73, 98, 112, 126, 233, 238, 243n
Dunstan, Willie: 117-118
Edward, Prince of Wales: 187
Emden, SMS: 71, 198
Euripides: 63, 64, 65, 67, 80
Fahey, John: 96, 97, 112, 126
Francis, Walter "Skipper": 69
Fullerton, Alexander: 114
Gallipoli: vi, 1, 67, 77, 86, 88, 90, 95, 100, 102, 103, 105, 106, 109, 110, 112, 116, 118, 120, 121, 122, 124, 131, 133, 134, 135, 137, 145, 147, 149, 152-153, 162, 164, 166, 181, 182, 185, 186, 189, 202, 225, 230, 234, 236, 241
Gammage, Bill: 59
Gault, James: 169, 238
George V of Great Britain: 152, 162
Gillison, Andrew: 74, 98, 117, 126, 238
Gladwin, Michael: 59
Green, James: 60, 79, 81, 93n, 112

Greene, Alfred: 123, 146
Haig, Douglas: 136, 146
Hay, James: 50, 64, 66, 71, 73, 74, 80, 82, 98, 155, 163, 179, 188, 192, 230
Hazell, George: 65, 247
Henry, Robert: 167, 170, 235
Higgins, Edward: 196, 211, 217
Hoepper, Carl: 37, 52n
Hoepper, Ferdinand: 37, 52n
Hoepper, Frederick: 37
Hoepper, Frederika: 37
Hoepper, Johann: 37, 52n
Hoepper, Mildred: 239
Hogan, Paul: 242
Holman, William: 189
Hore-Ruthven, Zara Countess of Gowrie: 222
Hughes, William Morris: 1, 76, 222, 236, 238
Hunter, David: 170
Idriess, Ion: 111
Irvine, William: 214
Jacka, Albert: 149, 152
Judaism/Jews: 89, 158
Kanakas: 16-17
Kuo, Ensign: 203, 205, 206, 207
Lang, Jack: 216
Laws, John: 240
Le Maistre, Frank: 182
Lady Musgrave: 15
Lake Michigan: 88, 89, 96, 97
Louise, Princess, Duchess of Argyll: 161
Lyons, Joseph: 223
Mackay, Iven: 67, 145, 152, 170, 218, 239
MacLaurin, Henry Norman: 55, 68, 71, 86, 90, 96
Macnaghten, Charles: 55, 96, 107, 109, 113, 124, 126, 129n, 151, 188
Mao Zedong: 198, 209
Mapp, Henry: 211
McAuliffe, Edmund: 60, 102, 112, 113
McGregor, James: 115, 119
McIlveen, Arthur: 229
McKenzie, Agnes (mother, nee Callan): 7, 15, 22, 28, 46
McKenzie, Alexander (uncle): 14
McKenzie, Alexander (brother): 6, 14
McKenzie, Anne (sister): 6, 14
McKenzie, Annie (wife, nee Hoepper): 37-39, 43, 44, 45, 62, 63, 64, 74, 75-76, 98, 105, 114, 117, 122, 124, 137-145, 150-151, 156, 158, 159, 160-166, 181, 184,

McKenzie, Annie (continued): 188, 190-191, 193, 201-203, 207, 211, 215, 217, 224-225, 227, 228-230
McKenzie, Archibald (brother): 6, 14
McKenzie, Colin Campbell (son): 43, 65, 141, 181, 190, 228
McKenzie, Donald (father): 6-7, 11, 14-18, 27, 28
McKenzie, Donald William Booth (son): 43, 75, 139-141, 184, 190, 225, 228
McKenzie, Ebenezer (Evan, great grandfather): 6
McKenzie, Evan (uncle): 14
McKenzie, Evan (brother): 6, 14, 17
McKenzie, F A: 84, 109, 153, 162, 165
McKenzie, Gordon Lindsay (son): 43, 141, 190, 228
McKenzie, Henrietta (sister): 6
McKenzie, Isabella (grandmother): 7
McKenzie, Isabella (sister): 6, 14, 17
McKenzie, James (uncle): 7, 14
McKenzie, James (brother): 6
McKenzie, Jane (aunt): 7, 14
McKenzie, Jean (aunt): 7, 14
McKenzie, Jean Gregor (daughter): 43, 47
McKenzie, later Newall, Jean (granddaughter): 247
McKenzie, later Mortimer, Mavis Hinemoana (daughter): 43, 45, 47, 64, 122, 141, 142, 190-191, 193, 194, 200-201, 203, 209, 210, 220, 224, 227, 228
McKenzie, Robert (brother): 6
McKenzie, Thomas: 161
McKenzie, William (grandfather): 6-7
McKenzie, William (cousin, son of Alexander): 17
McKenzie, William (cousin, son of Evan): 25n
McKenzie, William
- AIF appointments: 50, 59, 160
- Articles in *War Cry*: 41, 46, 187
- Boxing: 80
- Bundaberg: 17-24, 225
- Childhood: 6-11
- Conversion: 20-23
- Fatherhood: 43, 44
- Honours and awards: 110, 113, 145, 150-153, 162, 190, 224
- Imprisonment: 35
- Lone Pine, Battle of: 107-117
- Marriage: 38-41
- Migration to Australia: 14-15
- Mouquet Farm, Battle of: 149-151, 155-157
- Music: 30, 33, 45, 49, 50, 69-71, 76, 77-78, 89, 103-104, 132, 145, 146, 153-154, 158, 160, 161, 186, 219, 229
- Mystical experiences: 22-24, 155-157, 178

New Zealand: 47
Nick-names: 10, 15, 66, 170, 172, 185
Physical size: 18, 29, 63, 167, 204
Pozieres, Battle of: 147-149
Preaching: 1-2, 33-34, 40, 46, 81, 85, 86, 100, 120, 137, 163-164, 181, 184-186, 197, 200, 205
Retirement: 226
Salvation Army appointments: 30-33, 39, 41, 46-48, 47, 48, 183, 190, 193, 196, 211, 217
Salvation Army ranks: 30, 31, 41, 46, 48, 193, 217
Swearing, attitude to: 1, 19, 58, 64, 66, 82, 87, 189
Wassa riot: 83-85
McKernan, Michael: 192, 236
Methodist/Methodism: 19, 20, 28, 56, 58, 60, 112, 118, 158, 170
Merkara: 14
Miles, Frederick: 73, 106, 126, 228
Miltiades: 64, 66
Monash, John: 188, 217, 237, 238
Mongolia: 167
Mortimer, Kingsley: 210, 228
Murdoch, Keith: 109-110, 171
Non-Conformist/Non-Conformism: 13, 19, 56, 63
Orames, Benjamin: 159, 160, 208, 216
Presbyterian/Presbyterianism: 9-10, 13, 18, 20, 23, 28, 44, 56, 58, 74, 117, 224
Rafferty, Chips: 242
Reid, Sir George: 50
Returned Soldiers and Sailors Imperial League of Australia (RSSILA, now RSL): 193, 214, 217, 218, 220, 226, 230, 239, 242
Richards, Tom: 79, 92n, 124, 132, 145, 149-150
Rohr, Richard: 23
Roman Catholic/Catholicism: 56, 58, 60, 81, 87, 89, 137, 151, 158, 165, 168, 169
Rookwood Cemetery: v, 230
Salvation Army: 2-4, 17, 19-24, 28, 29, 30-31, 32-34, 36, 37, 43, 48, 50, 56, 58, 60, 62, 65, 66, 79, 81, 86, 88, 109, 123, 126, 154, 155, 158, 159, 162, 165-166, 171, 179, 181, 182, 188, 190, 192, 193, 200, 205, 208, 210-211, 214-215, 218-219, 221, 223, 227, 230, 234-235, 238, 240, 241
Sandells, George: 228
Schweitzer, Richard: 70
Scullin, James: 216
Simla, HMTS: 120, 122, 132
Simpson Kirkpatrick, John: 24n, 234, 240-242
Smyth, Neville: 119, 124
Stack, Walter: 109, 148
Stevens, Bertram: 222

Stewart, Christopher: 240
Street, Philip: 222
Stringer, Col: 3, 111, 240
Sun Yat-sen: 198, 209
Sunday keeping: 9-10, 20, 44, 48, 56, 68, 81, 221, 225, 242
Sydney, HMAS: 71
Taiping, SS: 225
Talbot, Albert Edward: 60, 68, 70, 71, 81, 93n, 102, 108, 113, 117, 126, 130n
Thompson, Astley John Onslow: 55, 72, 77, 96, 98
Unsworth, Isaac: 109, 117
Warrimoo, SS: 46, 53n
Wassa: 83, 85
Wilson, Graham: 111-112, 150, 233-234, 238, 240
Wolf, SMS: 167
YMCA: 82, 188

Publicity and Media Inquiries
projects@freshcontent.agency

The author and publisher would like to thank the following people who have supported the efforts of promoting this book: **Bevan Craig** for the author website, **Kristen Calculli** for project co-ordination, **Brenton Stacey** for public relations asssistance, and **Christina Hawkins** from Fresh Content Marketing for making some things happen.

With a doctorate in Australian war cinema, **Daniel Reynaud** is an Associate Professor, lecturing in History, Literature and Media at Avondale College of Higher Education in Cooranbong, New South Wales. He has been researching and writing on the topic of the Anzacs and religion for more than five years.

He has won a US Silver Angel Award 2011 in the National Television category, for Excellence in Media for one of his three television scripts on the Anzacs and religion, including an episode on William McKenzie. These have attracted an eastern Australian audience rating of up to 250,000 viewers per episode.

A feature article on William McKenzie has won an Australian Religious Press Association Bronze Award for Best Profile Story 2013.

As part of his research for this book, Daniel has travelled to all the key sites in McKenzie's war career: Egypt, Gallipoli, the Somme and Flanders, retracing the actions McKenzie was involved in.

For more stories and content like this book, visit:

www.danielreynaud.com

Daniel speaks frequently on topics of Anzac history, the life of William McKenzie, and the Anzacs and religion. Requests can be made to Daniel to deliver keynote addresses or half-day presentations. To find out more, please visit his speaking requests page at:

www.danielreynaud.com/speaking

You can also connect with Daniel Reynaud on Facebook:

Facebook.com/danielreynaudauthor